Praise for Simon Reynolds

'The foremost popular music critic of this era'
The Times Literary Supplement

'You'd be hard pressed to name a music journalist more adept at tracking and defining the zeitgeist' *The Guardian*

'A writer who manages to transmit the excitement he feels about the music into his prose – a rare gift, and one that makes him incessantly rewarding to read' *The Independent*

'Arguably the most provocative pop music writer of his generation'
The Boston Globe

'A gifted writer, able to do the impossible: put sound into the written word' *The Bookseller*

'Reading Simon Reynolds is like getting in a warm bath'
Jason Schwartzman

'He's peerless at coming at his subjects from fresh and unexplored angles and making hitherto unestablished connections between seemingly disparate elements' *Business Post*

'There has been no more authoritative music critic in Britain over the past thirty years than Simon Reynolds' *Irish Mail on Sunday*

FUTUROMANIA

Electronic Dreams, Desiring Machines,
and Tomorrow's Music Today

SIMON REYNOLDS

WHITE
RABBIT

First published in Great Britain in 2024 by White Rabbit,
an imprint of The Orion Publishing Group Ltd
Carmelite House, 50 Victoria Embankment
London EC4Y 0DZ

An Hachette UK Company

3 5 7 9 10 8 6 4 2

A CIP catalogue record for this book is
available from the British Library.

ISBN (Hardback) 978 1 3996 1833 5
ISBN (eBook) 978 1 3996 1835 9
ISBN (Audio) 978 1 3996 1836 6

Typeset by Born Group
Printed and bound in Great Britain by Clays Ltd, Elcograf S.p.A.

MIX
Paper | Supporting
responsible forestry
FSC® C104740

www.whiterabbitbooks.co.uk
www.orionbooks.co.uk

To Kieran and Eli

CONTENTS

CONTENTS

INTRODUCTION

Out of habit, I identify as 'rock critic', but in truth, by this point I have probably written more words about music made with synths and samples than with guitars. Of course, in a very real sense rock itself is electronic music. From pick-ups to effects pedals, electric guitars are dependent on, well, electricity. And electronically augmented unreality was present right at the primordial dawn of rock 'n' roll in the mid-1950s, with the slapback echo applied to Elvis's vocals during the Sun Sessions – an artificial effect created with the help of tape machines.

Still, as far as most people are concerned, electronic music means something other than rock. The term is reserved for music that sounds overtly synthetic – that has the clean, cold sheen that we customarily associate with the futuristic or the extraterrestrial. Partly this may be down to historical coincidence: both the development of synthesisers and the launch of the space race (the first satellites, the missions to the moon) occurred during the same post-WW2 period. But it's also an inherent quality of electronic tones: although the synth can sound dirty and gnarly, more often than not the sounds it generates tend to evoke either a heavenly perfection that transcends the human plane, or forbidding alien zones of unknowable otherness.

In many ways, this is a trick of imaginative projection. Nothing in electronic music recordings would exist without human decisions at every stage of the process, nor indeed without the human ingenuity and drive that in the first place led to the invention of synths, drum machines, sequencers, MIDI, digital audio workstations, programming software, Auto-Tune etc. Still, the inorganic sheen and mechanistic precision that characterises most electronic music does create a certain feeling of 'untouched by human hand' – an illusion, but a mind's-eye-activating one. For most of its history, electronic music has gone together with ideas of the posthuman and the inhuman.

Although some of the gentler and more beguiling approaches to electronic music are given due attention here (the melodic and emotive strains of eighties synthpop, for instance), mostly my focus and fervour is drawn to those tendencies that involve the new technology's capacity for the artificial and the abstract: synthesised sounds at their most disorienting and unfamiliar, machine-rhythms at their most relentlessly precise and physically testing, digitally sampled collages at their most jagged and jarring. Music that brings the hardest hit of futurity, the most jolting break with tradition.

Where does my intense investment in the idea of 'future music' originate?

It's probably three different things. At the start, there was the young person's patriotism about their own time, the desire to leave behind the past, to be always moving forward and looking to the horizon of tomorrow. That coupled with the young writer's desire to discover and explore new territories, a delight in the rhetoric of prophecy.

Another formative factor would be a kind of ambient modernism still lingering in the culture when I came of thinking age in my late teens and early twenties. Ironically, rather often this was based on the early decades of the twentieth century: the manifestos and rhetoric of movements like Futurism, Dadaism, Surrealism. Again, there's that young man's attraction to prose and pronouncements with a certain temperament and temperature (feverish in the case of Marinetti and crew).

The third factor was a teenage love of science fiction – directly in the form of novels and stories, films and TV, but also indirectly, through S.F.'s interface with cutting-edge music during the postpunk era. Before there was ever a new wave in rock, there had been a new wave of science fiction, with writers like J.G. Ballard and Philip K. Dick exploring 'inner space' and taking all kinds of formal leaps in style and structure that expanded the genre beyond its pulpy 'stories for boys' start. That was the kind of science fiction, set more often in the near-future and on Earth than in far-flung intergalactic scenarios millennia from now, that grabbed my imagination.

Some of the music in this book really is science fiction music, carrying themes of the futuristic or extra-terrestrial that are expressed not just through the sonics but in the lyrical themes, the artist's image and stage performance, and the artwork of records. Other music is vanguard in its sounds and rhythms but doesn't particularly have any truck with overtly futuristic imagery. Sometimes you'll have the paradox where the S.F. elements in the words and presentation are actually retro-futurist: already dated notions of tomorrow's world that hark back to the naive visions of the 1930s or 1950s. Thematically, Kraftwerk evoked the early twentieth century with their allusions to Fritz Lang and the autobahn. But in terms of their sonic architecture, in the 1970s they were already creating the building blocks of eighties and nineties music – electro, synthpop, techno, trance.

Although the technical aspects of electronic music figure in these essays, you won't find here a history of technology or a nitty-gritty delving into the inner workings of specific machines. The approach is actually rather like how I've grappled with guitar rock as a record reviewer. I've written hundreds of thousands of words trying to convey the overloaded textures and hallucinatory tone-colours produced by guitarists, but in truth have only a hazy sense of how those sounds were extricated from the instrument. With both rock and electronica, my interest leans more to the 'what?' and the 'why?' than the 'how?' – the cultural associations carried by the sounds, the sensations and emotions they trigger, the pictures created in a listener's mind. I'm also fascinated by how new mutations in sound open up social spaces and assemble subcultural tribes around them, the ways in which the evolution of music is propelled by individual desires and collective energies.

A word about *Futuromania*'s structure: the pieces are organised chronologically in order of their subject, not when they were written. Because some of the individual profiles move across an artist's career, there is an element of temporal slippage. But the overall direction of the larger arc is heading from back then (the 1970s) towards right now.

A word also about the contents: the pieces are mostly reproduced exactly as originally published, with the occasional error or infelicity fixed. In some cases, though, what appears is the 'director's cut' version. And on a few occasions, snippets of material that usefully provide context have been spliced in from another piece by me on the same subject. The overall selection is designed to avoid overlapping with *Rip It Up and Start Again* and *Energy Flash*, while still telling an overall story that encompasses the postpunk and rave eras covered in those books and resituates them within a larger narrative of electronic popular music.

Hopefully this book will work as a source of illumination but also as advocacy: an enthused listening guide to propel the reader towards adventures and discoveries. There is a lifetime of electronic listening here.

THE SONG FROM THE FUTURE: 'I Feel Love' by Donna Summer, Giorgio Moroder and Pete Bellotte, and the Invention of Electronic Dance Music

There are songs that divide pop history into Before and After. Some are incontestable: 'She Loves You', 'Anarchy in the U.K.', 'Rapper's Delight'. Others are up for debate. Sometimes a song splits pop time in half without that many people noticing its revolutionary implications: think Phuture's 'Acid Trax', the pioneering acid house track of 1987, whose impact fully emerged only later. Other times, the rupture in business-as-usual happens in plain view, at the peak of the pop charts, and the effect is immediate. One such pop-altering single that was felt as a real-time future-shock is 'I Feel Love'.

Released in early July 1977, 'I Feel Love' was a global smash, reaching No. 1 in several countries (including the UK, where its reign at the top lasted a full month) and rising to No. 6 in America. But its impact reached far beyond the disco scene in which singer Donna Summer and her producers Giorgio Moroder and Pete Bellotte were already well established. Postpunk and new wave groups admired and appropriated its innovative sound, the maniacal precision of its grid-like groove

5

of sequenced synth pulses. Even now, long after discophobia has been disgraced and rockism defeated, there's still a mischievous frisson to staking the claim that 'I Feel Love' was far more important than other epochal singles of 1977 such as 'God Save the Queen', 'Sheena Is a Punk Rocker' or 'Complete Control'. But really, it's a simple statement of fact: if any one song can be pinpointed as where the eighties began, it's 'I Feel Love'.

Within club culture, 'I Feel Love' pointed the way forward and blazed the path for genres such as Hi-NRG, Italo, house, techno and trance. All the residual elements in disco – the aspects that connected it to pop tradition, show tunes, orchestrated soul, funk – were purged in favour of brutal futurism: mechanistic repetition, icy electronics, a blank-eyed fixated feel of posthuman propulsion.

'"I Feel Love" stripped out the flowery, pretty aspects of disco and really gave it a streamlined drive,' says Vince Aletti, the first American critic to take disco seriously. In the club music column he wrote for *Record World* at the time, Aletti compared 'I Feel Love' to 'Trans-Europe Express/Metal on Metal' by Kraftwerk, another prophetic piece of electronic trance-dance that convulsed crowds in the more adventurous clubs.

The reverberations of 'I Feel Love' reached far beyond the disco floor, though. Then unknown but destined to be synth pop stars in the eighties, the Human League completely switched their direction after hearing the song. Blondie, equally enamoured, became one of the first punk-associated groups to embrace disco. Brian Eno famously rushed into the Berlin recording studio where he and David Bowie were working on creating new futures for music, waving a copy of 'I Feel Love'. 'This is it, look no further,' Eno declared breathlessly. 'This single is going to change the sound of club music for the next fifteen years.'

In the wake of 'I Feel Love', Giorgio Moroder became a name producer, the disco equivalent of Phil Spector. He even appeared on the cover of Britain's leading rock magazine, *New Musical Express*. The Moroder hit factory was widely considered the Motown of the late 1970s, with Donna Summer as its Diana Ross.

Summer and Moroder, with his iconic black moustache, were the public faces of the operation. But inside his Munich-based Musicland studio, Moroder led a team of brilliant musicians and technicians. Most significant of these was Pete Bellotte, Moroder's silent partner – silent in the sense that he never did interviews and shied from the limelight. But Bellotte played a crucial role as catalyst of song-concepts as well as musical and production ideas: it was he who had originally spotted Summer's vocal gifts. The crack squad also included man-machine super-drummer Keith Forsey; a series of keyboard players including Þórir Baldursson, Sylvester Levay and Harold Faltermeyer; the brilliant engineer Jürgen Koppers; and a slightly mysterious figure known as Robbie Wedel, whose occult command of the inner workings of the Moog made a crucial contribution to the construction of 'I Feel Love'.

In a business fuelled by ego, Moroder has always been unusually gracious and generous when it comes to acknowledging the collective nature of the magic that typically still gets attributed to him alone. Forsey recalls Moroder as being 'good at delegating, at finding talents that were compatible'. But he also stresses that Moroder called the shots. He 'was the leader, and you had to follow. Giorgio was boss.'

Step into Moroder's apartment in Los Angeles's upscale Westwood neighbourhood, and the scene screams 'Mr. Music'. There's a white grand piano, a special shelf for his Grammys and Oscars, and a wall laden with gold discs. Profuse with glass ornaments, the living room's predominantly white decor floats somewhere between *Scarface* (a movie Moroder

7

soundtracked, as it happens) and the sleek interiors of *10*, that seventies period piece in which Dudley Moore plays an LA-based songwriter undergoing a midlife crisis. In a corner there's a bronze Buddha draped in chiffon scarves, while an entire wall is mostly taken up with a gigantic and slightly garish painting of Elizabeth Taylor.

Twinkly and avuncular, Moroder still has his famous moustache, although it's now Santa Claus white. At seventy-seven, his memory is not what it used to be: he can recall some patches of history with crystalline clarity, but others – like the 1978 album *Once upon a Time*, the apex of the Summer–Moroder–Bellotte symbiosis, in my opinion – are totally blank.

Moroder grew up in the Alpine valleys of South Tyrol, a region of northernmost Italy that for five centuries was part of Austria until it passed into Italian control after the First World War. His native tongue is the regional Ladin language, although he is fluent in German and Italian. 'In my hometown Urtijëi, we would speak three languages during any day, depending on whoever you're talking with. But with my brothers, I would still to this day speak Ladino.'

In his youth, Moroder performed live in clubs, then started releasing and producing records from the mid-sixties onwards, scoring hits in a few European countries with bubblegum singles like 'Moody Trudy' and 'Looky Looky'. In the early seventies he partnered with Pete Bellotte, a British expatriate who'd spent much of the sixties clawing unsuccessfully for a commercial breakthrough as guitarist in the band Linda Laine and the Sinners while earning a solid living playing rough nightclubs in Germany. Although Moroder and Bellotte's bouncy, synth-laced ditty 'Son of My Father' became a smash in Europe when covered by Chicory Tip in 1972, there was little to indicate that the pair would become the presiding pop geniuses of the late seventies.

8

Along the way, Bellotte stumbled on the extraordinary voice of a black American singer who'd also moved to central Europe and stayed for the work opportunities. Boston-born LaDonna Gaines had graduated from fronting the rock group Crow in her hometown to musical theatre work in Europe as part of the cast of *Hair*, gigs at the Vienna Folk Opera in productions of *Porgy and Bess* and *Show Boat*, and studio work as a session singer. After marrying an Austrian actor, she took his name: Sommer. When her vocal on a Bellotte song demo unexpectedly led to record industry interest, she anglicised her married name to Summer and formed a three-way musical partnership with Moroder and Bellotte.

The team achieved modest success in Europe with singles and a debut Summer album, but the real breakthrough came with the disco-erotica epic 'Love to Love You Baby', which reached No. 2 in Billboard, No. 4 in the UK, and went Top 20 in thirteen other nations in 1976. Summer's gasps and groans had journalists nicknaming her 'the Black Panter' and 'the Linda Lovelace of pop' (after the star of the smash-hit porno movie *Deep Throat*). Crowning Summer the queen of 'Sex Rock', *Time* magazine counted no fewer than twenty-two simulated orgasms across the record's almost seventeen-minute-long span. Neil Bogart, boss of the legendary disco label Casablanca, had asked Moroder to extend the song to a full album side because – the story goes – he wished to soundtrack an orgy. Bogart enthused about the first side of the album *Love to Love You Baby* as 'a beautiful, great balling record' – in other words, a record to fuck to. He told people to 'take Donna home and make love to her – the album, that is' – and encouraged radio stations to play the track at midnight as a catalyst for home-listener romance.

Huge as it was, 'Love to Love You Baby' seemed like a sexed-up novelty single, something exacerbated by the sultry schlock of Summer's live performances of this era: she'd often be carried on stage by two men clad in loincloths, while backing-dancer couples simulated sex in ever-changing positions. Nor did the other songs on Summer's first three disco albums (lush, luxuriant, deftly executed but quite conventional in sound) presage any kind of giant musical leap forward from Moroder and Bellotte.

There was a clue to a secret experimental streak, though: a Moroder solo album quietly released in 1975 to almost zero attention. *Einzelgänger* (the title is roughly equivalent to 'lone wolf') teems with pitter-pattering drum machine beats and unsettling processed vocal-stutters that recall the ethereal whimsy of the three records Kraftwerk made before their pop move *Autobahn*.

But it's possible that Moroder's latent interest in electronic music might never have blossomed so spectacularly with 'I Feel Love' if not for the conceptual spark that came from Bellotte. The Englishman was in charge of lyrics, and his passion for literature drove him to organise Summer's early records around big themes. One of those concepts was an album in which each song stylistically corresponded to a different decade of the twentieth century. Almost as an afterthought, Bellotte and Moroder decided to end the album, titled *I Remember Yesterday*, with a song that represented the future: 'I Feel Love'.

Gaunt and sinewy, with long swept-back grey hair and light stubble, Pete Bellotte exudes a wry, semi-detached air sitting in the top-floor café of a London bookstore, as if faintly bemused by the abiding interest in the Moroder–Summer era. At the same time, the seventy-three-year-old self-described recluse is clearly proud of the achievements in which he played an indispensable role. This interview is a vanishingly rare occurrence: back in the day, Bellotte did no press at all, and there appear to be only a few photographs of him from that era, in which he sports an almost identical moustache to Moroder's.

10

Bellotte's love affair with the written word started at age nine, when his uncle gave him a copy of Charles Dickens's *A Christmas Carol*. By eleven, he'd read everything Dickens had written. Unlikely as it seems, Bellotte's bookworm tendency fed directly into Donna Summer's discography. *A Love Trilogy*, the 1976 follow-up to *Love to Love You Baby*, got its structure because he'd just read British fantasy writer Mervyn Peake's *Gormenghast* trilogy. *Four Seasons of Love*, the next album, was similarly shaped by Bellotte's reading of Lawrence Durrell's *Alexandria Quartet*, a tetralogy of novels looking at the same sequence of events from different perspectives.

Then, in 1977, came *I Remember Yesterday*. 'Originally it was going to be called *A Dance to the Music of Time*, because I'd just read Anthony Powell's twelve-volume cycle of the same name,' Bellotte explains. 'Those novels go through a whole period of British history, and from that I got the concept of the album: each song would relate to a different decade.' So the title track and opening number featured the swinging horns of a 1940s dance-band. 'Love's Unkind' jumped to the early-sixties girl-group era. Motown pastiche 'Back in Love Again' was a lovely lost cousin to the Supremes' 'Baby Love'. The seventies were represented by the Labelle-like funk of 'Black Lady' and the bang-up-to-date disco of 'Take Me', featuring unfeminist lyrics but gorgeous singing from Summer, a macho-man backing vocal that fills the mind's eye with chest-hair and gold chains, and a deliciously nubile groove of bouncy bass and chattering Clavinets.

The Anthony Powell-inspired concept for *I Remember Yesterday* tapped into disco's retro leanings as manifested by groups like Dr Buzzard's Original Savannah Band and the Pointer Sisters, whose early image and sound were steeped in forties nostalgia. But in a beautiful irony, the most famous track on this concept album proved to be 'I Feel Love', the reverse of retro.

11

For Moroder and Bellotte, the idea of a song and a sound from tomorrow meant synthesisers and machine-rhythm. So they called on a fellow whose services they'd used sporadically before: Robbie Wedel, an electronics wizard who assisted the Munich-based composer Eberhard Schoener with the operation of the Moog that the latter had bought. Wedel turned up, recalls Bellotte, with 'three big units, roughly two and half feet by two feet, full of oscillators and voltage controls, the wires hanging out like one of the old telephone exchanges. And he brought a fourth box too, which was the arpeggiator and trigger for the machine.'

The three men set to building the rhythm track. 'It was done in reverse,' says Moroder, referring to how he broke with his usual approach of writing a song first on a keyboard, then arranging in the studio. 'Donna came in later, and we composed the melody that would fit in. And "I Feel Love" is a difficult song to sing.'

While Moroder and Bellotte concentrated on building the tune's classic locomotive bassline, they didn't notice that Wedel had asked engineer Jürgen Koppers to lay down 'a reference pulse' or, as Moroder now calls it, the Click. 'We've laid the first track down, and Robbie says, "Would you like to synch the next track to this?" And we don't know what he means,' recalls Bellotte. 'So Robbie explained that because of the signal he'd put on track sixteen of the tape, each part of the tune created on the Moog will link up to exactly the same tempo. And the timing was exactly spot on. Robbie had worked out this methodology himself – it wasn't something the machine's inventor, Bob Moog, knew about. It was through Robbie that we managed to get the track – he's the reason why when you hear "I Feel Love" today, those sounds in there are so solid and fantastic.'

Session musicians drilled by hard taskmaster producers and seasoned bands led by disciplinarians like James Brown had often aspired to this level of unerring superhuman tightness; sometimes they'd got real close. But with the help of a machine and a German engineer, Moroder and Bellotte established a new paradigm for pop: a sound of such metronomic relentlessness it really did feel like it came from the future.

Another reason why 'I Feel Love' pummels along so propulsively is the bright idea that emerged somewhere in the process, probably from Wedel or Koppers, of putting a delay on the bassline: this created a strobing flicker effect, intensified by the equally clever trick of putting the original bass-signal through the left speaker channel and the minutely delayed pulse through the right speaker. The whole track seems to shimmer convulsively, like controlled and channelled epilepsy. Moroder recalls that the effect created problems in big clubs where the stereo separation was wide, because 'if you were dancing next to the left speaker, the groove emphasis was on the "up" and the feel was off'. But that glitch doesn't appear to have diminished the track's absolute dominion over disco dancefloors then and to this day.

Wedel also showed Moroder and Bellotte how to turn Moog noise into percussion by clipping it. 'You take white noise,' says Moroder, imitating the hissing sound. 'And you put it into an envelope, so it sounds like a hi-hat, or a snare.'

The only problem was that despite its famously fat, full sound, the Moog couldn't deliver the right punch for the kick drum and so, compromising their all-electronic conception for 'I Feel Love', Moroder and Bellotte were forced to call on the human, hands-on services of Keith Forsey. A veteran drummer who'd played with the chaotic acid-rock collective Amon Düül II before drifting into session work (and who would later achieve fame and fortune producing Billy Idol's eighties MTV smashes and writing Simple Minds' only US No. 1 'Don't You Forget about Me'), Forsey was renowned for his incredibly precise timekeeping. 'I was never one of those "chops" players,' Forsey says, meaning that he didn't go in for drum solos or flashy fills, but concentrated on ultra-taut groove maintenance.

Forsey recalls 'I Feel Love' as the start of a period in which Moroder recorded each drum in the kit individually for complete separation of sound: this 'totally clean sound, no bleed through, no overheads, no room sound' had more impact on the dancefloor. For Forsey, it was rather an unnatural, counterintuitive procedure, frustrating the natural way of playing. 'Your body has to dance if you want the people to dance,' he says. Forsey would find himself playing the kick, or the snare 'for fifteen minutes solid – the other guys would leave the studio booth and go off to make a cup of tea, leaving me to it'. Sometimes he'd put a phone book on the hi-hat so he could tap it silently, to preserve some element of groove and feel in his otherwise disembodied and deconstructed performance.

The rhythmic chassis of 'I Feel Love' now complete, it was time for the rider of the runaway train to play her part. Moroder and Bellotte both pay tribute to Summer's intuitive feeling for what a song required. A typical session, Bellotte recalls, involved the vivacious singer coming in and talking for several hours – she loved to gossip, joke, talk about what was going on in her life – before realising that time had flown and she had to dash off. She would then lay down her vocal in just one or two takes. Her variegated work experience – rock, gospel, musical theatre, light opera – gave her a wide range of modes to draw on, and 'she loved doing funny voices', recalls Bellotte. 'I've sung gospel and Broadway all my life and you have to have a belting voice for that,' Summer told *Rolling Stone* in 1978. 'They categorize me as a black act, which is not the truth. I'm not even a soul singer. I'm more a pop singer.'

For 'I Feel Love', Summer pushed beyond the softcore of 'Love to Love You Baby' with a vocal that sounds more unearthly than earthy. She uses what's known as a 'head voice', breathy and angelic, as opposed to the husky 'chest voice' you associate with grainy, groin-y R&B. The 'love' in 'I Feel Love' is closer to an out-of-body experience than hot between-the-sheets action. As Vince Aletti puts it, 'It's like she's coming from some other place.'

The song's feeling of suspension from time, of being lost in a loop of ecstasy or reverie, also comes from the incredibly simple and short lyric, in which phrases like 'heaven knows' or 'fallin' free' are each repeated five times. The hovering melodic plateau of the verse shifts to a gently ascending chorus of the title phrase – itself an odd utterance, since 'I feel love' is not really something you'd find yourself saying in any real-world amorous situation. Intransitive and open-ended, it's suggestive of a rhapsodic state of being in love with love.

Which is pretty much where Summer's head and heart were when the words were written. As Bellotte recalls, 'I Feel Love' was 'the first time Donna wanted to be involved in a lyric. She was in LA, so I'd gone round to her house one evening, and she answered the doorbell with a phone in her hand. She told me she was on the phone to New York, and I should come in, help myself to coffee, she'd be down in a second. I sat there with my notebook ready to write the lyric, and half an hour later, she came downstairs and said, "Won't be long!" So I waited and waited, and it went on for about an hour and half.' Finally, around 11 p.m., Summer finished her phone call, which had been to her astrologer.

Summer was a firm believer in the oracular power of horo-scopes and had once cancelled a private jet chartered by her manager because of a last-minute warning from her astrologer that she shouldn't fly. Forsey remembers sessions where he would be informed that 'Donna isn't coming to the studio today, her astrologer told her not to'. The reason for that night's intensive phone consultation was that she had just met Bruce Sudano, the guitarist and singer in Brooklyn Dreams, an R&B outfit who would later work as her backing group.

'Donna had fallen for Bruce, deeply,' recalls Bellotte. Summer and her astrologer had been examining her and Sudano's star signs, and comparing those alignments with the sign of her current – and, as it turned out, literally star-crossed – lover, Peter Mühldorfer, an Austrian. 'When she came downstairs, Donna announced that her astrologer had told her "This is the man." That was the night "I Feel Love" was written: when she'd changed her whole life. And it was the best thing that ever happened to her, she and Bruce were together for the rest of her life.' (Summer died in May 2012.) 'So when Donna flew back to Munich to record the vocal, that was the feeling she gave the song.'

That real-life, slightly kooky and very seventies story brings a human dimension to the genesis of this technologically turbo-charged track. But in other respects, Summer's performance has a woman-machine quality that looks ahead to the looped diva samples of house and rave music (tracks like Orbital's 'Halcyon', for instance, with its blissed spirals of trilling upper-octave feminine vocals), while also prophesying twenty-first-century fembots like Kylie and Britney. Summer's live performances of 'I Feel Love' sometimes played up this android aspect: *Rolling Stone*'s Mikal Gilmore described her dancing 'in angular, jerky motions', her face 'a dazed, mechanical mask'.

Many rock fans and critics seemed to believe that the electronic Eurodisco pioneered by Moroder and his team was actually robot music that literally played itself. Interviewed by *NME* in 1978, Moroder mocked the notion that the machines were in charge. 'Even if you use synthesisers and sequencers and drum machines, you have to set them up, to choose exactly what you are going to make them do. It is nonsense to

16

say that we make all our music automatically.' Sometimes it was easier to get the sound you were looking for with the new technology, he added, 'but as often as not it is at least ten times more difficult to get a good synthesiser sound than on an acoustic instrument'. On the cover of his 1979 solo album $E=mc^2$, Moroder appears with his white, rolled-up-sleeves jacket open to reveal a computer circuit board on his chest, as if having a little fun with the idea of electro-disco as machine-made, while also reinforcing the album's boast to be the first fully digital recording.

Still, there's no denying that it was precisely the *precision* of 'I Feel Love' that made it so stark and startling to listeners in 1977. Moroder and his team had assimilated the logic immanent within black dance music (think James Brown's 'Sex Machine') and German motorik rock (think Neu! and Kraftwerk), then taken it to the next level of clockwork exactitude. Human ingenuity and creativity drove the decisions at every step, but to listeners it sounded like the machines had taken over: a thrilling breakthrough for some, a disturbing development for others.

Revolutionary records like 'I Feel Love' carry a retrospective aura of inevitability, like they were ordained to be. And given the way technology was going, a track along the lines of 'I Feel Love' would have been made by somebody around that time. But, as we've seen, the precise shape the song took has an element of circumstance and accident: the convergence of Moroder's interest in synths with Bellotte's literary obsessions and Summer's heightened emotional state. The stars aligned and History happened.

Ironies abound in this tale. The first is that none of its creators thought much of 'I Feel Love'. Intended as an ordinary album track, the primary recording process for the song took just three hours. (The mixing took much longer.) 'It didn't

mean anything to us, in terms of us thinking we'd done anything special,' recalls Bellotte.

It was Casablanca boss Neil Bogart – an archetypal music-
biz 'record man', in so far as he was a non-musician but had
a matchless instinct for which songs had commercial potential
– who insisted that 'I Feel Love' should be released as a single.
In an echo of his intervention with 'Love to Love You Baby',
Bogart pinpointed three crucial edits that would extend the
song's length and expand its trippy, out-of-time feeling.

The other great irony of 'I Feel Love' is that its makers not
only failed to see the import of what they'd created, they didn't
really see its impact either. Moroder and Bellotte hardly ever
went to discotheques, so they didn't witness the frenzy it incited
on dancefloors across the world, the feeling of a sudden leap into
tomorrow. 'Neither Giorgio nor I can dance,' laughs Bellotte.
When asked how he had such a feel for dance music if he never
danced, Moroder says, 'I would just tap my feet in the studio.'

According to Bellotte, the pair were just too busy for clubbing.
In their heyday as hit-makers, they lived extremely regular
lives: starting work in the studio at around 10 a.m., they finished
promptly at six, and repaired to one or other of the finest restau-
rants in Los Angeles. (By mid-1978, the operation had moved from
Munich to the entertainment capital of the world.) Fine dining
was their solitary vice: although photos exist of Moroder wearing
a gold razor-blade necklace of the 'chopping out lines' type nestling
amid his chest hair, neither partner participated in the disco era's
rampant hedonism. Bellotte says they didn't smoke, drink or take
drugs. Moroder says he was in bed by the time fans of the music
were dervish-whirling to the sounds they'd made.

The impact of 'I Feel Love' on the sound of disco was immediate
and immense. A spate of electronic dance hits swiftly followed:
Space's 'Magic Fly', Dee D. Jackson's 'Automatic Lover',

Cerrone's 'Supernature'. The song, says Moroder, received a particularly strong response from the gay community. 'Even now, millions of gay people love Donna and some say, "I was liberated by that song." It is a hymn.'

The song's gay-anthem status was enshrined in 1985, when Bronski Beat covered 'I Feel Love' in a medley with 'Love to Love You Baby' and sixties melodrama pop hit 'Johnny Remember Me'. Frontman Jimmy Somerville's stratosphere-shattering falsetto entwined with the high camp of guest vocalist Marc Almond from Soft Cell, and the video was impishly homoerotic. 'Jimmy told me he became a singer *because* of "I Feel Love",' says Moroder. 'He heard that "oooh"' – he imitates Summer's helium-high soprano – 'and he said, "That's my career!"'

Another gay musician propelled on his journey by 'I Feel Love' was the producer Patrick Cowley. Described as the 'American Giorgio Moroder' – a tag that certainly fits his sound if not his mainstream impact – Cowley's work has been rediscovered in recent years by the hipster archival industry, with reissues of his Moog-rippling porno soundtracks. But his renown at the time came as a pioneer of Hi-NRG, the gay-club sound that would dominate the eighties and reach the mainstream with hits like Dead or Alive's 'You Spin Me Round'. Based out of San Francisco, Cowley supplied synths, sequencing and special effects for hits like 'You Make Me Feel (Mighty Real)' by trans diva Sylvester, co-founded the 'masculine music' label Megatone, and scored solo on the dancefloor with anthems like 'Menergy'. But his disco career actually started in 1978 with an unsanctioned fifteen-minute-long remix of 'I Feel Love' that circulated furtively on acetate among select favoured DJs on the gay scene. An inspired expansion, punctuated by hallucinatory breakdowns of swaggeringly inventive Moog-play and percussive delirium, Cowley's 'I Feel Love

Megamix' almost eclipses the original. Finally released officially in 1982, it made the UK Top 30.

By that point Moroder and company's innovations under-pinned large swathes of contemporary pop music in the UK and Europe. For some, hearing 'I Feel Love' was a life-changer. Phil Oakey told me that when Martyn Ware came round to his Sheffield flat in 1977 to recruit him into The Future – the group that became the Human League – Ware brandished copies of 'I Feel Love' and 'Trans-Europe Express' and announced, 'We can do this.' The group instantly shifted from its early Tangerine Dream-like abstraction towards poppy and boppy accessibility, as heard on the manifesto-like song 'Dance Like a Star', which bears more than a passing resemblance to 'I Feel Love'. Eight years later, and by then a pop star, Oakey would honour the debt by teaming up with Moroder for the hit single 'Together in Electric Dreams'.

Another outfit who had a Damascene conversion to elec-tronic disco was glam-era oddballs Sparks, who hooked up with Moroder for 1979's brilliant *No. 1 in Heaven* album and its UK hit singles 'No. 1 Song in Heaven' and 'Beat the Clock'. Originally from Los Angeles, the Anglophile brothers Ron and Russell Mael had become pop sensations in the UK in 1974, but by the time punk kicked off they'd lost their way. Looking for an aesthetic reboot, Sparks were the first established rock band to embrace disco at album length, as opposed to the one-off disco-influenced hits made by bands like the Rolling Stones. In interviews, Ron and Russell invented anti-rockism, loudly dismissing guitars as passé and deriding the very concept of 'the band' as exhausted. They burbled about the thrillingly modern impersonality of the Moroder–Summer sound, in particular 'I Feel Love' and its 'combination of the human voice and this really *cold* thing behind it'. Electronic disco, Sparks proclaimed, was the true new wave, whereas

20

most actual skinny-tie new wavers were merely retreading the sixties.

The Maels probably had the likes of Blondie in mind when they made that swipe. But Blondie themselves were converts to the new sound. Talking to *NME* in early 1978, Debbie Harry praised Moroder's sound as 'the kind of stuff I want to do' and the group covered 'I Feel Love' at a benefit concert later that spring. 'Heart of Glass' was their slinky first stab at disco, followed by tracks like 'Atomic' and 'Rapture', with its Summer-like swirl of a chorus. But 'Call Me', the Blondie track that Moroder actually produced, was brashly rocking in the Pat Benatar style.

Alongside obviously indebted postpunk and synthpop groups like New Order, Visage and Eurhythmics, the aftershocks of 'I Feel Love' reached into all kinds of odd corners. Progressive jazz-rock veterans Soft Machine, of all people, released the Moroder-style single 'Soft Space' in 1978. Apocalyptic goth doom-mongers Killing Joke underpinned several of their singles with clinical Eurodisco pulse-work. And while they were later synonymous with stadium-scale bluster, early on Simple Minds fused cinematic post-Bowie art-rock with hypnotic sequenced synth patterns on 'I Travel' and their Euro-infatuated lost masterpiece *Empires and Dance*.

Moroder took the 'I Feel Love' template further with Sparks and with his Academy Award-winning score *Midnight Express*, which produced the club hit 'Chase'. But surprisingly, he cut barely half a dozen tracks in the fully electronic vein with Donna Summer. *Once upon a Time* (1978) – another themed album, with a narrative updating the Cinderella story to the modern metropolis – dedicated the second of its four sides to synths. 'Now I Need You' and 'Working the Midnight Shift', the first two panels in a seamless side-long triptych, ripple with a serenely celestial beauty rivalled only by Kraftwerk's 'Neon

21

Lights'. Also a double album, 1979's *Bad Girls* shunted the synth-tunes to side four, frontloading the album with ballsy raunch and balladsy romance. But 'Our Love', 'Lucky' and the fabulous 'Sunset People' (an inexplicable failure as a single) made for a fine swan-song finale for the electronic style that made Summer famous and turned Moroder into an in-demand soundtrack composer.

Summer was eager to transcend the disco category, though, and *Bad Girls*' rock moves shrewdly repositioned her as a 'credible' artist in America. For the first time she received critical plaudits from rock journalists who'd previously belittled Eurodisco with descriptions like 'sanitized, simplified, mechanized R&B'. Now they were placated by Summer taking a more active role in the songwriting and by crossover ploys like the screeching solo from LA axeman-about-town Jeff Baxter that punctuated 'Hot Stuff', which reached No. 1 and remains Summer's biggest hit by far in the US.

'Donna Summer Has Begun to Win Respect' announced a 1979 *New York Times* headline. Respect ain't much use, though, when the magic vanishes. Breaking with the disco-tarnished Casablanca and signing to Geffen, Summer strove to become a radio-format-crossing all-rounder, resulting in a series of increasingly barren albums: the confused *The Wanderer*; one last Moroder/Bellotte-produced album, *I'm a Rainbow*, that Geffen suppressed and that finally saw release in 1996; and the dried-up gulch that was 1982's *Donna Summer*, a fraught and largely fruitless collaboration with Quincy Jones. In Britain, where popular taste preferred her clad in glistening synthetics, that self-titled album produced an unlikely hit with her last great single, a cover of 'State of Independence' by Yes-man Jon Anderson and Vangelis. With *Chariots of Fire* and *Blade Runner*, the latter was starting to eclipse Moroder in the Hollywood electronic-score soundtrack stakes.

In the early eighties, Moroder spent three years on his pet project: restoring Fritz Lang's 1927 futuristic dystopia *Metropolis* and finding lost footage, only to spoil the silent classic with colourisation and a score that recruited the unsuitable talents of Bonnie Tyler, Freddie Mercury and Loverboy. After the hostile reception that greeted the movie in 1984, he drifted away from music for many years, putting his energy and resources into quixotic ventures like the Cizeta-Moroder luxury sports car and a scheme to build a pyramid in Dubai. Meanwhile Bellotte had moved back to England, where he set up his own recording studio, but devoted most of his energy to parenting and to his literary interests: an unfinished biography of Mervyn Peake, a book of his own stories titled *The Unround Circle* and a CD of prose-poem 'rhythm rhymes', *The Noisy Voice of the Waterfall*.

But then – just like a classic-era disco album – came the reprise.

Moroder got a call from Daft Punk, then working on what would become their 2013 album *Random Access Memories*, a perverse vision-quest attempt to time-travel back to the seventies, the lost golden age when dance music involved shit-hot musicianship and heroic struggles to get results out of electronic technology crude and cumbersome by the standards of the digital today. Rather than collaborate with Moroder musically, though, Thomas Bangalter and Guy-Manuel de Homem-Christo had something more unusual in mind. They interviewed Moroder for a couple of hours, discussing the length and breadth of his career, and then isolated two short extracts: a vignette from his very early days as a struggling performer, and a potted history of the making of 'I Feel Love'. Sandwiching these soundbites between wedges of synth-burble modelled on the classic Munich sound, the result was 'Giorgio by Moroder': a poignant paean to the lost future that inevitably couldn't be sonically futuristic itself (indeed the Eurodisco

23

pastiche fashioned by Daft Punk is distinctly weak sauce). Instead, the song is conceptually innovative, inventing a new genre: memoir-dance.

'One day I'm going to type out the whole of that interview, all two hours, and that'll be my autobiography,' Moroder says, joking but half-serious. But rather than commemorate his past glories, what the collaboration with Daft Punk really did was restart his life as a producer. Since *Random Access Memories* came out, he's released his first solo album in twenty-three years, 2015's *Déjà vu*, teeming with collaborations with contemporary pop stars like Sia and Charli XCX. The critical response was mixed, the commercial performance lacklustre compared to his heyday (although the Britney-fronted cover of 'Tom's Diner' hit the Top 20 in Argentina and Lebanon). But Moroder is now an in-demand DJ: when we speak at his Westwood apartment, he's just about to head off to play a string of dates.

'They pay for your flights, and the money is *great*,' Moroder enthuses. In his set, he always plays 'I Feel Love' – a tweaked version in which he's finally fixed the left speaker/right speaker fluctuation in the bass-pulse that always bothered him. DJing is something that he never did at the time, and as a result – in a final irony – this means that nowadays he spends far more time in the clubs, up way past his customary bedtime, than he ever did back in the day. For the first time really, Moroder also gets to feel the love of his audience – three generations of them now – in the flesh.

Pitchfork, 2017

HOW KRAFTWERK CREATED POP'S FUTURE: A Florian-Centric Story

It has become a cliché to compare Kraftwerk to The Beatles, but if anything, their impact has been wider and more enduring. During their two decades of prime creativity, Kraftwerk intersected with and influenced a staggering array of genres and phases: progressive rock, glam, Krautrock, disco, postpunk, synthpop, industrial, hip hop, techno, trance. Artists in their debt are likewise bizarrely diverse, ranging from Human League to Spacemen 3, New Order to Stereolab, Prince to Daft Punk, Afrika Bambaataa to Big Black.

Florian Schneider, who died yesterday at the age of seventy-three, was the co-founder of Kraftwerk. For over thirty years, he produced the group's albums with fellow founder Ralf Hutter, contributed to the writing of songs and lyrics, played a number of instruments, conceived concepts and devised techniques. But in a funny way, one of Schneider's most significant contributions was his person. Schneider's aquiline features and smart attire manifested Kraftwerk's utter Europeanness. His aura of formality was the seed out of which grew the group's collective image of uniformity and discipline. Establishing distance between themselves and America, Kraftwerk opened up a future for pop that left rock 'n' roll far behind.

25

Kraftwerk operated within pop, yet remained somehow apart and above. When, in 1975, Lester Bangs jocularly enquired what kind of groupies Kraftwerk got, Schneider sternly snapped: 'None. There is no such thing.' His and Hutter's idea of rock star excess was buying lots of bicycles and taking up long-distance cycling (sometimes racing between cities on their tours). Their addiction to this virtuous vice inspired the sinewy 1983 single 'Tour de France'.

Drive and discipline are probably something Schneider absorbed from his upbringing. His father, Paul Schneider-Esleben, was a respected architect whose functional buildings and airport redesigns took their bearings from the 'New Objectivity' school of the 1920s. The parallel with Kraftwerk's balance of severity and grandeur is striking. It's almost as if Schneider imbibed minimalism from the ambient attitudes that surrounded him as a child.

It took Kraftwerk a while to arrive at the stark, stripped-down sound and uniform group image of their classic late-seventies albums *Trans-Europe Express* and *The Man-Machine*. They started, in the final years of the 1960s, as post-psychedelic progressives with long hair to match. In 1968, Hutter and Schneider met at the Academy of Arts in Remscheid, near Düsseldorf, where they studied piano and flute respectively. Sharing an interest in improvisation and avant-garde electronics, as well as a fondness for The Velvet Underground, The Doors and the multimedia provocations of Fluxus, they joined with three other musicians and recorded the album *Tone Float* under the name Organisation. While the name points ahead to their technocratic image to come, the music was freeform in typically late-sixties style. Hutter and Schneider developed a strong relationship with *Tone Float* producer Conny Plank, which continued when they broke away to form Kraftwerk. They also worked for a while with guitarist

Michael Rother and drummer Klaus Dinger, who would go on to become Neu!

At a time when nearly all European bands had English names and sang English lyrics, the choice of Kraftwerk as a name was a statement. For many years, Hutter and Schneider used German song titles. They would also play with stereo-types of a German genius for order and efficiency, starting with the name 'Kraftwerk' itself, which means power plant. Schneider talked in interviews about how the clipped precision of their music had a relationship with the national character and 'the feeling of our language . . . Our method of speaking is interrupted, hard-edged . . . a lot of consonants and noises.'

In the early days, though, Kraftwerk's music neither referenced nor evoked the robotic. Its rhapsodic lyricism owed more to Schubert, and Beethoven's 'Pastoral' Symphony than to the Bauhaus or Fritz Lang. Schneider's flute was prominent in the instrumental palette. (He also contributed keyboards, violin, slide guitar, percussion, effects, xylophone.) Listening to the group's first three albums – *Kraftwerk*, *Kraftwerk 2*, *Ralf und Florian* – and knowing how their sound would evolve, it's possible to hear the flute as a kind of proto-synthesiser. The Elysian serenity of the billowing and entwining patterns on 'Tongebirge' and 'Heimatklänge' look ahead to Eno's ambient and nineties IDM like Seefeel and Aphex Twin. 'Ruckzuck', conversely, combines overblown rasping texture and percussive-propulsive riffs to sound almost like a sequencer.

A small contingent of contrarian aficionados regard the three 1970–73 albums as the best stuff Kraftwerk ever did. Certainly their fascinating and beguiling mixture of *musique concrète* soundscapes, Steve Reich-like systems music, and idyllic ambi-ence is ripe for rediscovery. Bootleg versions circulated on CD in the nineties but an official reissue never happened. Schnei-der himself dismissed their interest value as 'archaeology'.

27

Kraftwerk might justifiably feel that the story really begins with *Autobahn*. That is the point at which they went from a Krautrock curio to a world-historical force, when the single edit of the twenty-four-minute title track became an international hit in 1975. Even then, though, twinkling guitar and wafting flute feature alongside synth pulses and drum machine. 'Autobahn' offers a pastoral vision of the motorway, entranced as much by the verdant landscape rolling by as the tarmac and traffic. The metronomic putter of the rhythm is steady and serene, a controlled cruise that couldn't be further from Steppenwolf's highway anthem 'Born to Be Wild'. Where most rock imagines the motorised vehicle as an extension of phallic power, Kraftwerk were interested in the Zen aspects of driving, a symbiotic merger of man and machine. In 1975, Schneider told *Melody Maker* the trance state created by 'Autobahn' was nothing to do with a druggy speed-rush but 'very clear-minded. It is like when you are driving a car, you can drive automatically without being consciously aware of what you are doing.'

A hit single in Britain, the US and eight other countries, 'Autobahn' also won Kraftwerk a famous fan. David Bowie became a vocal supporter, turning on his own audience by playing the album before concerts on his *Station to Station* tour and gushing to magazines like *Playboy* about how 'my favorite group is a German band called Kraftwerk – it plays noise music to "increase productivity"'. Bowie would actually credit *Autobahn* with redirecting his cultural focus away from America and R&B towards Europe and electronic music, ultimately causing him to move to Berlin, where he would make the most adventurous music of his life and produce two career-changing albums for Iggy Pop, *The Idiot* and *Lust for Life*.

Bowie admired the way that Kraftwerk avoided 'stereotypical American chord sequences'. He also loved their un-rock 'n' roll image – something that started with Schneider and then spread to the entire group. In their early days, Kraftwerk had resembled other Krautrock groups in their scruffy appearance and emphasis on musicianship rather than showmanship. That began to change with the cover of *Ralf und Florian*. Hutter still sports shoulder-length lank hair, an open-neck check shirt and chemistry-teacher glasses, but Schneider is dapper in an understated and out-of-time style: neatly groomed short hair, tie and suit. This presaged the look that would become Kraftwerk's trademark image: four men with slicked-back short hair and identical spotless shirt-and-tie uniforms.

Schneider also profoundly influenced Kraftwerk's direction by befriending an artist called Emil Schult, who became the group's image-consultant. The styling and packaging of Kraftwerk on stage and on record vaulted forward in coherence and impact, transforming them into fellow travellers of British glam artists like Bowie and Roxy Music, inhabiting their own parallel universe of retro-futurist chic. In the artwork for 1977's *Trans-Europe Express*, photography and a portrait painting by Schult make Kraftwerk look like a troupe of singing stars from between the wars, while the black-and-white video for the title track features the group in hats and leather gloves, gentlemen travelling in style in the private compartment of a 1930s train. *The Man-Machine* (1978) casts further back in time, its red-and-black colour scheme and slant-wise typography paying homage to the graphic innovations of Soviet modernists like El Lissitzky and Malevich. The design of these peak-Kraftwerk albums matched the themes of the songs, which evoked Fritz Lang ('Metropolis'), the naive wonder of electricity ('Neon Lights') and a bygone 'elegance and decadence' ('Europe Endless').

But even as the imagery and allusions harked back to the lost futurism of early-twentieth-century movements like Suprematism and Bauhaus, the music itself pushed forward into the future. Kraftwerk were inventing the 1980s, building the foundations of synthpop and sequencer-propelled club music. Acoustic instruments, including Schneider's flute, were now fully jettisoned, and the sound pared down to the sparse purity that we associate with classic Kraftwerk. Crucially, it was music stripped of individualised inflection and personality, with no hint of a solo or even a flourish. 'We go beyond all this individual feel,' Schneider told *Sounds*. 'We are more like vehicles, a part of our *mensch machine*, our man-machine. Sometimes we play the music, sometimes the music plays us, sometimes . . . it plays.'

By 1981's *Computer World*, the subject matter (the microchip revolution) caught up with the state-of-art sound. Kraftwerk captured both the unease of the computer's potential for surveillance and disconnection (the eerie shivers of 'Home Computer') and the tender human longings mediated still through new systems of telecommunication (the heart-flutter tremblings of 'Computer Love'). Despite the odd dated reference ('Pocket Calculator', which came about when Schneider brought a musical calculator to the studio), the album's concerns still resonate in a present in which we're even more symbiotically merged with and dependent on computer technology.

By the early eighties, Kraftwerk had created such a forcefield of influence that the pop world suddenly swarmed with groups modelled on the Germans' sound and image. The Human League originally found their path after the twin 1977 revelation of hearing 'Trans-Europe Express' and the Munich electronic disco of Donna Summer's Giorgio Moroder-produced 'I Feel Love', and by 1981 had finally become huge international pop stars in their own right. Gary Numan stole the android image and with 'Cars' came up with a more neurotic take on 'Autobahn'. Formed out of the orphaned remainder of

Joy Division, New Order loyally followed through on their late singer Ian Curtis's love for Kraftwerk, forging electronic dance-pop veined with doubt and gloom. Although increasingly over-shadowed by their own offspring, Kraftwerk managed to score their own megahit with the jaunty 'The Model', but – being a four-year-old *Man-Machine* tune – it didn't direct attention to their current masterpiece *Computer World*.

Meanwhile, this most Teutonic of outfits was achieving an implausible level of impact on black American music. Hatched out of the South Bronx hip hop culture, Afrika Bambaataa's 'Planet Rock' has been described as 'the Rosetta Stone of electro' by disco historian Peter Shapiro. If so, one of the inscribed languages is German, since the track is in large part a collage of Kraftwerk, layering the stirring chords of 'Trans-Europe Express' over the synth-bass groove of 'Numbers'. Over in Detroit, Juan Atkins of Cybotron and Model 500 pioneered techno with tracks like 'Cosmic Cars' and 'Night Drive (Thru-Babylon)'. Atkins's ally Derrick May described Detroit techno's wintry electro-funk as 'George Clinton and Kraftwerk stuck in an elevator with only a sequencer to keep them company', while their young associate Carl Craig pinned down the paradox of the Germans' appeal with his famous tautology: 'Kraftwerk were so stiff, they were funky.' Most surprising of all was Kraftwerk's influence in the South, where Miami bass, New Orleans bounce and other local styles took their clean, cold electronic sound in an incongruously lascivious direction. How strange to think of Florian Schneider – fan of Bach and Schubert, a man who looked a bit like Prince Philip – being a catalyst for generations of booty-shake sounds.

Faced with all this competition they'd spawned, Kraftwerk struggled to locate the new edge that would keep them ahead of the pack. Where 'Tour de France' was a last blast, 1986's *Electric Café* was already surpassed by young contenders like

31

Mantronix. Then came the rave revolution. When Kraftwerk issued the 1991 'remixed greatest hits' package *The Mix*, the contents brilliantly remodelled their old tunes for the contemporary dancefloor. But the surrounding tour set the pattern for the rest of their career, in which Kraftwerk would release no new music (apart from an album-length elaboration upon 'Tour de France' in 2003) but sporadically tour with increasingly visually spectacular presentations of their past material.

I saw Kraftwerk play in 2014 during one of these mobile 'museum of the future' jaunts. By this point, Florian Schneider had long left the group (he stopped performing live in 2006, quit formally a few years later – the culmination of a long process of fading creative involvement). The show at the Disney Concert Hall in Los Angeles was stunning (it required the wearing of 3D spectacles) and the sense of love in the audience was palpable. But neither this concert, nor the two previous times I've seen the group – 1998 and 1991 – is my most vivid memory of hearing Kraftwerk.

That is when I was travelling in a car on the actual autobahn, somewhere between the Black Forest and Cologne, about a dozen years ago. Like many men, crying doesn't come easy: personal tragedy or torment is less likely to produce a torrent than particular pieces of music, or certain films. As the pastures rolled by the passenger window, the lush scenery punctuated by gently gyrating electrical windmills, the motorik CD of Neu!, La Düsseldorf and Kraftwerk I'd prepared for this moment reached one of Kraftwerk's peak tunes. It might have been 'Trans-Europe Express', or 'Neon Lights', or 'Autobahn' itself – I had to turn my face away and look fixedly out of the window to hide my tears. I'm not sure why their music, so free of anguish and turmoil, has this seemingly paradoxical effect. Partly it's a response to the grandeur of ambition, the achieved scope of the Kraftwerk project. But it's also to do with what Lester Bangs called the 'intricate balm' supplied by the music itself: calming, cleansing, gliding along placidly yet propulsively, it's a twinkling and kindly picture of heaven.

NPR Music, 2020

THE FINAL FRONTIER: The Analogue Synth Gods of the 1970s

Ask people about synthesisers in pop music, and the first names to trip off most lips will be the Human League or Depeche Mode. The more techno-savvy and dance-music-attuned will nominate Kraftwerk as the source or mention Giorgio Moroder's Eurodisco productions such as Donna Summer's 'I Feel Love'. The chances are pretty slim, however, that names like Isao Tomita and Evangelos Odysseas Papathanassiou will come up, and not just because they're tough to pronounce. The fact is that an entire swathe of 1970s synthesiser-based music – pioneered by Tangerine Dream, Klaus Schulze and Wendy Carlos, popularised by Tomita, Jean-Michel Jarre and Vangelis (that's the aforementioned Mr Papathanassiou) – has been pretty much written out of the history of electronica.

This neglect partly stems from the nature of the music, which doesn't fit either of the subsequently established images of electropop (catchy ditties in the early eighties Depeche mould or beat-driven dance music in the techno/ trance continuum). From its epic scale (compositions that often took up the whole side of an album) to its cosmic atmosphere (albums were typically inspired by outer space or natural grandeur, astrophysics or science fiction), the genre wasn't exactly poppy. But it was hugely popular all across the world during the seventies: Tangerine Dream's 1974 breakthrough album *Phaedra* went gold in seven territories, while Tomita's Debussy-goes-synth *Snowflakes Are Dancing* received Grammy nominations in four different categories. After his worldwide hit single 'Oxygene, Part IV', Jean-Michel Jarre embarked upon a career that has sold over sixty million albums to date, with the debonair Frenchman also staging ever more grandiose outdoor spectaculars of music and lasers in cities across the world watched by audiences that ran into the millions.

Jarre's music was as close as the space music genre got to conventional pop, its brisk programmed drums and melodious synth-lines making it accessible and catchy. Mostly the genre was closer to ambient mood-music. Replacing pop's driving backbeat with placid pulse-rhythms or amorphous swathes of texture, it was designed to conjure eyelid-movies for the supine, sofa-bound and, more often than not, stoned. At its most abstract – solo albums by Klaus Schulze and by Tangerine Dream's leader Edgar Froese – these were clouds of sounds to lose yourself in, a Rorschach mindscreen for projecting fantasies onto. Yet unlike the kosmische rock of their German contemporaries Can, Faust and Neu!, which has been credible with hipsters ever since those groups were first active, and unlike the more esoteric (i.e., unsuccessful) sixties electronic outfits like Silver Apples, the cosmic synth voyagers have rarely been namedropped by contemporary bands as a cool reference point.

Until now, that is. In the last few years bands have emerged who have unabashedly cited Tangerine Dream as an influence. France's M83 take their name from the spiral galaxy Messier 83 and make eleven-minute-long tracks like 'Lower Your Eyelids to Die with the Sun' that resemble the missing link between My Bloody Valentine's woozy shoegaze and Tangerine Dream's *Phaedra*. In New York, the ultra-hip DFA label released Delia Gonzalez and Gavin Russom's *The Days of Mars*, an album whose four long instrumentals flashed listeners back to Klaus Schulze epics like 'Floating' and 'Mind-phaser'. Jim Jupp of Belbury Poly, whose second album *The Owl's Map* came out late in 2006 on supercool London label Ghost Box, identifies Wendy Carlos, Schulze and Tangerine Dream as a major inspiration: 'I think it's the fact that they were exploring what must have been mind-blowing technology, and giving free rein to musical ideas that had no pre-existing language,' Jupp explains. 'There's also something supernatural in the sound of modular synths and mellotrons; they always seemed the natural soundtrack for a golden age of science fiction and that Erich von Däniken-era pop culture of ancient astronauts and earth mysteries.'

Dance culture too has recently taken a turn towards the kosmische, with the fad for 'space disco', as pioneered by Norwegian producers Hans-Peter Lindstrom and Prins Thomas. Lindstrom made a track called 'I Feel Space' and Thomas named a tune 'Goettsching' in homage to cosmic-rocker-turned-techno pioneer Manuel Göttsching, who collaborated with Klaus Schulze. These producers are obsessed with an obscure late-seventies scene in northern Italy where disco and space rock collided. At the lakeside club Cosmic, DJ Daniele Baldelli layered rippling and wafting electronics and heavily processed guitar textures, taken from records by Göttsching, Schulze and other German kosmonauts, over disco instrumentals and African percussion records, blowing the minds of Italian youth who trance-danced all night long in an LSD-spiked daze.

The seventies cosmic synth genre was very much an exten-sion of psychedelia and that whole late-sixties mindset of 'taking drugs to make music to take drugs to' (the catchphrase of a much later band, the UK late-eighties trance-rock outfit

Spacemen 3). The first deployments of electronic sound in rock came from 'synthedelic' bands like United States of America, Silver Apples, White Noise and Fifty Foot Hose, who were looking for ever more otherworldly textures. The Beatles were also interested in *musique concrète* and avant-garde classical composers who used electronics: Paul McCartney recorded a fifteen-minute Stockhausen-influenced track called 'Carnival of Light' (never officially released) while George Harrison recorded a whole album of Moog-synth doodlings titled *Electronic Sound*, released in 1969 via Apple's experimental side label Zapple.

'When the synthesiser arrived, it was clearly going to be a major new weapon in the psychedelic arsenal,' says Steve Hillage, who spent the early seventies playing guitar in Gong alongside British synth pioneer Tim Blake, before embarking on a solo career dedicated to 'the mixture of guitar and electronics' in partnership with his synth-twiddling lover Miquette Giraudy. Hillage cites the pioneering all-electronic album *Zero Time* by an American outfit called Tonto's Expanding Head Band as the record that 'blew my mind' and woke him up to the synth's potential. He eventually tracked down Malcolm Cecil, the co-designer of the TONTO synthesiser, to produce his 1977 album *Motivation Radio*.

Tonto's Expanding Head Band was a duo, Malcolm Cecil and Robert Margouleff. The name Tonto was short for The New Timbral Orchestra, which was not so much an all-new invention by Cecil as the adaption and customisation of Robert Moog's Moog Series 3 synthesisers to create a warmer and polyphonic sound (synthesisers at that point being monophonic, incapable of playing chords). Cecil and Margouleff ended up providing technical assistance for Stevie Wonder, who pioneered the use of synthesisers in R&B. The history of electronics in black music is a story beyond the remit of this essay, but

38

we should note the presence of exotic and otherworldly synth textures in the jazz-fusion of the period (Herbie Hancock's *Sextant*, featuring ARP synth played by Dr Patrick Gleeson; the spacey and abstract synth-daubings of Weather Report founder Joe Zawinul, and others) as well as the electronic keyboard work of Bernie Worrell in Parliament-Funkadelic.

The general public mostly first encountered electronic music not through pop music, however, but through the fad for Moog-ified versions of themes by the great composers that rampaged through the world of popular classical music in the late sixties and early seventies. The craze was kickstarted by American composer Wendy Carlos with the 1968 million-selling album *Switched-On Bach*. In the early part of the sixties, Carlos had been an avant-garde composer, working at the famous Columbia-Princeton Electronics Center under Vladimir Ussachevsky. After forming a connection with synthesiser inventor Robert Moog, Carlos launched the company Trans-Electronic Music Productions and converted Bach's baroque compositions for the Moog. *Trans-Electronic Music Productions, Inc. Presents: Switched-On Bach* – to give the album its full title – was a huge success and was swiftly followed by *The Well-Tempered Synthesizer* (a play on Bach's *Well-Tempered Clavier*). Carlos then set to working on a double album of original compositions, 1972's *Sonic Seasonings*. Each of the four long-player sides evoked one of the four seasons. The music's placid atmospheric textures and use of environmental found sounds arguably pre-empts Brian Eno as inventor of ambient music. That same year Carlos recorded the score for Stanley Kubrick's controversial movie *A Clockwork Orange*, mixing baroque adaptions with eerie originals like 'Timesteps' and 'Country Lane'.

Around this time a Carlos-inspired TV and film theme composer in Japan called Isao Tomita was deeply immersed in recording his own debut album of electronicised classical. After hearing *Switched-On Bach*, Tomita bought a Moog III synth, created a home studio and started his own company, Plasma Music, modelled on Trans-Electronic Music Productions, Inc. and dedicated to creating 'music by electronic means'. Released in 1974, *Snowflakes Are Dancing*'s otherworldly translations of Debussy made the album a worldwide success. The album combined calligraphic delicacy of detail with a vivid verging on garish palette of electronic tone-colours.

In a gesture that would become typical for the synth epic genre, Tomita included a long list of all the equipment used in the making of the record on its back sleeve (including every single component of his Moog and the number of each that he possessed: 'extended range fixed filter bank – 1; envelope generator – 4; bode ring modulator – 1; sequential controller – 2 . . .' etc.). Also a defining element of the genre's emerging iconography was the back cover photograph of the maestro in front of a bank of dials, knobs, potentiometers and cables. Subsequent albums grappled with Mussorgsky and Stravinsky, and the arc of Tomita's career peaked creatively and commercially with 1977's version of Gustav Holst's suite *The Planets*. This was Tomita's most playful translation of classical music for the space age, the glistening otherworldly tones of the synths suiting the extraterrestrial evocations of Holst's music. The update is full of exquisite touches, like the use of stereo panning on the 'Mercury' movement to accentuate the darting, quicksilver spirit of the messenger god.

By this point, though, a certain grandiosity had taken over in Tomita Land. On the front cover of the vinyl album and its spine, the title actually reads 'The Tomita Planets'. Holst's name only appears on the back cover in tiny, barely legible, blue-on-black letters above the 'The' in 'The Planets', with the font used being much smaller than the one used for the prominent statement 'electronically created by Isao Tomita'.

This apparent assertion of co-authorship is affirmed even more boldly with a further note that reads 'this album was produced, arranged, programmed for synthesisers, performed, recorded and mixed down by Isao Tomita'. Clearly somebody's ego was in danger of going supernova!

Talking of egomania, in rock music during the first half of the seventies synthesisers became widespread but tended to be little more than an expensive toy for exhibitionist rock stars. Typically, they served as an exotic embellishment to established styles, as opposed to instigating a radical overhaul of the way the music moved and was structured. Performers like Keith Emerson of ELP and Yes-man Rick Wakeman played their synths like glorified organs, all grandstanding bombast and arpeggiated folderol. Apart from Tonto's Expanding Head Band, the first group to go all the way into a radically all-electronic and un-rock sound was Tangerine Dream. The group originally spawned out of Berlin's Zodiak Free Arts Lab, a club started by Hans-Joachim Roedelius (later of Cluster and Harmonia) and Conrad Schnitzler, who would go on to make a series of experimental and forbiddingly dissonant electronic albums.

'Zodiak was an avant-garde club during the late sixties, a large white-and-black room where various concerts and hap-penings took place,' says Edgar Froese, who had first moved to Berlin as an art student, doing sculpture and also spending a period of time in 1967 with Salvador Dalí ('It was a fantastic experience having had the chance being for some weeks in his auratic atmosphere and playing for him at his surrealistic garden parties in Cadaques,' Froese recalls). The spirit of Zodiak was totally sixties, all multi media based 'total art' and anything-goes extremism: 'In the absurd often lies what is artistically possible,' as Froese put it in one interview. It was here that Froese met Klaus Schulze, who had been drumming in a freak-rock band called Psy Free. Together with Schnitzler they formed Tangerine Dream and started a Zodiak residency, their freeform performances often lasting for five or six hours.

Tangerine Dream recorded their debut album *Electronic Meditation* for Germany's leading psychedelic rock label Ohr. Despite the 'electronic' in the title, the group was not yet synthetic; the sound-palette included organ, drums, guitar, cello and flute, and the overall vision bore the heavy imprint of Pink Floyd's extended trance-rock tracks based around guitar glissandi, hypno-drone basslines and Rick Wright's spacey Farfisa keyboards. Gradually, Tangerine Dream's sound became more electronic, especially after the arrival of Chris Franke, an avant-garde music fan who admired Ligeti and Stockhausen. On the title track of Tangerine Dream's second album, 1971's *Alpha Centauri*, a beatific flute insinuates its sinuous melody between unsettling drones and electronic whooshes (the famous EMS VCS3 Synthi) conjuring the scenario of an idyllic forest glade that has suddenly become the landing strip for a flotilla of flying saucers.

When Peter Baumann joined for 1972's *Zeit*, Tangerine Dream stabilised as a trio. The album, a double, was their most formless and disorienting yet, the missing link between Floyd's *Ummagumma* and Brian Eno's *On Land*, the sound woven out of spacey whispers, low humming bass-drones, clouds of cymbal spray and bubbling Moog-ripples. *Atem* (1973) added a Mellotron to the group's armoury. A sort of primitive sampler popular with prog rockers like the Moody Blues, the Mellotron contained swatches of pre-recorded tape that enabled rock bands, especially in the live context, to imitate the sounds of string sections and symphony orchestras.

This first avant-garde freeform phase of Tangerine Dream's music is known by fans as the 'Pink Years', because the Ohr logo was a pink ear. The era came to an end in part because John Peel, the BBC's token hippie who championed the music of the underground (i.e., post-psychedelic and progressive bands) on his Radio 1 late-night show *Top Gear*, was a huge supporter of *Atem*, hailing it as his 'Import of the Year'. This endorsement helped to turn Tangerine Dream into a major cult band in the UK, such that Virgin Records, in those days a mail-order company specialising in import albums from Europe, noticed that they'd shifted over 15,000 Tangerine Dream albums in Britain purely through the post. Richard Branson, the boss of Virgin, was looking to start his own record company and decided Tangerine Dream, along with another German experimental outfit, Faust, were perfect candidates to launch Virgin Records and shape a distinct identity that set the label apart from others catering to the long-hair underground, such as Island and Charisma.

Edgar Froese recalls Simon Draper, Virgin's A&R chief and aesthetic helmsman, 'telephoning me in Berlin to say this radio guy Peel was playing *Atem* to death on his programme. Two days later I sat with Branson on the stairs of his record store in Notting Hill Gate, London, and signed a contract which was in power from 1973 to 1983. Ten years of roller-coaster experiences began!'

The shift from Ohr to Virgin coincided with Tangerine Dream wholeheartedly embracing electronic technology. *Phaedra*, their debut for Virgin, was propelled by Moog-bass pulsations and laced with washes of VCS3 and Mellotron. 'No one as far as I know had made use of the big Moog synth as the first sequencer,' recalls Froese. 'That became Tangerine Dream's trademark. It was associated with Bach's idea of a *basso continuo*.'

Another influence was the minimalist aesthetic of American composers like Terry Riley (whose partly electric keyboard-driven *A Rainbow in Curved Air* had been a big hit with the 'heads' of the hippie counterculture). Their use of hypnotic

43

repetition, their cellular approach of multiple ultra-simple pulses and refrains interlocking to create complexity, their bright timbres and embrace of tonality and consonance after years of avant-classical atonality and dissonance, their music's paradoxical mood of tense serenity and its influence from Eastern spirituality – all these shifts gave birth to a new approach in modern classical music, the genre known variously as 'new music' or 'systems music', as popularised by Philip Glass and Michael Nyman, especially through their later work for movie soundtracks like *Koyaanisqatsi* and *The Draughtsman's Contract*. 'Terry Riley and Steve Reich, the founders of minimal music, had discovered a new way of describing the world with sounds and playing techniques, a kind of "atomic structure" in music,' argues Froese. 'What seemed to be an endless repeating structure of single notes could be discovered as a floating, always changing pool of sound molecules – very hypnotic and fascinating if you could concentrate yourself on the deeper meaning of it.'

Phaedra was a gold record in seven countries, doing particularly well in France and in Britain, where it fulfilled Virgin's hopes by crashing into the Top 10. Tangerine Dream followed it with the equally successful *Rubycon* and *Ricochet*, the latter a live document of a tour of European cathedrals. In this pre-punk golden era for Tangerine Dream, Virgin also put out in swift succession three solo albums by Edgar Froese, 1974's *Aqua*, 1975's *Epsilon in Malaysian Pale* and 1976's *Macula Transfer*. *Aqua* was notable for its use of Manfred Schunke's 'Kunstkopf' or 'artificial head' recording system, at a time when the record industry (post-*Dark Side of the Moon*'s mega-success) was obsessed with the idea of surround sound and trying to launch quadraphonic sound as the ultimate listening experience. 'Kunstkopf was a recording technique using a human dummy with an inbuilt microphone system,' recalls Froese. 'Listening

44

back to the recording, you have got the natural impression listening with your human system to a 360-degree audio signal. It did not become very commercial, however, because it did not work properly with a normal stereo speaker system.'

Epsilon in Malaysian Pale, largely based around textures from the Mellotron, won admiration from someone high up in the rock star aristocracy: David Bowie. A fan of Kraftwerk, Cluster, Harmonia and Neu!, Bowie described Froese's *Epsilon* as 'the most beautiful, enchanting, poignant work . . . That used to be the background music to my life when I was living in Berlin.' All the German electronic and un-rock sounds of the day informed the famous trilogy of albums – *Low*, *"Heroes"*, *Lodger* – Bowie recorded in Berlin with Brian Eno as his principal accomplice. 'In a way, it was great that I found those bands, because I didn't feel any of the essence of punk at all in that period, I just totally by-passed it.' Bowie 'had absolutely no doubts where the future of music was going, and for me it was coming out of Germany'.

Of all the German groups of the era, Tangerine Dream had the biggest worldwide impact. 'We did tours all over the globe and received gold status in seven countries,' recalls Froese. 'Not bad for some "strange knob switchers from Germany", as the UK music papers called us!' In those days, touring with synthesisers was a major headache. The machines were bulky and heavy, but also fragile and temperamental. They could even be dangerous: a travel-damaged Moog gave Franke a severe electric shock at one gig in Australia. 'Transportation was horrifying. We spent 30 per cent of our income for insurances and repair of instruments,' recalls Froese. 'Voltage-controlled oscillators and other devices were completely unstable,' he adds, because their extreme sensitivity to room temperature meant that 'any given tuning of the oscillator stayed "in tune" for maybe ten minutes'.

45

This problem confronted all progressive musicians using electronics. One reason Steve Hillage had three synth players in his live band during the mid-seventies was to 'guarantee we could deliver the goods sonically!' Klaus Schulze recalls how the settings on his synthesisers would constantly drift. 'Nobody could make the same sound two days in a row. With my big Moog, when the spotlights went on, the heat affected the tuning. At the same time, the Moog needed two hours just to warm up; you had to plug it in as soon as you lugged it into the hall.'

Schulze's version of electronic space music was darker and even more abstract than Tangerine Dream's, his albums *Irrlicht* and *Cyborg* often conjuring images of barren moonscapes and fog-shrouded alien planets. Where Tangerine Dream averaged four long tracks per album, a Schulze LP typically featured just two side-long compositions that stretched the sound-fidelity limitations of the vinyl album by running to twenty-five or even thirty minutes. These epic tracks were typically recorded in a single take. 'I would play until the tape ran out,' Schulze recalls. 'I was recording in my living room or, perhaps it would be better to say, living in my studio!'

According to Schulze, the impulse to do extended compositions originally came out of sixties drug culture. 'We were all smoking and drifting into long-term moods. Four-minute songs were over too quick. It wasn't relaxing music, not like a dream. We wanted to do music that was like a classical piece, with leitmotifs, codas.' The title of his 1973 album *Picture Music* pinpoints the genre's aspirations to be an inner-space version of movie scores. 'It's for short movie clips in your head,' says Schulze. 'The music doesn't entertain you so much as it's forcing you to use your imagination to make it complete. It's not really "entertainment", because the listener has to complete the music and, if you're not willing to add some of your own fantasy, it's quite boring!'

'Boring' and 'soporific' were epithets frequently hurled by hostile rock critics at the cosmic synth artists, especially in the live context, where Tangerine Dream's shows were so lacking in showiness (the group motionless behind their banks of synths) that audiences (the reviewers claimed, anyway) were in danger of falling asleep. In a 1974 interview, Peter Baumann retorted, 'Exactly, we play as a group but the distinction between us and a rock band is that they put on a show – we put on a mind show.'

The sort of rock critic who spent the entire 1970–75 period waiting for punk to happen – like Lester Bangs, who famously and hilariously slagged off a Tangerine Dream concert – may have hated the electronic mindscape groups, but during the mid-seventies, this sort of music had a massive worldwide following. Indeed 1976–77, supposedly the years of punk, were actually the peak of space music's popularity. In 1977, Schulze played at the Planetarium in London, showcasing *Mirage*, probably his all-time masterpiece. 'That was the first time a concert was given in a planetarium,' Schulze says, audibly beaming with pride down the phone line. 'But I don't know if a planetarium is really the ideal place for music, because its hemisphere shapes create echoes and sound reflections from all sides.'

That same year Tangerine Dream embarked on its debut traipse across America, performing to sold-out crowds with a surprisingly multi-racial aspect – black youth being as wowed by the group's alien synth sound as they were by the similarly futuristic noises made by Kraftwerk on 1977's *Trans-Europe Express*. 'From talking to a lot of black fans in the US, I believe it is the pulsating deep rhythm attracted them in the first place,' says Froese. 'They also told me that not using words gives them a huge span of emotional freedom to experience themselves in a different way than happens with other music. At least it's all soul music, isn't it?'

47

Electronic space music's non-verbal nature is crucial, helping to explain one of the most striking aspects of the genre: this was a style of music led by, even dominated by, Europeans. Pop music in the 1970s was an Anglo-American hegemony. There was a strong sense that rock especially was innately anglophone, and this created a huge disadvantage in the international market for bands either for whom English was a second language or who chose to sing in their native tongue. The space synth genre, being instrumental, levelled the playing field and allowed European – above all German and French artists – to make serious inroads into the rock markets of the UK, USA, Canada and Australia. Journalists noticed and started to call the new genre 'techno-rock'.

Tangerine Dream's 1977 American tour was documented on the double album *Encore*. That same year the group recorded a high-profile soundtrack for the movie *Sorcerer*, made by *Exorcist* director William Friedkin. Seeing the boom of instrumental long-form works by these artists and others like Virgin's superstar Mike Oldfield, the record companies went on a cheque-book spree, signing up synth-twiddlers like Michael Hoenig, Bo Hanson, Clearlight and Vangelis.

The commercial high profile of synthesiser music and its associations with long-haired 'progressives' were why most punk rockers initially regarded keyboards as a no-no. Playthings for rich rock stars, synths like the Moog were simply too pricey – and too expensive to transport – for young guttersnipes getting a band together. 'Technoflash' was *NME*'s sneering designation for the genre, the flash referring both to the ostentatious display of nimble-fingered virtuosity and to the over-the-top stage costumes and expensive lighting that prog rockers like Rick Wakeman often opted for. When Wire's second album *Chairs Missing* appeared in 1978, the presence of synths led one reviewer to complain that they'd gone from *Pink Flag* to Pink Floyd in less than a year.

Then, abruptly, cheaper and more portable synths like the Wasp came on the market. In mid-1978 a spate of synth-based singles emerged from the postpunk do-it-yourself underground, including the Human League's 'Being Boiled', The Normal's 'Warm Leatherette', Throbbing Gristle's 'United'. But these artists were at pains to differentiate themselves from the cosmic synth bands. The Normal – Daniel Miller, founder of Mute Records – complained that the trouble with most prog synth players was that they were musicians who played the synth pianistically rather than treating it as a noise-generating machine. Yet only a few years earlier, Miller had been a huge Klaus Schulze fan. Even the Human League had been recording ninety-seven-minute electronic soundscapes like 'Last Man of Earth' only a few months before shifting in a dance-pop direction with 'Being Boiled'. In 1978, though, it was crucial to avoid any taint of hippie. So 'Trans-Europe Express' and 'I Feel Love' were cited as revelations, but no one gave the nod to Jean-Michel Jarre's 'Oxygene IV', a huge hit globally around the same time that 'I Feel Love' was a worldwide No. 1 smash.

Jarre's homeland France was the European country that most ardently embraced the new techno-rock. Kraftwerk were bigger there than in Germany, while Klaus Schulze achieved a mainstream prominence way beyond the cult-figure status he enjoyed elsewhere. *Timewind* (1975) won a Grand Prix du Disque award in the 'contemporary music' category and the following year's *Moondawn* sold a quarter of a million copies and planted itself in the Top 5. There were numerous homegrown French electronic rockers, outfits like Clearlight and Heldon, but none of them had the mass impact of Jean-Michel Jarre. Although he originally came from an avant-garde background, having studied under the direction of *musique concrète* pioneer Pierre Schaeffer at the Groupe de Recherches Musicales,

Jarre's work aimed straight for the middlebrow jugular, fusing nineteenth-century classical melodiousness and scale (*Oxygene* the album consisted of six movements, 'Oxygene I' to 'VI') with electronic textures and sequenced rhythms.

All the principles on which Jarre's music was organised – theme, variation, harmony, euphony, codas and counterpoint – harked back to the era before twelve-tone serialism, atonality, Varèse and the rest of the twentieth-century modernist vanguard. His monstrous success in large part stemmed from the deftness with which he applied a space-age patina to what was essentially the musical fare of his parents' generation (literally, in the sense that his father, Maurice Jarre, had been a famous composer of stirring and stately movie scores for epic films like *Lawrence of Arabia* and *Doctor Zhivago*). Yet like Kraftwerk's equally euphonious hymns to the modern world, Jarre's music had an undeniable appeal, brimming with a wide-eyed optimism and excitement about technology, space exploration and all things futuristic. This naive anticipation for tomorrow's world was already looking slightly dated and kitschy by the mid-seventies, but it was very much part of popular culture, from the success of science magazines like *Omni*, futurologists and popular science writers like Alvin Toffler and Carl Sagan, and the pseudo-science/paranormal fringe of UFO-logists like Erich von Däniken.

Oxygene was followed by 1978's *Equinoxe*, a more rhythmically propulsive album that made heavy use of sequenced basslines and made the charts in thirty-five countries, and then *The Magnetic Fields*, a Top 10 album in every country in Europe. Playing purely instrumental music, Jean-Michel Jarre had become one of the biggest pop stars in the world. Perhaps inflated by his worldwide success, the hallmark of Jarre's career became a gigantism verging on overkill. Starting with a 1979 Paris concert that drew one million fans to the Place de

la Concorde, Jarre staged a series of increasingly spectacular
hi-tech extravaganzas. He became the first Western pop
musician to perform in the People's Republic of China, played
at NASA's 25th Anniversary celebration in Houston, threw a
huge 1988 event in London called Destination Docklands, and
drew 2.5 million to Paris's La Défense district in 1990. This
run of Guinness record-breaking mega-concerts peaked with his
performance in front of 3.5 million Russians at Moscow's 850th-
anniversary celebrations. Jarre also received an honour to make
the other spacetronica pioneers green with envy – having an
actual heavenly body named after him, the asteroid 4422 Jarre.

With the exception of Tangerine Dream, the major figures
in the analogue synth epic genre were solo artists like Jarre.
Something about the tableau of the solitary composer flanked,
on stage or in the studio, by banks of electronic gear seems to
go to the core of the genre, conjuring an aura of 'Great Man,
Alone' grandiosity. Vangelis is a supreme example of this
syndrome. He started out in the Greek prog-rock band Aphro-
dite's Child and was later offered the chance to become Yes's
keyboard player. But Vangelis turned it down, feeling that the
compromises involved in the group situation would constrain
his vision. Instead, he built a recording studio in the centre
of London, near Marble Arch, filling it with statues, figurines
and exotica to create an inspirational atmosphere, and calling
it Nemo because, he says now, 'it was sort of cut off from the
conventional studios in London and quite different. It looked
a little bit like Captain Nemo's submarine in Jules Verne's
20,000 Leagues under the Sea.' Here Vangelis composed his
music on the spot, surrounded by a huge array of keyboards,
improvising straight to tape.

Signing to RCA, Vangelis released a stream of solo albums
from the mid-seventies onwards, along with a series of collaborations with Yes vocalist Jon Anderson. Most of the Vangelis

solo LPs – *Spiral, Albedo 0.39, China* – showcased his gift for melody and his trademark synth-palette of limpid and numinous tones. One exception was 1978's *Beaubourg*, a sinister, atonal affair named after the building that houses the Centre Pompidou, and which Vangelis characterises as a kind of prank. 'At the time I was doing something I considered totally absurd, and I borrowed the name Beaubourg from the Paris so-called museum. I felt that if it had a voice it would sound like this.'

RCA's hope for a *Tubular Bells*-scale smash from Vangelis didn't materialise, but his work began to appear in movies and TV themes, where the music's aura of majesty and scale lent itself to things like Carl Sagan's TV series *Cosmos*. Then the breakthrough came with his 1981 Oscar-winning score for *Chariots of Fire*, followed a few years later by Vangelis masterpiece, the score for *Blade Runner*, where his droopy pitch-bent synth-tones possess the quality of glistening gas settling on the horizon's rim. Vangelis composed the score live, improvising as video-taped scenes from the film unfurled on a screen in his recording studio: 'Nothing was pre-composed, everything was composed with the images.' From the colossal thudding pillars of percussion that open *Blade Runner* to the climactic twinkles of 'Tears in Rain', everything is drenched in reverb – an effect as contrivedly atmospheric and infallibly seductive as director Ridley Scott's over-reliance on shadow and drizzle. Soundtrack and cinematography together create a sense of immense expanse – space that isn't empty but as filled with feeling as it is with droplets of moisture. The result was a movie that you see-hear – an audiovision for the ages.

While some went into the New Age genre, movie soundtracks are where most of the cosmic synth artists really came into their own. Here was a field in which their lack of onstage showiness or pop charisma was not a drawback. Composing scores allowed them to give up the unprofitable and wearisome routine of touring in support of albums. After doing the *Sorcerer* O/S/T, Tangerine Dream went on to compose over thirty more movie scores. 'It gave us the freedom to do what we wanted to do without being suppressed by a record company,' says Froese. 'Plus there was the chance to work in one of the most bizarre art forms one could think of.' Alternating between film scores and his own solo albums, Vangelis abandoned Nemo for a new studio, the Epsilon Laboratory, built almost entirely from glass and situated on the top of a tall building in Paris. But soon he abandoned it for a peripatetic existence, enabled by the increasingly portable nature of synthesiser technology.

The soundtrack direction was something of a saviour, for the eighties were wilderness years for many of the synth epic pioneers. The increasing ubiquity of electronic sounds and rhythms in pop music diminished the future-shock aura of their own work. A hardcore of fans kept the faith during the eighties, many of them becoming cult artists in their own right, such as Steve Roach. Although Tangerine Dream and others remained popular in Germany, in the rest of the world these artists' profiles slipped dramatically. But the faith was kept by an organisation called Ultima Thule, a record store and mail-order company based in Leicester, England, and founded by two brothers, Steven and Alan Freeman. The name 'Ultima Thule' came from a Tangerine Dream single from the Pink Years. The Freeman brothers also put out *Audion*, a magazine dedicated to all things kosmik and European. As well as the omnipresence of synthesisers in eighties music, the synth gods' own shift from analogue technology to digital keyboards, Fairlight samplers, sequencers and MIDI technology was an uneasy transition, with the results often sounding clinical and standardised compared to their classic analogue work. Jean-Michel Jarre disrupted his run of monstrous success in 1984 with *Zoolook*, an album that heavily deployed the Fairlight sampler with very mixed results, and never quite recovered as a recording artist, although he continued to stage ever more massive live events.

In 1989, the legacy of the seventies synth gods surfaced in an unlikely place: London's dance scene. A DJ called Dr Alex Paterson was operating the pioneering chill-out zone Land of Oz, attached to Paul Oakenfold's famous acid house club Spectrum. Ravers frazzled after hours of nonstop dancing to acid's hypnotic beats and mind-bending basslines could retreat into Oz and get their synapses soothed by ambient music – things like Steve Hillage's *Rainbow Dome Musick*, originally recorded for a 1979 New Age festival. 'The first time I went down to Oz, Alex was playing *Rainbow* but he was mixing it over beats,' recalls Hillage. Another Paterson favourite was *e2-e4*, an album recorded in 1981 by Ash Ra Tempel's Manuel Göttsching just after he'd come off a tour playing with Klaus Schulze, and released a few years later via Schulze's Inteam Records. One long sixty-minute track of softly pittering electronic beats and fluttering synths, *e2-e4*'s gentle euphoria fitted the Ecstasy mood perfectly, if quite accidentally. Then in 1989 a house-ified version of the track entitled 'Sueno Latino' became an anthem on the rave scene.

Rainbow Dome Musick and *e2-e4* bridged the gap between the seventies synth gods and the post-rave culture of chill-out zones and 'electronic listening music' that flourished in the early nineties. A new breed of artists emerged – Mixmaster Morris, Sven Vath, Biosphere, The Future Sound of London, Pete Namlook and above all Alex Paterson's own group The Orb – audibly indebted to Schulze, Tangerine Dream and the rest, inheriting not only their textures but their love of concept albums and long tracks, their grandiose ambition and tendency towards cosmic kitsch. After hearing his electronic tapestries layered over kicking beats at Land of Oz, a lightbulb went off above Hillage's head, and with partner Giraudy he plunged

54

into the techno fray with a new outfit called System 7. Schulze worked with Pete Namlook, who in the eighties had played in the electronic New Age/jazz-fusion outfit Romantic Warrior before becoming a techno DJ. The duo recorded a series of Pink Floyd-homaging albums released via Namlook's Frankfurt-based label Fax under the title *Dark Side of the Moog*. 'Suddenly I was the godfather of trance and ambient, or the Pope,' recalls Schulze. 'I was honoured.' Although the chill-out boom faded after a few years, the influence of the seventies synth gods continued in trance. Chris Franke contributed to the global dance culture in a quite different way, leaving Tangerine Dream in the late eighties to work with the electronic company Steinberg and helping to create the CUBASE virtual studio technology, one of the most significant forces in electronic music-making during the nineties.

Being embraced and validated by a young generation of drug-addled technophiles gave the seventies survivors a fresh lease of life, and this galvanising boost has yet to fade. Most remain active in music. Hillage and Giraudy still record under the names System 7 and Mirror System. Tangerine Dream continue to release a steady stream of records, following 2005's *Jeanne d'Arc* with this year's fortieth anniversary of Tangerine Dream marking album *Madcap's Flaming Duty*. Vangelis sporadically records movie scores. Jean-Michel Jarre regularly stages his mega-concerts, albeit on a reduced scale (relative to his own past exploits, anyway), most recently playing to 100,000 Poles for the twenty-fifth-anniversary celebration of Solidarity, an event staged at the Gdańsk shipyard where the movement first started. As for Klaus Schulze, he recently released *Moonlake* – his 101st album. Size – of individual opus and entire oeuvre – clearly remains the hallmark of the synth epic genre!

Observer Music Monthly, 2007

TECHNOPOP: Yellow Magic Orchestra and Ryuichi Sakamoto

Asked to identify the birthplace of techno, most people would answer Düsseldorf or Detroit, hometowns of Kraftwerk and Cybotron respectively. Some might make a case for Sheffield and its scions Human League and Cabaret Voltaire. One city that almost never comes up is Tokyo. Yet Yellow Magic Orchestra, the trio of Haruomi Hosono, Yukihiro Takahashi and Ryuichi Sakamoto, has arguably the strongest claim of all to the 'Godfathers of Techno' title.

Not only was YMO's sound centred around synthesisers and largely aimed at the dancefloor, but also, unlike any of the other contenders above, a substantial proportion of their early recordings consisted of instrumentals – which is one of the hallmarks of techno. On the other hand, it's true that those early albums used Takahashi's hands-on drumming rather than programmed machine beats. But perhaps what ought to sway the decision in the Japanese group's favour is that they were the first to use the word 'techno' in connection with their music. Their second album, 1979's *Solid State Survivor*, kicks off with 'Technopolis' and the record's huge domestic success spawned a Japanese form of new wave known as technopop. Their fifth album, released in 1981, was called *Technodelic*.

And then, clinching the contest, YMO released a flexi-disc EP called *The Spirit of Techno* in 1983 – a year before Cybotron's single 'Techno City' and while Kraftwerk struggled in their Kling Klang studio on an album with the working title *Techno Pop* (eventually released in 1986 as *Electric Café*).

'We invented technopop,' Sakamoto declared in a 1988 interview with *Elle* magazine. The tone of insistence hinted that – despite his own solo successes and Oscar-winning soundtrack composing – YMO's failure to conquer the West and get the credit still rankled. Still, there was consolation in the form of recognition from fellow musicians overseas. UK techno duo LFO namechecked YMO as 'pioneers of the hypnotic groove' in an ancestral roll-call that appeared in 'Intro', the opening track of 1991's *Frequencies*, and again in the single 'What Is House'. The following year LFO joined with other leading UK rave producers for a tribute album of remixed YMO tunes titled *Hi-Tech/No Crime*. Inventors of Detroit techno, the Belleville 3 – Juan Atkins, Derrick May, Kevin Saunderson – had listened to YMO's albums as teenagers in rapt reverence. 'All the YMO albums were amazing,' May told a Red Bull Music Academy audience in 2010, recalling 'sitting in the car . . . pumping it really loud, like it was the latest Run DMC'.

The black American connection to YMO is particularly striking. 'Firecracker', the trio's debut single, reached No.18 in the Billboard R&B chart. The group appeared on *Soul Train*, America's leading black music TV show, to play 'Firecracker' along with their cover of 'Tighten Up' (a late-1968 hit for Texas R&B outfit Archie Bell & the Drells). The bass-propulsive electro-disco groove of 'Firecracker' featured in an Afrika Bambaataa 1979 live DJ performance at a Bronx high school, a recording of which circulated for years on tape under the title 'Death Mix' before finally coming out on vinyl in 1983. YMO's innovations are as much part of the DNA of electro as Kraftwerk's.

While its futurism triggered the imagination of young producers-to-be like Mantronix, 'Firecracker' also revealed another equally important side to the YMO project: retro-kitsch irony and a love of playing games with pop history. Far from being beamed into 1978 from the twenty-first century, the song itself dated back to 1959. Based around melodic intervals that sound vaguely Chinese, the original 'Firecracker' first appeared on Martin Denny's exotica album *Quiet Village*. Wielding marimbas and mallets, Denny's ensemble trafficked in clichéd travel-brochure images of geishas parting bead curtains and hula girls in grass skirts and floral leis. Rather than seeing such associations as offensive, YMO found amusement in 'that fake image of Asian culture, exotic, typical stereotype image . . . created in Hollywood!' as Sakamoto put it. The inauthenticity appealed to their highly sophisticated sensibility. So YMO took Denny's orientalism and exported it back to the West with an extra layer of twice-removed simulation glazed on top.

Alongside the whimsy, though, a sincere ideal of sonic cosmopolitanism runs through both YMO's work and the members' solo careers. Validating the idea of audio tourism, Hosono talked of creating 'sightseeing music'. Sakamoto likewise titled one solo record *Esperanto*, after the invented language that its makers hoped would bring about interna-tional understanding, and coined the concept 'Neo Geo' as the title of another album, heralding a post-geographical One World music of the near-future.

Japanese pop has long been peculiarly open to imported ideas, from not just the anglophone sphere but Europe, Latin America and other parts of the world. Sometimes that has resulted in immaculately accurate pastiches; other times, it's led to only-in-Japan hybrids and composites. YMO's work, and Sakamoto-solo, leans far more to the latter: it's hard to imag-

59

ine any other country in the world coming up with a techno-
ska cover of Elmer Bernstein's Western theme 'The Magnificent
Seven', like YMO did on their third album ×∞*Multiplies.*

Speaking to *The Fader* in 2015, Sakamoto traced the roots of
YMO's sensibility back as far as 1868, when Japan, after 250
years of self-enforced isolation, opened up to the outside world
and underwent rapid industrialisation. 'It almost destroyed the
traditional music because . . . the Japanese government thought
only Western culture and music was good . . . We lost a stream
of our traditional music – since then musically we are flowers
without root . . . That's probably a big reason for me endlessly
seeking what I have to do.'

In the beginning, the spark was as classically Western as imaginable: Johann Sebastian Bach. Learning piano from a pre-school
age, Sakamoto fell in love with a succession of European composers, starting with Bach, moving on to Claude Debussy, and later,
as a student at the Tokyo National University of Fine Arts and
Music, embracing the avant-garde cutting edge of John Cage
and Iannis Xenakis. By this point, aged eighteen in 1970, he was
also exploring the dizzying possibilities offered by synthesisers
like the Buchla and Moog. But he was also, prefiguring YMO's
doubled interest in the futuristic and the exotic, studying Indian
and African music and for a while entertained ambitions to be an
ethnomusicologist.

It was through session-musician work that he encountered
Hosono, five years older and a veteran of various Japanese
avant-pop outfits such as The Happy End. Yellow Magic
Orchestra, in the beginning, was Hosono's conception,
something for which he recruited Sakamoto and Takahashi
(formerly of Sadistic Mika Band, one of the few Japanese rock
groups to make any waves overseas, thanks to their affinity
and friendship with Roxy Music). But although Hosono was

the leader and the only member credited as producer on the first four albums, Sakamoto quickly emerged as a potent counterforce, resulting in both creative sparks and personal friction that ultimately split the group. 'I arranged the tracks,' Sakamoto told Geeta Dayal in 2006, adding that the group nicknamed him the Professor, because 'I studied in a conservatory. I knew harmony, counterpoint, how to write a sonata, a fugue.'

Although appearing as a trio in photographs and album artwork, YMO as a working unit was more like a quartet, because of the crucial role of programmer and sound engineer Hideki Matsutake, the former assistant to Isao Tomita (whose electronic renderings of classical music by the likes of Debussy and Holst had caught the ears of Western listeners). For a time there was a shadowy fifth member-of-sorts, lyricist Chris Modsell, an Englishman. The anglophone nature of most of the lyrics and titles indicated the group's ambition to invade the Western pop sphere.

In many ways, YMO took their cues from Kraftwerk, who similarly produced English-language versions of their albums outside Germany. 'We wanted to make a Japanese Kraftwerk,' Sakamoto declared in a 1998 interview. Just as Kraftwerk played on Germanic clichés of discipline and stiffness, YMO deliberately 'used a lot of stereotyped images about Japanese people'. For instance, the cover of 'Tighten Up' starts with the greeting 'We are YMO from Tokyo, Japan/We don't sightsee, we dance!' and when they appeared on *Soul Train*, they placed their manager Youichi Ito in the audience, dressed in the stereotypical uniform of a Japanese tourist – salaryman jacket and a big camera round his neck. The US cover of the self-titled debut album was illustrated with a geisha holding a fan, but with wires (symbolising Japanese advanced technology) exploding out of her head.

This notion – Japan as the vanguard of electronic technology, just that little bit further into the future than the rest of
us – was actually grounded in economic realities. When YMO
launched their career, their native land was already leading
the world in the research, development and exporting of
consumer electronics, from colour televisions to music centres.
Everyone remembers the famous battle for dominance between
VHS and Betamax as video formats, but this was a war
between two Japanese companies, Sony and Panasonic. The
Japanese government poured a fortune into the R&D of microchips – the same integrated-circuit technology celebrated in
YMO's album title *Solid State Survivor*. On the debut album,
'Computer Game: "Theme from *The Circus*"' and 'Computer
Game: "Theme from *The Invader*"' nodded to Japan's domi-
nance of the world's arcades: Space Invaders was developed by
Taito, Pac-Man by Namco, both Japanese companies.

So another reason to think of Japan as the birthplace of
techno is that it was the place where most of the foundational
technology behind electronic dance music was developed:
synths like the Yamaha DX7 and Korg MS-20, Akai's samplers
and MPCs (a crucial tool used in early hip hop), the Technics
1200 turntable (invented by Matsushita Electric). Above all,
Japanese expertise gave the world of dance music the Roland
range of iconic instruments: the Roland 808 and 909 drum
machines, the 'acid house' bass machine the Roland TB-303,
pioneering sequencer Roland MC-4 Microcomposer, and the
Roland Juno 106 synth (synonymous with the searing sounds
of hardcore techno in the 1990s). Thanks to programmer Matsutake, YMO were plugged into the state of the technological
art: their recordings often featured the earliest public appearance of a new piece of music technology.

A case in point is the group's fourth album *BGM*, released
in 1981 and the first album to prominently feature the Roland

808 drum machine, subsequently a cornerstone of hip hop and rave subgenres like bleep and jungle. *BGM* actually features a mutant Japanese twist on hip hop in 'Rap Phenomena'. As much as the crunching beats and denatured percussion sounds, it's the smeared synth-timbres and edge-of-dissonance tonalities that make *BGM* the group's most experimental album. The next album *Technodelic*, also released in 1981, added an early version of the digital sampler, custom-built for YMO by a Toshiba engineer. They used it to turn Indonesian chants, gamelan sounds and vocal snippets into track components. Two years ahead of the most advanced Western pop artists, YMO were already developing the sampladelic vocabulary of FX and stabs that would be used by Fairlight-wielding musicians such as Kate Bush and Art of Noise.

The five-album run from the 1978 debut to *Technodelic* is a feat of sustained evolution as impressive as the similar sequence of Talking Heads recordings in that same time period, or David Bowie's journey from *Low* to *Scary Monsters*.

Amazingly, while making these giant steps with each album, every member of YMO maintained a prolific and equally adventurous solo career. Having already debuted with *Thousand Knives of Ryūichi Sakamoto* in 1978, Sakamoto recorded his second solo LP *B-2 Unit* in 1980, establishing a pattern of collaboration with musicians outside the home islands by recruiting XTC's Andy Partridge and dub producer Dennis Bovell. A record that still sounds futuristic today, over forty years later, *B-2 Unit* resembles a synthetic jungle, skittering with odd-angled beats and rubbery sound-slithers. Tracks like 'Participation Mystique' suggest a religious ceremony on an alien planet – structured, elegant, but unreadable. As opaque as its cryptic title, *B-2 Unit* bypassed most listeners at the time. The exception was the single 'Riot in Lagos', a cult hit in the more daring clubs. Loosely inspired by Nigerian rhythm god Fela Kuti and drawing on Bovell's spatial sorcery, the track propels Afrobeat's syncopations far into a posthuman tomorrow: the flanged screeches, folded drones and zig-zagging streaks of tone-colour have the delicacy of Japanese calligraphy and the precision savagery of modern warfare.

B-2 Unit's angular rhythms infused Sakamoto's next major achievement outside YMO, a collaboration with David Sylvian, the singer of Japan. When the South London glam rockers chose their name, it was a placeholder, not indicative of any particular interest in Japanese culture. But success in Japan, initially based on the group's androgynous image, led to tours there and sure enough they became infatuated with all things East Asian, resulting in songs like 'Life in Tokyo' and 'Visions of China'. For Japan's 1980 album *Gentlemen Take Polaroids*, by which time their sound had evolved into an exquisitely subtle art-pop centred around synths and unusual tonalities, Sakamoto co-wrote and played keyboards on 'Taking Islands in Africa'. Then in 1982, Sylvian and Sakamoto recorded the astonishing double-A-sided single 'Bamboo Houses'/'Bamboo Music', roping in Sylvian's brother and Japan drummer Steve Jansen for the jolting rhythms. As the title hints, the core of the sound is a kind of synthetic simulation of the shakuhachi, a bamboo flute. But the way the textures are used – folded planes of blurry translucence, like origami made of frosted glass – propels ancient tradition into the disorienting future. Amazingly this double portion of avant-pop cracked the UK Top 30 in 1982.

A larger hit followed in 1983 with the exquisite 'Forbidden Colours', Sylvian adding an achingly poignant vocal to Sakamoto's fluttery theme for the Second World War movie *Merry Christmas, Mr. Lawrence* (in which Sakamoto also acted, playing a Japanese officer who develops a homo-erotic fascination for a British prisoner of war, played by David Bowie).

The success of the soundtrack plunged him into a long career composing for movies, working alongside directors like Bertolucci (whose *The Last Emperor* earned Sakamoto an Academy Award).

The delirious experimentalism of *B-2 Unit* and the Sylvian collaborations recurred in flickers on later Sakamoto albums – most strongly on the dense sampladelic thickets of *Esperanto*. But increasingly, Sakamoto solo work slipped into a mould of chic tastefulness, overly polished and overloaded with overseas guests (1989's *Beauty*, for instance, featured Youssou N'Dour, Robert Wyatt, Brian Wilson, Sly Dunbar, Robbie Robertson, Jill Jones . . .). By 1995's Latin-influenced *Smoochy*, the output got a bit too adult and easy on the ear.

Then, in the early twenty-first century, Sakamoto entered a new phase of recharged creativity, catalysed by a new collaborator. 'In the 1980s David Sylvian was a huge influence on me. But after 2000, Carsten Nicolai . . . has a huge impact,' he recalled in one interview. Sakamoto and Nicolai, better known as Alva Noto, together made a series of brilliant ambient records, merging the former's Satie/Harold Budd-esque piano with the wisps and clicks of the German producer's sound design: 2004's *Vrioon*, 2005's *Insen*, and then, after a gap, 2011's *Summvs* (featuring a surprising and lovely cover of Brian Eno's 'By This River' from *Before and After Science*).

The reorientation brought on by his partnership with Noto can be detected in much of Sakamoto's purely solo work these past two decades, from the underscores he created for *L.O.L.: Lack of Love* (an evolutionary life-simulation game) to the aqueous wonderland of *Plankton* (a collaboration with a biologist and a visual artist) through to his acclaimed solo album *Async*. Recorded after an up-close brush with death, in the form of throat cancer, the 2017 album is perhaps Sakamoto's equivalent to Bowie's *Blackstar*: a twilight meditation on

memory and mortality and a twilight resurgence in experimental risk-taking. Sakamoto marshalled a unique palette derived
from found urban sounds (and some non-urban – 'walker' uses
the rustle of his footsteps through a leaf-thick forest floor)
and prepared instruments (in one case, the 'preparation' was
nature's work – a tsunami-drowned piano, decayed and out-of-
tune). These raw sonic ingredients were simultaneously sheerly
textural but also freighted with personal meaning, evoking the
fragile preciousness of existence.

Two *Async* pieces brought the theme of transience into
painful clarity via recitation. On 'fullmoon', the voice of Paul
Bowles, who died in 1999, is heard reading a passage from
his own novel *The Sheltering Sky* (the movie version of which
Sakamoto scored). 'Because we don't know when we will die,
we get to think of life as an inexhaustible well, yet everything
happens only a certain number of times, and a very small
number really . . . How many more times will you watch the
full moon rise? Perhaps twenty . . . and yet it all seems limit-
less.' Friends of Sakamoto's from all over the world then read
out Bowles's words, each in their own language.

But on 'LIFE, LIFE', the feeling is more radiant, a blend of
defiance and acceptance. 'I was, I am, and I will be/Life is a
wonder of wonders,' intones David Sylvian, reading the words
of Arseny Tarkovsky, Russian poet and the father of Andrei
Tarkovsky (Sakamoto's favourite filmmaker, paid direct homage
on the *Async* tracks 'solari' and 'walker').

From the early nineties onwards, Sakamoto lived in New
York. This relocation, to the most cosmopolitan and polyglot city
on the planet, seemed to reflect a statement he'd made a few
years earlier: 'I don't know what I am. I was born in Japan, but I
don't think I'm Japanese. To be a stranger – I like that attitude.
I don't like nationalities and borders.' The ideal, latent in all
of Sakamoto's work – with YMO, solo and his many collabora-

tions – crystallised in 2003 as a kind of poetic manifesto. In the wake of 9/11 and the attack on his new home city, at the height of the Iraq War, he teamed up with Sylvian to release a beautiful single titled 'World Citizen' that was not so much a protest song as simply a plaint: 'Why can't we be/Without beginning, without end? . . . I want to travel by night/Across the steppes and overseas . . . I want to pronounce all their names correctly/World citizen'.

Pitchfork, 2023

DUB REGGAE: Keith Hudson, Creation Rebel, Dub Syndicate

Keith Hudson – *Pick a Dub* (Blood & Fire)
Creation Rebel – *Historic Moments Volume 1* (On-U)
Dub Syndicate – *Classic Selection Vol. 3* (On-U)

Originally recorded in 1974, Keith Hudson's *Pick a Dub* gets Jon Savage's vote (in the discography to *England's Dreaming*) for greatest dub album of all time. Certainly, it's up there with *King Tubby's Special* or Joe Gibbs's *African Dub Chapter 3*. There's a glow, a spiritual halo, to this music that even the best of today's digi-dub and ambient-dub units can't get close to. While the primitive two- or four-track recording and self-cobbled echo-chambers used by Tubby, Hudson, etc., have a lot to do with mid-seventies dub's blurry magic, another crucial factor is the pulsing presence of flesh-and-blood musicians inside the refractory, hall-of-mirrors vortex of the mixing desk. Classic dub involves the fusion of 'feel' (a live, interactive rhythm section) with the kind of disembodying, disorientating effects that antici-pated today's digital, sampladelic music. Rhythm is spatialised so that it oscillates 'vertically' (within the soundscape) as well as 'horizontally' (through time). And so in 'Black Heart', the chicken-scratch guitar doesn't just mark the after-beat, it leaps periodically out of its niche in the mix to buffet you about the face, while in 'Dread Than', the rhythm guitar is a smeared bloc of sound, as sculptural as it's kinetic.

Like psychedelia, like ambient, dub is about nostalgia. Its Promised Land on the temporal horizon is really a *return* – to a lost golden age (womb-time, when all sound reached us through the echo-chamber of the mother's body?). Dub's repetition incarnates an abolition of Time; it prefigures the end of our exile in History. Van Morrison was speaking the same inarticulate speech of the heart when he sang 'and it stoned me, just like going home'. But while Morrison expressed his homesick yearnings lyrically with his allegory of Caledonia, dub depicts Zion using space and light. In tracks like 'Part 1&2 Dubwise' and 'Black Right', reverbed, quicksilvered hi-hat and cymbals are all it takes to conjure up synaesthetic visions of an enfolding vastness. It's a sensation of being at home in infinity that the philosopher Gaston Bachelard called 'intimate immensity'.

Historic Moments Volume 1 is taken from 1977's *Dub from Creation* and 1978's *Rebel Vibrations*, albums that Creation Rebel recorded, with Adrian Sherwood at the controls, for his proto-On-U label Hit Run. More technically advanced than *Pick a Dub*, but pre-digital, these tracks are even more disorientating in their mix of human touch and studio-warped virtuality. Dub's use of echo on the drums, so that each part of the kit is fed through a different acoustic ambience, turns rhythm into a labyrinth. Stand-outs on this splendid collection include 'Vision of Creation', with its ghost-town piano and squeaky-bedspring drums, and 'Rebel Rouser', where the rhythm is doubled with a quasi-military beat that gradually deliquesces into a vapour trail of reverberance.

Some of the Rebels went on to play in Dub Syndicate. Mostly consisting of unreleased or drastically revamped tracks, *Classic Selection Vol. 3* dates from the late eighties. This music's high-definition gloss and inelastic programmed rhythms seem paradoxically more dated than Keith Hudson or Creation Rebel. Above all, despite the advances in recording technology, there seems to be less *space* in this dub than in Hudson and Tubby (who, like Can, achieved miracles with only two track). Or, at least, it's a different kind of space, more precise and geometric, less halcyon and exalted. The difference between classic dub and digi-dub is like the difference between a stained-glass window and a computer graphic.

Perhaps that spiritual aura is irretrievable, at least until contemporary dubsters renounce digital technology, sequencers, MIDI and the rest, and turn Luddite, like US lo-fi rock or techno's analogue-fetishists (like Aphex Twin). In the meantime, dub's legacy lives largest not with the purists and upholders-of-the-faith, but as a rogue chromosome in other genres: Saint Etienne's 'London Belongs to Me', AFX's 'Analogue Bubblebath 3', Scorn's 'Deliverance', drum and bass, jungle . . .

The Wire, 1994

ELECTRONIC DREAMERS: UK Synthpop

The UK synthpop era really kicked off in June 1979 when´ Tubeway Army's 'Are "Friends" Electric?' hit No. 1. Soon the charts were teeming with thin white dudes caked in Max Factor 28 Pan Stik and playing one-finger melodies on Korg keyboards. The sound and visuals owed a substantial debt to David Bowie's Berlin trilogy and his stranded alien in *The Man Who Fell to Earth*. Chuck in some Europe Between the Wars atmospherics and you had the recipe for Visage's 'Fade to Grey' and 'The Damned Don't Cry', Japan's 'Nightporter' and 'Ghosts', Ultravox's 'Vienna', and the rest of the scene known (confusingly) as both Futurists *and* New Romantics. Bowie himself resurfaced with the synth sorrow of 'Ashes to Ashes'. And bringing up the rear were the pioneers, the chaps who'd coined the whole Mittel Europa/*Mensch-Maschine* shtick in the first place: Kraftwerk, No. 1 in February 1982 with their 1978 tune 'The Model'.

Synthesisers in popular music actually go back much further than the mandroid melancholy of Gary Numan. All the way back to the psychedelic sixties, when American groups like Silver Apples, Fifty Foot Hose and The United States of America ditched guitars for oscillators. German cosmic rockers Tangerine Dream gradually streamlined their Pink Floyd-wannabe grandeur into a minimal, darkly pulsing, all-electronic sound. Floyd themselves forayed into full-blown synth-rock with *Dark*

Side of the Moon's 'On the Run', whose brain-searing wibbles anticipated acid house, while other proggers like ELP's Keith Emerson and Yes's Rick Wakeman performed behind massive banks of electronic keyboards and hammed it up with a Bach-style bombast of arpeggiated variations. Far more unearthly electro-tones could be heard on television S.F. series like *Doctor Who* (thanks to the BBC Radiophonic Workshop) and *The Tomorrow People*, or at the cinema courtesy of dystopian movies like *A Clockwork Orange*, *The Andromeda Strain* and *Logan's Run*. Black music too had its complement of visionaries besotted with the synth's cornucopia of otherworldly tone-colours, from fusioneers Weather Report and Herbie Hancock to funkateers Stevie Wonder and Funkadelic.

Black or white, these precocious knob-twiddlers all had a freakadelic, proggy mindset: they dug synths for the 'far out, man' noises they generated, so they let rip long noodling solos or oozed out abstract dronescapes. Few stood much chance of troubling the hit parade. In some ways the crucial word in synthpop isn't 'synth' but 'pop'. The British groups who took over the charts at the dawn of the eighties were catchy and concise. Here they followed the lead of Kraftwerk, who were not only the first group to make a whole conceptual package/ *Weltanschauung* out of the Electronic Age but were also sublime tunesmiths.

Equally inspiring to the synthpop artists was Kraftwerk's formality: their grey suits and short hair stood out at a time of jeans and beards and straggly locks, heralding a European future for pop, a decisive break with America and rock 'n' roll. Perhaps even more of a portent here was Giorgio Moroder's Eurodisco, whose clockwork-precise sequencers and icily erotic electronics forged the connection between synthesisers and the dancefloor. Released in 1977, Donna Summer's Moroder-produced 'I Feel Love' and Kraftwerk's 'Trans-Europe Express' divided pop time in two as profoundly as 'Anarchy in the U.K.'. The eighties begin there.

Conveniently, these singles arrived at a time when synths got vastly more affordable, portable and user-friendly. As revealed in the new BBC Four documentary *Synth Britannia* (which you can find on YouTube and in which I appear), what once cost as much as a small house (and therefore stayed the preserve of prog superstars) became something you could buy for a few hundred pounds, or cheaper still if you mail-ordered a build-your-own-synth kit and were prepared to spend weeks assembling the bloody thing. Groups who'd been inspired by punk's confrontational rhetoric and sartorial provocations but who found the actual sonic substance of punk rock to be too ye olde rock 'n' roll seized on the cheapo synth as the real coming of do-it-yourself.

Synthpop went through two distinct phases. The first was all about dehumanisation chic. That didn't mean the music was emotionless (the standard accusation of the synthphobic rocker) but that the emotions were bleak: isolation, urban alienation, feeling cold and hollow inside, paranoia about surveillance from the sinister forces of control. On the postpunk underground that meant Cabaret Voltaire and Throbbing Gristle, both of whom ironically used a fair bit of guitar but heavily treated it with electronic effects. On the pop overground it meant John Foxx and Gary Numan. Gary also used guitar prominently on his early hits under the name Tubeway Army. The secret of his success was that his music, for all its majestic canopies of glacial synth, *rocked*. Even when he dropped the guitar along with the name Tubeway Army and went fully electronic on 'Cars', he kept his flesh-and-blood drummer (the wonderfully named Cedric Sharpley, formerly of the prog-rock band Druid).

The second phase of synthpop reacted against the first. Electronic sounds now suggested jaunty optimism and the gregariousness of the dancefloor – they evoked a bright, clean future just round the corner, as opposed to J.G. Ballard's desolate seventies cityscapes. And the subject matter for songs mostly reverted to traditional pop territory: love and romance, escapism and aspiration. The prime movers behind synthpop's rehumanisation were appropriately enough the Human League (just check their song titles: 'Open Your Heart', 'Love Action', 'These Are the Things That Dreams Are Made Of'). Soft Cell were also crucial with their songs of torrid passion and seedy glamour. Their line-up – male diva Marc Almond, keyboard wiz David Ball – set the template for the first half of the eighties. The new compact synths resembled an orchestra in a box; you didn't need to have a whole band of instrumentalists. Suddenly pop was packed with duos who divided labour neatly between the composer/technology-operator and the singer/lyricist: Eurythmics, Yazoo, Tears for Fears, Blancmange, Pet Shop Boys. The shape of a synthpop outfit was subversive, or at least enough to make rockists uneasy: the rock band's gang-like structure replaced by same-sex 'couples' plus the occasional female diva/male boffin partnership.

Yazoo were a classic example of this fire-and-ice combo: Alison Moyet's proto-Joss Stone soulfulness matched with Vince Clarke's pristine perkiness. Clarke had been the brains behind Depeche Mode, or so everybody thought. Yet while he went on to commit a spree of cultural crimes under aliases like The Assembly and Erasure, it was Depeche who unexpectedly grew into Major Artists, leaving behind dinky ditties like 'Just Can't Get Enough' for the musically sophisticated, politically engaged/enraged *Construction Time Again* and *Some Great Reward*. The anti-monetarist smash 'Everything Counts' caught the melancholy of that moment after the 1983 re-election of Thatcher, while 'Master and Servant' combined an S/M-inspired personal-is-political allegory about power ('it's a lot like life', so 'forget all about equality') with a pop translation of Einstürzende Neubauten/Test Dept-style metal-bashing. Best of all was the haunting 'Blasphemous Rumours', a jibe at the Almighty which suggested 'God's got a sick sense of humour'.

One running theme in *Synth Britannia* is voiced repeatedly by Daniel Miller, the founder of Depeche's record label Mute, and this is the notion of electronic music being essentially un-British. But that would seem to beg the question of why the UK became the world's leading nation for synthpop, and later the major force in electronic dance music all through the nineties. The truth is that the real kingdom of synthphobia was the United States. But this also meant that American misfits could express their deviance by spurning standard high school fare like Mötley Crüe for 'faggy' English electropop. Depeche's cult following in the States expanded as they turned out to be surprisingly kick-ass live performers on the arena circuit, peaking with a 1988 show at the Pasadena Rose Bowl that drew 70,000. They were bigger still in Central and Eastern Europe, almost Beatles-level in Germany where to this day there are Depeche raves that play Mode music all night long. In Tallinn, Estonia, I came across the DM Bar, which offers cocktails named after songs by Mode and their contemporaries like Orchestral Manoeuvres and Visage.

A curious thing that comes through watching *Synth Britannia* is how the futuristic-ness of this music is largely irrecoverable to us, precisely because we live in the future that the synthpop era helped to bring about. Electronic tonalities are omnipresent to the point of banality, thanks to nineties techno-rave and noughties R&B, videogames and ringtones. 'Electro' in the early eighties meant cutting-edge, the future-now; nowadays 'electro' refers to the kind of sounds that lit up hipster bars in Hoxton all through this past decade and then unexpectedly went mainstream this year with La Roux and

77

Lady Gaga, which is to say synthetic pop that *isn't* state-of-art, *doesn't* use the full capacity of the latest digital technology, and is therefore almost as quaint as if it were made using a harpsichord.

With the future-shock aspect depleted, what comes through now is the *pop* in synthpop: OMD's pretty tunes, the aching plaintiveness of Numan and Human League. Oddly, what have made this music last are the same things that made The Beatles and Motown immortal: melody and emotion.

Guardian, 2009

INDUSTRIAL DANCE AND ELECTRONIC BODY MUSIC

Tyranny for You, the new album by Front 242, sounds like business as usual for the Belgian electronic outfit. It features their usual trademark features: juddering, girder-like beats, seismic sequencer pulses, bombastic synthesiser flourishes and domineering, chanted vocals. These days Front 242 aren't so fond of the samples that used to punctuate their techno-mantras (snatches of political oratory, televangelist preaching or trash-movie dialogue). But their aura is still overbearing and ominous.

There's one crucial difference about *Tyranny for You*, though: it's Front 242's first release for a major label. After nearly a decade of 'covert operations' in the independent sector, Front 242 have signed to Epic Records and are making a bid for a mass audience. Where once they likened themselves to a terrorist unit, now they talk of how 'terrorism aspires to tyranny'.

Nobody can agree on what to call the kind of music that Front 242 play: 'industrial disco', 'dancecore', 'electronic body music' are just some of the names that practitioners disown more frequently than pledge affiliation to. But after ten years as the soundtrack for a burgeoning cult scene, this sound may be on the verge of going overground. The recent grim turn in

79

world events could even help it on its way, as clubgoers react against the New Age 'positivity' of current dance music and turn to something more in tune with the chaos of the age. For industrial disco is danceable but it isn't funky, and it doesn't correspond to most people's idea of 'fun'. If disco is escapist, industrial disco is 'no escape'-ist. Drawing on media images of conflict and calamity, it doesn't so much document as *amplify* the tension and chaos of the outside world.

The international network of producers and consumers of this music stretches from Yugoslavia to Belgium to Britain to Canada and the USA. But the market is dominated by a triumvirate of record companies. First and foremost is Chicago's Wax Trax! label, whose output includes records by Revolting Cocks, My Life with the Thrill Kill Kult, KMFDM and Front Line Assembly. Wax Trax!'s public image has come to be defined by the notorious figure of Al Jourgensen, who at thirty-one has been dubbed 'the world's best-paid juvenile delinquent'. Jourgensen is a mainstay of the industrial super-group Revolting Cocks as well as his own band Ministry. Then there's Belgium's Play It Again, Sam label, who have pioneered 'electronic body music' with groups like Front 242, à;GRUMH, Borghesia and The Young Gods. Finally there's the Vancouver-based Nettwerk, whose roster includes Skinny Puppy, Severed Heads, Consolidated and SPK. The three labels are loosely allied, often licensing each other's records in their own terri-tory, while members of their groups frequently collaborate on sideline projects.

Industrial dance's musical 'roots' (the term seems inappropri-ate for music so inorganic and assembled) lie in the Eurodisco sound invented in the late seventies by producer Giorgio Moroder and popularised with tracks like Donna Summer's 'I Feel Love'. Moroder's aim was to create a pulse-based dance music that would be easier for white people to shake their stuff to than funk's tricksy syncopation. Another critical influence is the early-eighties German group D.A.F., who replaced the flash and dazzle of symphonic disco with a precise and rigorous grid of synth pulses. D.A.F.'s version of dance was less about flamboyant self-expression and more about 'absolute body control' (as one of their songs put it).

The 'industrial' side to the genre originates in a term adopted by one of the factions that emerged in the aftermath of punk. 'Industrial' groups like Cabaret Voltaire and Throbbing Gristle believed that punk was about disturbing the individual listener, rather than rallying youth in raucous solidarity behind political slogans. Challenging the listener involved tampering with traditional musical structures, experimenting with new technology and exploring subject matter that undermined comforting truths rather than shored up a consensus. These groups combined traditional avant-garde techniques (tape loops, found sounds, electronics) with the new spatial possibilities opened up by disco and dub reggae (using the studio as an instrument). The industrial aesthetic also drew on influences outside music, in particular the apocalyptic visions of cult writers like William S. Burroughs and J.G. Ballard. From Burroughs, they derived an obsession with 'control' (an almost superstitious paranoia about networks of surveillance and mind-manipulation) and the technique of 'cut-up' (the use of quotes and soundbites from the media). From J.G. Ballard, they drew an interest in aberrant sexuality and a fascination with scenarios of social collapse.

Industrial dance groups still work in this interface between pornography and pathology. For some, it's purely a question of voyeuristic kicks. Others have more honourable motivations: Skinny Puppy rub our noses in the horror of vivisection in order to enlighten and arouse compassion. But most groups on the scene tend to have a morbid attraction to extremist

81

thought and behaviour: the arcane rituals and 'discredited knowledges' of occult groups, the warped notions of conspiracy theorists, vigilantes and psychopaths.

Industrial dance music is enthralled by the outer limits of human experience, and in particular with the extremes of male psychology: the outlaw, the survivalist, the terrorist, the serial killer, the dictator, the technocrat. Industrial's aura is supremely masculine. The key adjective is 'hard', as in hard beats, hard living, hardcore. London's major club for this kind of music is simply called Hard Club. Dance is less a fun-time release and more like an endurance test. Standard disco phrases like 'work that body' are taken literally. The pumping-iron rhythms and unflagging repetition of groups like Nitzer Ebb and Die Krupps evoke a mood of aerobic triumphalism: like working out or marathon running, this is an aimless strength that exists only to flex itself. Promo videos for industrial tracks often incorporate images of glistening, tensed musculature reminiscent of the heroic realism of totalitarian art.

A key influence here is the rhetoric of the Italian Futurists and Soviet Constructivists, with their faith in technology, their formal brutalism and their suspicion of the 'feminising' aspects of civilisation. Industrial dance music particularly resembles Futurism in its worship of speed: not the illicit drug but the tempo of the twentieth century as it hurtles towards the apocalypse. (Wax Trax! group Lead into Gold wittily summed up the aesthetic with the title of their recent LP *Chicks & Speed: Futurism*). And like the original Futurists, the industrial dance groups have an ambiguous relationship with totalitarianism. For some, the flirtation is aesthetic rather than ideological (the sub-Wagnerian monumentalism of In the Nursery). Others make more explicit allusions. The German group KMFDM talk of their dream of a 'positive fascism' – an army of youth marching in one direction for peace and love, and working to build a society in which images of violence are banned. Or there's Front 242, who propound a survivalist philosophy that some critics have dubbed 'micro-fascism' (organising your own mind and body like a police state).

Even if you can't endure the music, industrial dance music is fascinating because it displays the full gamut of male psychology – from the sociopathic 'rebel without a cause' to the fanatic's will-to-power and paranoid worldview. Like rap, industrial can function as a glimpse into the void at the centre of the male ego. It provides a hyperbolic expression of two opposed masculine impulses. On the one hand, there's the outlaw who revolts against God and whose rampages range from rampant egoism to feats of self-destruction.

The other tendency involves the will-to-order in the face of chaos. The best representative of this approach is a San Francisco group called Consolidated, who have been described as a 'white Public Enemy'. Their brilliant album *The Myth of Rock* savages the notion of rock rebellion, which they diagnose as a symptom of arrested development. Consolidated dismiss rock as a regressive cul-de-sac whose main effect is to keep people from changing the world. The group are painfully aware of the problematic aspects of the scene from which they've emerged (they talk disparagingly of 'white aerobic supremacism'). Although their music shares much of the brutal exhilaration and galvanising rigour of the industrial genre, Consolidated claim they're inspired by a different, matriarchal model of strength. In that sense, they've done everyone a big favour: excising the unsavoury aspects of industrial while preserving the excitements of the form, they've brought the genre over to the side of the angels.

New York Times, 1991

INTO THE PHUTURE: Acid House

House music is disco-ultimate, assembled not born – an extraction of the most dance-effective elements from Hi-NRG, Moroder, Euro-synthpop and early-eighties New York electro-funk. The gimmicks, special effects and extended breaks once added to spice up disco have become the *whole body* of house.

Acid house is the purest, barest distillation of house, the outer limit of its logic of inhuman functionalism. With acid, black music has never been so *alien*ated from traditional notions of 'blackness' (fluid, grooving, warm), never been so close to the frigid, mechanical, supremely 'white' perversion of funk perpetrated by early-eighties pioneers like D.A.F. and Cabaret Voltaire.

Acid house is not so much a new thing as a drastic culmination of two tendencies in house: the trance-inducing effects of dub production and repetition; a fascination for the pristine, fleshless textures and metronome rhythms of German electropop. Pure acid tracks like Tyree's 'Acid Over' and Armando's 'Land of Confusion' recall the brute, inelastic minimalism of D.A.F. – these tracks consist of nothing but relentless machine-beats and eerie inflections.

Tyree claims never to have heard or heard of D.A.F., but acknowledges the influence of Liaisons Dangereuses, a D.A.F. offshoot operating in the same techno-primitive realm ('Oh

MAN, they were BIG in Chicago. Since '81.') as well as Kraftwerk, Telex and Trilogie.

Other acid house tracks suggest even more arcane references: Suicide, The Normal ('Warm Leatherette'), Die Krupps (proto-metalbashers and a precursor group to Propaganda). Ex-Sample's 'And So It Goes' combines cut-ups ('Heroin Kills'), unidentifiable bursts of distorted samples and human cries torn from their context (agonies of desire or distress) in a manner not unlike Front 242.

On Reese's 'Just Want Another Chance', Detroit producer Kevin Saunderson sets a guttural, Stephen Mallinder-style monologue of desire over the spookiest of Residents synthdrones – an ectoplasmic bassline much slower than the drum track. On a different tack, 'Strings of Life' by Rhythim Is Rhythim (Derrick May, also from Detroit) takes the sultry swing of Latin disco and clips it into a spasmodic tic that's deeply unsettling. On the flipside, 'Move It' is a perimeter of trebly rhythm programs that restlessly orbit the black hole where the song should be. It strangely recalls one of those lost, desolate Joy Division B-sides.

Phuture's 'Acid Trax' is the track that launched the acid house phenomenon with its warped and wibbling Roland 303 bassline. But weirder still is the flipside, 'Your Only Friend'. The 'Cocaine Mix' is *ill*. A treated voice midway between a dalek and the Voice of Judgement announces: 'This is Cocaine speaking'. Spectral eddies of a disembodied human wail, reminiscent of nothing so much as Public Image Ltd's 'No Birds Do Sing', simulate the soul languishing in cold turkey. Then we're launched on a terror-ride that again reminds me of PiL, this time 'Careering' or 'Death Disco'. 'I can make you lie for me/I can make you die for me/In the end/I'll be your only friend.'

Where disco was always about escapism, acid house is about no-escapism. In this, it takes after the postpunk avant-funk of

86

the early eighties. Like avant-funk, it sounds *inhibited*. Acid house departs from the trad disco idea of dance as good-times celebration and embraces the avant-funk idea of disco as trance, a form of sinister subjugation. Expansive and expressive gestures are replaced by a precise and rigorous set of movements, *demands* on the body, flamboyance and improvisation by a discipline of pleasure. Perhaps there's liberation in submitting to the mechanics of instinct, soldering the circuitry of desire to the circuitry of the sequencer programs.

As for the connotations of 'acid', all involved in the Chicago scene deny that hallucinogens have anything to do with the sound. However, many clubgoers do take Ecstasy, a drug which provides a euphoric sense of communion without causing hallucinations . . .

House has been bordering on the psychedelic for some time anyway, with the spaciness of its dub effects, its despotic treatment of the voice and its interference with the normal ranking of instruments in the mix (encouraging 'perceptual drift'). On one mix of Nitro Deluxe's 'On a Mission', a single phrase of female voice is vivisected, varispeeded and multitracked into a psychedelic babble of sub-phonemes and vowel particles, becoming an airborne choir of lunatic ecstasies, a locust swarm of placeless peaks and plaints spirited free of their location in the syntax of desire.

On the Kenny Jones mix of Ralphi Rosario's 'You Used to Hold Me', stray sibilants from Xavier Gold's vocal flake off to bob inhumanly in their own parallel slipstream, until her vocal is absorbed into the backing track, with one spasm of passion turned into a jack-knifing rhythm effect. On the 'Devil Mix' of Master C&J's 'In the City', Liz Torres' voice is distorted and distended in a manner uncannily akin to Butthole Surfers.

With *pure* acid house, however, it's not really a question of acid rock's twenty-four-track technicolour overload, of a

dazzling opening of the doors of perception, but more like
a contraction or evacuation of consciousness. Not a matter
of being saturated by TOO MUCH but of being compelled
to focus on too little, reduced to a one-track mind. If people
do drop a tab or two to 'Acid Over' they must have strange
digital visions, enter Mondrian phantasmagorias, Spirograph
inner orbits.

What the berserk strobe-flicker of acid house is most reminiscent of is an episode from *Star Trek*: miscreants are punished by
being subjected to a strobe-like flashing lightbox which clears the
brain, leaving them suggestible and capable of being literally re-
formed. But one deviant is left in the machine, brainwashed but
un-reprogrammed, lost in a terrifyingly blank catatonic limbo.

Like D.A.F.'s new savagery, like psychedelia's orgiastic
utopianism, house incites a superhuman/inhuman insatiability.
With the jettisoning of the song-as-story, sex loses narrative
and context, becomes asocial and fantastical. There's no sense
of trajectory (courtship/seduction/foreplay/union), no sexual
healing, no communication. Nothing is ever resolved: house
is the beat that can never satisfy or be satisfied. The stutter-
beats, the costive basslines, sound *neurotic*: the music's a
repetition-complex, a symptom of some unstaunchable vacancy
of being. Every bar of the music becomes orgasmic, making the
idea of climax meaningless.

And where acid rock imagined utopia as a garden of pre-modern
innocence, acid house is futuristic, in love with sophistication
and technology. Acid house imagines a James Bond/Barbarella
leisure paradise of gadgetry and designer drugs. House is a kind
of pleasure factory and, as Marx wrote, the factory turns human
beings into mere appendages of flesh attached to machinery.

*

Tyree, rising producer . . . explains the origins of the acid sound.

'The actual sound has been around a long time. Mike Macharello had it on a cut called "Single Girl" he had out in '84 [as "Knight Action"]. But acid really started happening when DJ Pierre thought up the name when he put out "Acid Trax", under the name Phuture. People were wild for that track.

'The crucial element in acid is that the bassline really carries the song, not so much the drum track. It's the modulation of the frequencies of the bassline that keeps the track moving, keeps it hot.

'It has nothing to do with drugs, it's just a name that fits because the music's crazy. But it affects you like a drug; it takes you over. People go into a trance, they just lose it! It makes everything seem so fast, it's like an upper.

'There aren't that many people doing acid music yet – most of them, Mike Dunn, Bam Bam, Two of a Kind, myself, are friends. But as an influence, acid house is spreading.'

Farley Jackmaster Funk says that the Acid Machine (a piece of Roland equipment called Bassline) 'is an obsolete, old-fashioned piece of technology that no one had ever thought of using that way before. I get a lot of my original sounds from outmoded technology.'

This reminds me of Dinosaur Jr's preference for quaint guitar effects because they provide 'harsheties rather than subtleties': the gauchely moderne effects of the acid machine, once laughable, now seem otherworldly.

Other directions for Tyree could be New Age ('I like to listen to that when I want to chill') and mixing rap and acid house. 'At my parties I mix house trax with hip hop records on 45 rpm – makes LL Cool J sound like a chipmunk!'

Melody Maker, 1988

RAVE: Acen's Trips II the Moon

Acen – 'Trip II the Moon 2092' (Kniteforce)

There are many examples of box sets that collate all of an artist's singles, complete with the original picture sleeves. But I've never before encountered a box dedicated to a *single* single. If ever there was a tune that could withstand this degree of inflation, though, it's 'Trip II the Moon'. Not only is this breakbeat hardcore classic widely considered the greatest anthem of the rave era, there was already a certain grandiosity to the way Acen and his original label Production House rolled out the track across the summer of 1992.

The record came out in three successive versions, the second and third not so much remixed as re-produced: 'Trip II the Moon, Part 1', 'Trip II the Moon, Part 2 (The Darkside)', 'Trip II the Moon (Kaleidoscopiklimax)'. Giving remixes, when done by the original artist, titles that involved words like 'Part' or 'Volume' would become a hallmark of the jungle scene. Most likely this trend took inspiration from Hollywood pulp franchises with their sequels, itself an echo of the sprawling sagas of Tolkienesque fantasy and Frank Herbert-style S.F. But in '92, a track that came out three times over several months was virtually unheard of. A sales-driving strategy designed to extend a tune's currency and possibly rocket it into the pop charts, it also reflected artistic ambition: a growing confidence from some operators within a scene then sniffed at by techno-cognoscenti that they were not in the business of trashy, ephemeral floor-fodder but crafting popular art that would pass the test of time.

And here we are in 2021, almost three decades later, the original 'Trip'tych A-sides plus excellent B-sides arrayed across six slabs of vinyl, where they jostle alongside new interpretations by Acen and nine guest remixers. The box title's reference to '2092' gestures at a posterity even further down the temporal line. It suggests both aesthetic durability and the implication that this music comes from the future. A sensation that felt absolutely real back in the early nineties and still somehow clings to these tempestuous tracks even now.

The sheer solidity of the attractive if pricy box is a demonstration of maximal respect. 'Maximal', as it happens, is the right word for Acen's sound and peers like Hyper-On Experience. Before hardcore, and indeed after it during the later nineties, techno and house generally cleaved to a minimalist aesthetic, sometimes taking a single riff or vamp and inflecting it subtly over five, six, seven minutes. UK rave producers, conversely, 'get busy', action-packing their tracks on both the linear axis and the vertical. Tracks unfold through time as multi-segmented epics hurtling through bridges and breakdowns, intros and outros. But each passing moment is layered with simultaneous sound-events, resulting in a stereo-field infested with audio-critters bouncing around like in some crazily detailed animation.

Listening again to all three 'Trips' is a reminder of just how unique and curious an animal was hardcore. There's hardly a trace of Detroit or Chicago audible here. Most UK producers, including West Londoner Acen Razvi, were former B-boys, electro fans who spent their teen years breakdancing and spraying graffiti. Acid house (and attendant chemicals) flipped their heads, but soon they reverted to type. But while sped-up breaks and samples are the foundation, hardcore's hyperactivity is a world away from nineties rap like Wu-Tang Clan. No British rave producer would drag out a single break-loop across six sombre minutes of stoned monotony like RZA. There are hardcore tracks from this era that contain a rap album's worth of ideas crammed into six minutes.

One thing hardcore did share with East Coast hip hop is soundtrackism. The centrepiece sample in 'Part 1' is an impossibly stirring swathe of orchestration from 'Capsules in Space' off John Barry's *You Only Live Twice* score; 'Part 2' likewise lifts a serene ripple of strings from the same Bond movie's 'Mountains and Sunrises'. Actually, that's not quite accurate: the copyright holders blocked sample clearance, obliging Production House to hire a mini orchestra to replay Barry's themes. Acen tells me that he 'sampled both pieces of music with the exact same low-resolution bit rate I did with the vinyl', in order to replicate the particular grainy quality the original samples had. 'We used those settings to save space for memory, because we always used to max out the very limited memory on these early samplers.' Acen's fetish for movie scores manifests also on the brilliant B-side 'The Life and Crimes of a Ruffneck', which heists the heart-spasming staccato melody of Morricone's 'Chi Mai'.

Other raw ingredients came mostly from rap, R&B and ragga: Rakim's sped-up squeak 'I get hype when I hear a drum roll', Chuck D's threat/promise 'here come the drums', Topcat boasting he's 'phenomenon one'. The electrifying diva shriek 'I can't believe these feelings' that supplies the hypergasmic hook on 'Trip' hails from obscure Britsoul outfit Tongue 'n' Cheek, while Prince protégé Jill Jones supplies erotic gasps for another terrific B-side, 'Obsessed'. As for that eerily familiar goblin voice murmuring 'in my brain' – that's a witty bit of self-citation, pulling from Acen's previous single 'Close Your Eyes', which sampled and sped up Jim Morrison off The Doors' 'Go Insane'.

Nowadays, it's easy to identify the constituent parts of beloved tunes thanks to websites like whosampled.com and the collective nerd knowledge of old skool message boards. But back in the day, the music barraged your brain as a kinetic collage jumbling the instantly recognisable, the faintly familiar and the wholly unknown. (Whether you spotted stuff depended also on your listener competency – age, musical background, level of intoxication). Hardcore was technically postmodern, in its procedures. But as a sonic outcome, and in terms of motivating spirit, it hit with the juddering force of full-bore modernism. The conceit felt true: this *was* music from the future, built from mutilated and mutated shards of past. That's one reason why the idea of the space race – man's greatest adventure, a surge into the unknown – resonated with rave and supplied Acen with not just the 'Moon' title but the name of his next single, 'Window in the Sky'. Drugs played a part too (understatement of the century). Rave was modernist but it was also psychedelic.

If the main meat here is Acen's extended spurt of original genius, the remixes are mostly splendid. Kniteforce boss Chris Howlett (aka Luna-C) and old skool legend NRG manage to stay true to, yet also intensify, the original 'Trip' blend of cinematic and epileptic. Retro-jungle youngblood Pete Cannon offers a pell-mell scratchadelic take on 'Ruffneck'. The only misfire comes from doyen of scientific drum and bass Dbridge. If only he could have reinhabited the mindset of his own teenage hardcore identity, The Sewer Monsters! Instead, 'Obsessed' gets flattened into a dank neurofunk furrow à la Jonny L's 'Piper'. It sounds obsessive, for sure, but the emphasis on sound design and moody monotony has nothing to do with the larcenous free-for-all and cartoon delirium of the early nineties.

The Wire, 2021

GABBER AND GLOOMCORE: The Mover and PCP Records

At the dawn of the nineties, a Brooklyn DJ named Leonardo Didesiderio stood on a Frankfurt street clutching his record box in the rain. The organisers of the party at which he'd just played had failed to fix up a hotel for him. A local DJ noticed his plight and offered him a place to stay. That night the twenty-two-year-old German played his guest a track he'd made: 'We Have Arrived', a stampede of pounding techno with distorted kick drums and a blasting blare of a riff. The American sat there for hours playing it over and over, then announced to his host that the track was the future of electronic dance music and that he would put it out as the debut release of a record label he'd been planning to start.

True to his word, Lenny D – as he's better known – launched the Brooklyn-based label Industrial Strength Records in 1991 with 'We Have Arrived', credited to Mescalinum United, coupled with the double-A-side track 'Nightflight (Non-Stop to Kaos)', credited to The Mover. Both aliases belonged to Marc Acardipane, the DJ who'd rescued Lenny from the downpour. A native of Frankfurt – Germany's bustling and modern-looking financial centre and in the early nineties the country's leading city for electronic dance music – Acardipane had apprenticed in punk, moved into industrial, even dabbled in hip hop. By the start of the nineties, though, he'd noticed that techno was turning into a computer-era update of rock, based on similar sonic principles: distorted riffs and mid-frequency noise, attack and attitude. Acardipane decided to push those tendencies further. Push them to the limit.

Although New York club music was already shifting into a harder-faster mode, thanks to epochal techno tracks by Brooklyn's own Joey Beltram like 'Energy Flash' and 'Mentasm', the style that Acardipane developed was a quantum leap forward into a cold, dark, future-rave sound. Reminiscing in the comments section of Discogs's entry for that debut Industrial Strength 12-inch single, Lenny D's associate Frankie Bones hailed Acardipane as a foundational figure: 'We built our scene in the Brooklyn Underground from tracks like this. Music made for large spaces . . . It made perfect sense in an old warehouse. Tracks like this did not sit well with most people that were playing house music. Way too abrasive, loud and gritty. The beats were relentless. They held back for nobody, consuming everything in their path.'

New York producers like John Selway, Oliver Chesler and Sal Mineo hurled themselves down this pummelling new path for techno and, by 1992, were releasing tracks on Industrial Strength under names like Disintegrator, Temper Tantrum, DJ Skinhead and Strychnine. Many came from industrial music or hardcore punk backgrounds, rather than the dance scene: what they made wasn't club music so much as music that *clubbed* the listener. At the harder East Coast parties like Storm Rave and Mental, dancefloors started to resemble mosh pits.

Meanwhile, back in Frankfurt, Acardipane and his business partner Thorsten Lambart released 'We Have Arrived' and a torrent of belligerent, high-velocity tracks via their own label Planet Core Productions (aka PCP). Alongside an insane volume of music (hundreds of tracks, scores of releases), Acardipane created a legion of alter egos – Ace the Space, Rave Creator, Freez-E-Style, Protectors of Bass – that would eventually number in the region of sixty. Each fictitious persona had its own distinctive style. Alien Christ tracks like 'Art of Shredding', for instance, were inspired by Suburban Knight's twitchy Detroit techno classic 'Art of Stalking'. T-Bone Castro specialised in lewd, crude tunes like 'Bitches' (off 1993's *Sex Drive* EP) while his 'brother' Nasty Django slammed out rowdy anthems like 'Let It Roarrrr!!!' and the Lemmy-from-Motörhead-sampling 'Ey Fukkas!'. Acardipane and Lambart even resorted to using an Atari computer and police software designed to construct identikit images of suspected criminals to create imaginary faces for their roster of non-existent artists.

The partners also spun off from PCP a miniature swarm of sub-labels, each with a subtly different sound and concept. Dance Ecstasy 2001 was their populist outlet for 'peak of the night' anthems, a slightly more punitive version of the trance sound for which Frankfurt was globally famous. Cold Rush, conversely, was for cognoscenti: a cavernous and glacial sound that lived up to the imprint's slogan 'music created somewhere in the lost zones'. Speaking over the phone from his current home, Hamburg, Acardipane tells me that 'with Cold Rush, my idea was that if you were dying on the dancefloor, these would be the last tracks you heard!'

At home, on headphones, listening to Cold Rush classics like 'Thru Eternal Fog' and 'Marchin' into Madness', you feel like you're inside a vast cathedral space carved out beneath the frozen methane crust of Pluto. This 'gloomcore' style of gabber taps into the history of sacred echo, from Gothic churches designed to swathe the listener in non-localisable low-frequency reverberance, all the way back to the prehistoric audio-technics of pagan rites conducted in caves and grottoes. Piteous melodies whimper, wilt and waver in the air. Although the kick drum is still pretty fast, around 180 bpm, the dirge-like droop of shimmery atmospherics and sickly synth-drones makes gloomcore feel slower than it actually is.

For a long while, virtually every release via the PCP label cluster was entirely made by Acardipane or featured him as a co-producer. But then spiritual kinsmen turned up. From France came Guillaume Leroux, whose work under names like Renegade Legion and Dr Macabre married brutality and atmosphere in a way that rivalled Acardipane's own productions (and with the strobing death-ray synth-stabs of 'Torsion', possibly even surpassed him). There was also Miroslav Pajic, a Frankfurt man with a Serbian name, whose collection of alter egos rivalled Acardipane's but whose most cinematic and haunting tracks – 'Skeleton's March', 'Hall' – came out under the alias Reign.

The artist names and track titles were crucial, framing the music and creating pictures in your mind (invariably dystopian or desolate) before you even dropped the needle into the groove. Most of the titles came from the non-musician Thorsten Lambart, whom Acardipane describes as 'a genius', even though their partnership fell apart in the late nineties owing to an undisclosed personal disagreement.

But back in their mid-nineties heyday, PCP were an unstoppable force. Crowd-pleasing monsters like 'Stereo Murder' and 'Six Million Ways to Die' made them hugely popular in the Netherlands, where an entire subculture called gabber had sprung up in the wake of 'We Have Arrived'. Punning artist aliases like Pilldriver indicate how PCP targeted the Ecstasy-gobbling hordes of northern Europe. But the label explored more experimental directions too. Having started with a banger, Mescalinum United veered off into abstract noise with the 'Symphonies of Steel' EPs, eventually abandoning the beat altogether for what Acardipane called 'sick ambient': a vaporous sound that he says was an attempt to conjure the inhospitable surface of a planet like Jupiter.

In Germany itself, PCP had been hip early on, but by 1994 they found themselves languishing in a sort of no man's land. Their sound was too doomy and aggressive for the rave mainstream of fluffy trance associated with rave promoters like Low Spirit and the annual Love Parade in Berlin. But it was also too pulpy in its horror and sci-fi references to be acceptable in the snooty world of German minimal techno. After PCP disintegrated, Acardipane did record a Mover album for the ultra-hip label Tresor, 2003's *Frontal Frustration*. But any credibility he might have garnered through that was thrown to the winds when he teamed up that same year with the pop-rave outfit Scooter for a remake of his Marshall Masters shout-a-long 'I Like It Loud'. The single 'Maria (I Like It Loud)' went Top 5 in Germany and Hungary and reached No. 1 in Austria. Its Oompa Loompa-like chant also became a jock jam crowd-inciter at a number of European soccer stadiums. In the glossy big-budget video for the Scooter remake, Acardipane appears at various points, looking slightly awkward, as if inwardly contemplating the underground's reaction to seeing their hardcore hero on MTV Europe. Still, the smash single earned him a sustaining stream of publishing money that carried him through a twenty-first century that proved to be much quieter than his hectic, hyper-productive nineties.

Unlike the Industrial Strength release, the PCP version of 'We Have Arrived' featured a different tune on the flipside: a sinister track titled 'Reflections of 2017'. That year – impossibly far off and futuristic in 1991 – became a running theme through Acardipane's work, triggering a mind-swirl of dystopian *mise en scène* out of *Blade Runner*, *Terminator* and *Robocop*. 'Well, you know I'm a machine, I'm wired up,' Acardipane told *Alien Underground* zine in a rare interview. 'I'm roaming the earth and it's nice and doomy here.'

'See you in 2017' was The Mover's slogan. And sure enough, after a long period of near inactivity, 2017 saw Acardipane get busy again: he played raves as the techno equivalent of a 'legacy act' and reissued some of his best-loved Mover tracks in remastered form. An all-new album, his first in fifteen years, was also planned for 2017. But dissatisfied with his first attempt at the comeback record – he felt it was 'too polished-sounding' – Acardipane scrapped it completely. Finally, bearing the somewhat clunky title *Undetected Act from the Gloom Chamber*, the long-player was released in late March 2018.

The spur to remobilise came in 2016 when a promoter fixed Acardipane up with a rare date in Berlin. The setting – an old crematorium – was perfect for The Mover's reverb-soaked sound and mournful melodies. Acardipane discerned a renewed appetite for techno's harder and darker side in the young crowd, most of whom would not have been born yet when PCP got started. Gamely, he'd brought along specimens of contemporary electronic music that he liked. But he noticed that when he drew for his own tunes from back in the day, 'the kids really went wild. It became like a real rave. If I play something like "Nightflight", the people go nuts.'

Acardipane feels that these young ravers are 'looking to the past because they don't like the new stuff'. His nickname for today's electronic dance music is 'highway techno': there's a sort of cruise-control quality to it. The production and sound-design glisten with intricately textured detail, but there's no propulsive drive, no hard *core* to these tracks. 'People like me want back the energy, the futurism, the darkness, the power, the emotion.'

Undetected Act is a strong restatement of the classic Mover sound. Motored by a Moog-synth bass-grind, 'Stealth' – one of the highlights – harks back to Acardipane's baptismal rave experiences in Frankfurt clubs like The Omen and Dorian Gray. Laced with lachrymose piano, 'Lost' – another gem on the album – took a while to find the atmosphere he sought. A prototype version was 'not lonely enough', he says.

Acardipane played that piano motif himself. Surprisingly, given that the barbarian style of techno he did so much to spawn is regarded by many even within the EDM world as anti-music, his conventional training runs deep. As a boy he sang in a professional choir for several years. Between the ages of eight and eighteen, he studied classical guitar. He also received electric guitar lessons from a member of the Frankfurt punk band Strassenjungs. After forming several punk groups himself, Acardipane started to dabble with synths and drum machines in the mid-eighties, during the heyday of industrial and electronic body music.

But there were also attempts at hip hop, an enduring passion: Acardipane loved Public Enemy and to this day hero-worships Dr Dre for his sound engineering. 'But there came a time when I had to look in the mirror and realise, "You don't come from Compton!" We had to look for the street sound of Europe.' Acardipane found it in, of all places, Belgium, which around the turn of the eighties into the nineties was spawning a baleful and bombastic hybrid of house rhythm and industrial textures. The ignition point for The Mover vision really lies with forgotten Belgian producers like The Mackenzie, 80 Aum and T99, whose tunes were like lobotomised rave updates of Wagner's 'Ride of the Valkyries' and Carl Orff's *Carmina Burana* movement 'O Fortuna'.

It was around this time – end of eighties, start of nineties – that Acardipane began to have a recurring dream. Not exactly recurring: he describes it as like a movie or TV series, with each dream as the next episode. The dreams were set in 2017.

101

That's where 'Reflections of 2017' came from, and the whole Mover mythos of that remote-in-time year. The year 2017 seemed to figure for him as a sort of imaginatively projected singularity pulling him and his music towards the future like a tractor beam. Now that Acardipane has gone right past his Year of Destiny, he sometimes sounds a little bemused by what his role might be today.

That year certainly turned out to be apocalyptic, and 2018 may yet top it, but it's not how we imagined things back in the early nineties. Meanwhile, the electronic dance culture has spent much of the twenty-first century succumbing to technostalgia, revisiting genres from the nineties and even exploring the prehistory of rave culture, with a huge resurgence of interest in eighties industrial and EBM. In such temporally confused circumstances, The Mover can be forgiven for going back to the future rather than trying to reinvent it.

Director's expansion, *Village Voice*, 2018

JUNGLE: The Breakbeat Symphonies of Omni Trio

A ripple runs through it. The peal of piano – reflective or rhapsodic, elegiac or euphoric – is the lineament that marks almost all of Robert Haigh's music across his nearly forty years of recording. You hear it on his eighties releases, when he aligned with the esoteric industrial underground but had more in common with Harold Budd. You hear it as a Morse signal summoning dancers to the ravefloor in the series of Omni Trio EPs recorded by Haigh for peerless jungle label Moving Shadow in the early nineties, and again – but now more serene and slinky – on his cinematic drum and bass albums from later that decade. Finally, in the twenty-first century, you hear the piano naked and unadorned once more, with the flurry of albums Haigh recorded after parting ways with UK dance culture, culminating with the quiet triumph of 2017's *Creatures of the Deep*.

When I enquire just what it is about the instrument that speaks to him so deeply and persistently, Haigh gathers his thoughts slowly over the phone from his home, a tiny town near Truro in Cornwall. 'I think it's just the fact that you can – on your own – make a really wide sort of sound with the piano. You can create chords and the basslines as well. What attracted me in the beginning was that I could do the whole thing myself.' Later, dissatisfied, Haigh returns with clarifications via email: 'The piano is essentially a percussive instrument but it's capable of the most fluid extended voices. It can produce thunderous bass tones alongside the most intimate and fragile top notes. I also like the fact of its self-containment and independence. This makes it a great tool for improvisation, which is the basis for most of my writing.'

As for initiating raptures that made him notice the instrument's potential, Haigh mentions the title track of Bowie's *Aladdin Sane*, featuring Mike Garson's famously jagged, dissonant and somehow decadent solo, and the 'strange discordant piano' on *The Faust Tapes*. In his late fifties now, Haigh is old enough to have experienced that album as a real-time astonishment, thanks to his older sister, who bought Virgin Records's 49p bargain only to be baffled by it, and passed it on to fourteen-year-old Rob. Beyond the piano element, Haigh attributes a profound formative impact to this early exposure to *The Faust Tapes*. 'Initially I couldn't make much sense of it either, but because I only owned two or three albums at that point, I persevered. If you listen to my stuff you wouldn't immediately think "This guy's influenced by Faust." But there's a seam of experimentation in my music and it probably started with the way Faust's music is all cut up and juxtaposed, with beautiful melodies next to atonal chaos.'

Haigh's first hands-on encounter with the piano came much later, though, when he was a student at London's Central School of Art. 'There was a room in the back, with a piano in it, and I used to go in there sometimes and plonk about. I never really thought "*This* is what I wanna do." The piano was just something I kept being drawn to.'

Before the piano, though, there was the electric guitar – and the voice. Considering how camera-shy and publicity-averse

Haigh has been during his career, it's a jolt to learn that he once fronted a glam-rock group called Labyrinth. 'It's a cliché to say how much Bowie influenced your life, but my first single was actually "Starman."' More than a mere amateur band, Labyrinth gigged heavily in Yorkshire (Haigh grew up between Barnsley and Sheffield) and entertained serious hopes of being signed. 'We got all sorts of promises: "Oh yeah, we'll record you."'

Nothing came of it, though, and Haigh headed down south to art school. But instead of painting, most of his creative energy got siphoned into the roiling ferment of postpunk. He formed the avant-funk outfit Truth Club (later renamed Fote) which bore the heavy imprint of the Pop Group and This Heat and would support groups like Clock DVA and Cabaret Voltaire. Haigh was still playing guitar at this point, but in an unorthodox fashion: using a dildo instead of a plectrum. 'I'd seen This Heat doing something similar,' he laughs. Attracted by both the visual provocation and the possibilities for making strange sounds, Haigh procured his own plastic phallus and soon found that if he 'put it near the pick-ups and just moved it an inch away, it made a buzzing tone. I even cut a little notch in the end of it, and I could put that over a string, move that along the fretboard and that made a really cool sound.'

Postpunk contained an abundance of the same qualities Haigh had first thrilled to in Faust: contrasts and collisions, discipline and disorder. 'Such a music of possibilities' is how he fondly remembers the 1979–81 period. 'Instead of being based around chords, like rock was in the sixties and then again in Britpop, postpunk was more like counterpoint: a more spacious way of composing. So with a band like PiL, there was a repetitive deep bassline and almost Steve Reich-like patterns played on a scratchy guitar.'

By the early eighties Haigh had quit art school and was working at a Virgin record shop on Oxford Street – not the

famous Megastore but a branch further up the road. The
basement became a hang-out for London's industrial-aligned
musicians. Former employee Jim Thirlwell would bring his
Foetus releases, Nurse with Wound's Steve Stapleton visited
regularly and likewise came bearing strange sounds, and all of
it got played on the big sound system. After recording a solitary Truth Club/Fote single, Haigh had by this point launched
Sema, a 'dark ambient' solo project, which in rapid succession
generated three albums (*Notes from Underground*, *Theme from
Hunger*, *Extract from Rosa Silber*) during 1982–3, all issued
through his own Le Rey imprint. 'Steve was into the Sema
stuff. We would hang out at his graphics design office, just
down the road from Virgin. Then he invited me to some Nurse
with Wound sessions.'

Haigh contributed to the Faustian frolics of mid-eighties
Nurse with Wound albums such as *The Sylvie and Babs Hi-Fi
Companion* and *Spiral Insana*. Meanwhile, he put out the EPs
Juliet of the Spirits and *Music from the Ante Chamber* via
the Belgian label L.A.Y.L.A.H., joining a roster of industrial
luminaries that included Coil, Current 93, 23 Skidoo, Organum
and Hafler Trio. In an echo of Throbbing Gristle's 'dis-concerts',
L.A.Y.L.A.H. talked about putting out 'anti-records', while the
label's name was an acronym for the Aleister Crowley dictum
'Love Alway Yieldeth: Love Alway Hardeneth'. But Haigh says
he never had too much truck with the magic and ritual element in industrial culture, responding more to its cut-up and
Dada side.

Besides, Haigh's own music was steadily drifting away
from the industrial zone. Sema started as disquieting abstract
ambience sourced in various processed instrumental sounds,
but the piano gradually emerged as the principal voice, and
a calming one. A pivotal release was 1984's *Three Seasons
Only*. Credited to Robert Haigh and Sema, the Haigh side was

piano only. Satiesque sketches like 'Two Feats of Klee' pointed ahead to *Valentine out of Season* (released on United Dairies in 1987) and 1989's *A Waltz in Plain C*. Both came out under his own name.

The Sema moniker was borrowed from an artists' organisation co-founded by Paul Klee. 'I was a Klee fan from my art school days and I think I just literally opened a book on him, saw the word "Sema" and thought "I'll have that!"' Other homages include 'Rosa Silber' (a reference to Klee's painting *Vocal Fabric of the Singer Rosa Silber*) and 'Concrete and the Klee' (presumably a play on 'Concrete and Clay', the 1965 hit for Unit Four Plus Two). 'Some of Klee's work is probably not far off a visual representation of Satie's music,' Haigh says. He relates the juxtaposition of 'figurative and nonfigurative' in Klee's work with the blurring between tonal and atonal that fascinates him in music. 'When I'm doing a tonal piece, I'm trying so hard to pollute it with wrong notes, notes that aren't meant to be there, because I find that's what makes the music stick. If it's all tonally correct, I lose interest.'

Allusions to high culture pepper Haigh's output of the eighties (which was reissued several years ago by Vinyl on Demand as the box sets *Time Will Say Nothing* and *Cold Pieces*). There's the Fellini nod of 'Juliet of the Spirits', the Chopin reference of 'Berceuse' and the John Cage title pilfered for *Valentine out of Season*, while 'Empire of Signs', from *Three Seasons Only*, is named after Roland Barthes book about Japan. 'I was young then,' Haigh says with a self-deprecating chuckle. True, the trying-a-bit-hard comes over slightly jejune. What's more striking about all these serenely sad etudes for solo piano and their highbrow framing, though, is how there's minimal indication that within just a few years Robert Haigh will be making intensely rhythmic music at the pulsating heart of a working-class drug culture.

*

By the late eighties, Haigh was still working at Virgin but he
and his wife had moved out to Ware in Hertfordshire and were
raising the first of three children. Increasingly frustrated by the
commute and the way it cut into his parenting time, Haigh and
his partner decided to start their own record store in nearby
Hertford. 'She'd worked at Virgin too, so between us we knew
the retail game inside out.' Or so they thought: opened in 1989,
Parliament Music's first year proved to be a real struggle.

'Going into it, we had the attitude of, "we'll make it work".
But it wasn't working, and it was a very depressing time.
And then what came along and helped us make it work was
this axis of rave music: the house and techno 12-inches that
a certain faction of kids came into the store looking for. I
realised that if we could get more of that stuff, we'd have the
edge on the other, more mainstream record store in Hertford.
And then when I started to listen to that stuff, I found myself
falling in love with it.' Haigh discovered not just sonic affini-
ties with postpunk – rough-hewn DIY music released on tiny
labels – but that figures from the scene in which he'd been so
passionately involved were cropping up as significant players
in the new movement. Cabaret Voltaire's Richard H. Kirk, for
instance, reappeared in Sweet Exorcist, leading lights of the
northern bleep 'n' bass sound. 'Not only did rave save my business, it opened up a whole new way of thinking about music.
Because my direction at that point had started to wane a bit.'

One thing that caught Haigh's ear was the way this
insane-sounding and radically futuristic music prominently
featured – of all things – the piano, an instrument that dated
to the eighteenth century. In 1989, a wave of Italo-house
anthems built around rattlingly rhythmic piano breakdowns
had conquered the UK scene and would permanently place

the piano vamp at the core of hardcore's sonic arsenal. 'It's that juxtaposition thing again: tracks would have this tough beats-and-bass work-out, and then in would come the uplifting melodic piano.'

The oscillating flicker and rictus-like optimism of the piano vamp are synonymous with the sensations and emotions catalysed by MDMA. Amazingly, given the supremely Ecstasy-attuned records he would soon be making, Haigh never experienced that side of rave culture. 'I got a taste of it, though, from certain days in the shops,' Haigh says, referring to Saturdays when local kids, still buzzing from the night before, would congregate to hear the latest white labels. He says that his only vice really was alcohol. Besides, as a parent in his early thirties, he was a generation older than most everybody else involved in rave. Haigh recalls Andy C of 'Valley of the Shadows' legend coming into the shop and realising that the sixteen-year-old DJ/producer was young enough to be his son.

Many leading rave labels started out of record shops (think Warp in Sheffield, or Romford's Boogie Times, which spawned Suburban Base). Retail awareness of what's selling turns into an A&R instinct for where the music wants to go next; relationships develop between the staff and local DJs and producers. So it was that Parliament Music became PM Recordings, as young customers started to show Haigh their own stabs at making techno. Blown away by the results achievable on an extremely basic set-up, Haigh invested £300 in an Amiga 500 and got hold of the ultra-rudimentary ProTracker software. 'It was just 8-bit, whereas the minimum anyone would use nowadays is 16-bit. And ProTracker just had four tracks, scrolling down the screen, into which you would drop events that would trigger a breakbeat or a sound. So it was very primitive indeed.'

Released on PM Recordings in 1992, the first of Haigh's hard-core forays came out under the name Splice. They include the aptly named 'Pianism', the bonus track '7 Original Piano Breaks for DJ Use' and numerous collaborations with a Parliament Music employee who went by the name Rhodes K. But Haigh would rather draw a discreet veil over this early phase. Indeed, when I first interviewed him back in '94 – a conversation conducted via the Royal Mail and written in capital letters, as if lower case would be too intimate – Haigh did not even mention Splice or PM Recordings. For sure, while tracks like Syko and Mak's 'Recognise' or Splice's 'Falling (in Dub)' have the nutty, made-in-two-minutes charm of the era, there are no lost classics to be found here. Indeed, there's a palpable quantum leap with the first release as Omni Trio: the *Mystic Steppers* EP, initially released on PM sub-label Candidate, and then, in refurbished form, as his debut record for Moving Shadow.

If piano is the instrument of Haigh's life and remained a melodic signature through all his rave-era discography, he rapidly manifested two other forms of mastery: vocal science and breakbeat science. Haigh's deployment of diva samples was inspired, his choices often locating emotional resonances that escaped the enclosure of rave (all primary-colour explosions of E-lation and collective celebration) to connect with real-world feelings of anguish, self-doubt and fragility. Case in point: 'I know I'm not that strong enough', the main vocal lick in the *Mystic Steppers* track 'Stronger'.

Haigh attributes this to the advantage of working in a record store and accessing 'a lot of a cappella albums that other people couldn't get their hands on, import records . . .' He also talks about using vocal samples as the starting point for his tracks, which he'd fashion around them (partly because of his obsession with everything being in key). But you can't help thinking that being so much older than most of his producer peers – and a parent too – Haigh might also have had a deeper feeling for how challenging life can be.

As for breakbeat science, Haigh's rhythmic finesse first surfaced on 'Mystic Stepper (Feel Good)' with its slip-and-slide drums (some psychedelically reversed for extra instability) and blossomed with the epochal 'Renegade Snares', the lead track on 1993's *Vol 3* EP. 'One of the things important to me was personalising a break as much as I could. I think I was one of the first to chop up a break into its constituent parts.' Taking anywhere from a bar to four bars of a drum break, Haigh would slice it into sixteen components and essentially write them into new breaks. 'Once you've chopped it, you can move any bit to any position – and that's where the fun is because you can really mess about. For me it was all about *owning* the break.'

Suddenly, a whole new 'future frontier' (the title of a track on *Vol 3*) opened up for Haigh and his music. As heard on tracks like the 'Roasted Rollin'', mix of 'Renegade Snares', the result involved an inversion of standard musical priorities. Instead of a steady background foundation to the track, the rhythm section became the focus of listening, grabbing the ear with its baroque contortions, the ultra-crisp intricacy of the meshwork of snares, kicks, hats and shakers complicated further by detonations of bass syncopating against the drum groove. Meanwhile, other elements in the track – piano motifs, synth pads, orchestrations modelled on or sampled from film scores – might be childishly naive in their heart-tugging insistence. Drum patterns became primary hooks, the melodies that sang in your memory. Like the intro to *Vol 4*'s 'Original Soundtrack', a vertigo-inducing beat-sequence that feels like a video loop of a swimmer plunging into a pool only to reverse out of the splash surface and back onto the board. Or like the stiletto stitch-work of the breakdown in 'Soul Freestyle' (off 1994's *Vol 5*), a ballet of exquisitely controlled violence.

111

As jungle crested to a peak of unexpected musicality in 1994 – only a year earlier it had been widely dismissed as sub-music, chaotic drug-noise for kids so pilled-up they'd lost any sense of discrimination – the genre achieved that oxymoronic coexistence of opposites that Haigh always craved: frenzied and chilled, minimal and maximal, street and avant-garde. Another paradox about the scene was that while it was accurately associated – in terms of both its imagery and its demographics – with the inner city, there was a surprisingly strong suburban contribution. Having grown up in that county myself, it always tickled me that Hertfordshire was such a major player: along with the Hertford-centred Parliament Music nexus, Moving Shadow was based out of Stevenage, while Source Direct and Photek hailed from St Albans.

As his series of EPs kept on intensifying the Omni sound-clash of fierce and filmic, as heard on tracks like 'Living for the Future' and 'Thru the Vibe', Haigh released *The Deepest Cut Vol 1*: one of the first drum and bass full-lengths, and still one of the best ever. Then came a style switch. On 1995's *Vol 6*, Haigh bid farewell to the explosive mode (shredded Amen breaks, hypergasmic divas) that made his name with the dazzling B-side track 'Torn', a play on the junglist superlative 'tearing'. Meanwhile the A-side 'Nu Birth of Cool' showcased a new direction: rolling, jazz-tinged, glistening with a sheen of luxury. Abandoning what he now deemed the Pavlovian pyrotechnics of the 'Renegade Snares' era, Haigh sought a more 'fat' sound, as he termed it, on the second Omni album *Haunted Science*. The shift paid dividends on 'The Elemental', a miracle of restraint, with a bassline as delicately poised as beads of condensation trickling down a blade of foliage in a rainforest, set against a second low-end pulse thudding like distant thunderclaps. But later albums like *Skeleton Keys* and *Byte Size Life* steadily eased into background listening.

From being at the centre of jungle, Omni Trio had gradually slipped into the subgenre known as liquid funk, as had other leading Moving Shadow artists like EZ Rollers and Flytronix. Meanwhile, the genre's mainstream had gone in the opposite direction: crowd-pleasing rampages of roaring bass and treadmill beats like an interminable chase-scene. 'The drums got pared down to a big heavy kick and a big heavy snare,' Haigh recalls of these disillusioning days at the turn of the millennium. 'The beat became just a vehicle for the bassline, and those were getting more and more outlandish, verging on comical. But it worked on the dancefloor and DJs loved those tunes. That stuff would just fly out of our shop. Even a poor DJ could mix those tunes, 'cos it was all the same beat and there were no tricky, intricate rhythms.'

For a producer like Haigh, the ascendancy of the 2-step, bass-blast style of drum and bass 'really narrowed down the possibilities . . . you couldn't really explore a musical phrase. I really felt like I couldn't compete with producers doing that type of drum and bass, and I didn't want to. I was being drawn into working in other areas. It was a wrench at the time, but I just felt, "Go on, be brave." I had to have a little conversation with myself.' He also had to have a conversation with his wife, for jettisoning the Omni Trio name would jeopardise their livelihood (the early albums especially having sold very well internationally). 'But it had been building in me, and I felt I had to be honest and move into a different sphere. It wasn't really a choice – I could continue and fake it, but that would have blotted the memory of something that people still talk about affectionately.'

Rogue Satellite, the final Omni album, came out in 2004, and its closing track bore the symbolic title 'Suicide Loop'. To this day he gets regular requests from old skool rave promoters asking him to do an Omni Trio PA (something he never did even in his heyday) but he always declines. 'I don't think I've cut up a break in over twelve years now.'

Since closing that chapter of his life, music has been pouring out of Robert Haigh, with eight albums of solo piano in the past decade. *Creatures of the Deep*, released towards the end of 2017 by experimental-music label Unseen Worlds, is different from the sparse, piano-only watercolours of earlier albums like *Written on the Water*. It would be a massive exaggeration to suggest there's something faintly Omni-like about *Creatures*, but it does sound significantly more produced. The backwards sounds on 'From the Mystery' made me flash momentarily on the psychedelically reversed beats of 'Mystic Stepper', while 'Winter Deeps' actually features a bassline of sorts. 'It's this simple motif that doesn't quite repeat itself,' explains Haigh. 'It's shifting slightly as it moves along, almost forming a drone for the piano motifs to weave in and out of.'

'I Remember Phaedra' harks back further to Sema and that wintry postpunk/industrial vibe, its hovering drones and indeterminately ethnic woodwind vaguely reminding me of *Eskimo* by The Residents. Overall, *Creatures of the Deep* teems with unidentifiable wafts of texture, subliminal smudges and an intense attention to sculpting the ambience through subtle adjustments of reverb halo or stereo placement. 'It's like painting pictures,' says Haigh, referring to the compositional balance, the contrast and the shaping of empty space in his pieces. 'I don't set out to be experimental but it always creeps in, because I'm always looking for a fresh way of doing something. I don't know if I have a lot to say but I look for new ways of saying it.'

Entirely self-taught as a pianist, avoiding notation (except occasionally for his own self-devised diagrams), Haigh composes through a process of improvisation and editing. He once said

114

that it would be more accurate to say that he uncovers music rather than writes it. 'I'll just play and play – and then I'll come back to it. It's like chipping away at something, rather than building it up.'

Haigh once argued that 'all genuine music is to some extent autobiographical'. That's an intriguing assertion, especially from someone who's avoided the public eye and about whom most of his fans know very little. What is his lyric-less music telling us about Robert Haigh the man? 'I don't think there is a narrative coming through, except perhaps on a subconscious level. But I do wonder sometimes what is attracting me to a Lydian-type scale that I seem to be drawn to, or a Dorian minor scale in some of the tunes.'

The closest Haigh has got to autobiographical music in the commonly understood sense was his 2015 album *The Silence of Ghosts*. That came out of a period of illness, the sort of perpetually sapping malaise that makes normal functions of life (eating in this case) difficult, and that in turn triggered a depression. 'The last thing you wanna do when you've got some kind of ailment is obsess about it. But when it's that sort of intimate ailment, you keep coming back to it. It coloured everything I did through that period.' Thankfully the condition eventually improved and Haigh's equilibrium was restored.

More generally, though, there's a feeling that runs through most of Haigh's work – the post-Sema records, the breakbeat era, the last decade's run of solo piano – that was beautifully caught by Kodwo Eshun in his phrase 'the kindness of Omni Trio'. A feeling of benediction and grace that shone through even when the beats were at their most frenetic. And now the beats have been taken away, that cloudless blue-sky serenity is, as Haigh says, 'more exposed now'.

Another factor that's possibly brought this reflective and soul-soothing aspect to the fore is that Haigh has been practising meditation for almost two decades now. 'I was a bit of a mess by the end of the nineties,' he says, referring to the twin attrition of overwork and drinking to unwind. 'I was turning into an anxious wreck. Because I was drinking in the evenings, my days were a bit foggy for a while. I was looking for an alternative to living like that and one day I just came across a book, in W.H. Smith's I think. A really cheesy, commercial book on meditation, but there was something in there about mindfulness of the breath. "Watching the breath" – that caught my eye and I thought, "I'll give that a go." And surprisingly on my first attempt, a little switch went off in my head. So meditation is something I try to do to keep my spirits up. And I've had varying degrees of success with it, but I've stuck with it for eighteen years. I do it practically every single morning.' He pauses. 'Please don't turn me into a beanbag hippie!'

The Wire, 2018

ARTCORE: A Guy Called Gerald's *Black Secret Technology*

In many ways, Gerald Simpson has the absolutely archetypal profile of your average artcore junglist. Steeped in early-seventies jazz-rock (Herbie Hancock, Chick Corea, etc.), Gerald flipped for electro (Afrika Bambaataa, Mantronix), then tripped out to acid house and Detroit techno.

His first creative efforts were in the Hit Squad, a Manchester hip hop collective from whose cadres 808 State coalesced. Gerald was briefly a member of 808 and actually co-wrote their biggest hit 'Pacific State'. By then, Gerald had his own thing going, having scored a Top 20 smash with 'Voodoo Ray'. This slinky acid-samba reappears in drastically remodelled form as 'Voodoo Rage', on Gerald's brand new, unspeakably brilliant album *Black Secret Technology*. It turns out that the song was always meant to be called 'Voodoo Rage', but Gerald didn't have enough memory in his sampler and had to chop the 'g' off the soundbite (originally, and bizarrely, from a Peter Cook and Dudley Moore sketch satirising white bourgeois British 'experts' pontificating about the blues).

After 'Voodoo Ray', the logical thing for Gerald would have been to follow all the other Detroit buffs up the funkless cul de sac of 'electronic listening music'. Instead, after a frustrating

117

period signed to major label Sony, Gerald discovered the glory of the breakbeat. Originated by James Brown and the Meters, sampled by hip hop producers, breakbeats are what enabled a generation of post-rave producers to move beyond the 4/4 monotony of house, into the multi-tiered, hyper-syncopated rhythmic psychedelia of drum and bass.

'Originally, I was into drum machines. I used to hate breaks. But then I discovered that with a sampler you don't just have to take a break and loop it, you can chop it up into segments, recombine it, enhance and stretch the sounds. Basically you can turn a couple of hits into a whole drum solo!'

Metalheadz man Goldie had contacted Gerald, dragged him down from Manchester to Rage, London's legendary early-nineties 'ardkore club. Gerald realised that hardcore was an emergent subculture that was totally British, and he wanted in. 'The whole vibe was totally different to what was going on in Chicago. I realised there was no point in me trying to sound like American house. Jungle was also like touching ground with my own personal roots, 'cos my parents are from the West Indies. For me it was like "I'm still a real person. I've not been castrated by Sony." 'Cos they'd wanted me to make Hi-NRG-style club tracks.'

Gerald's first efforts were tough tracks like '28 Gun Bad Boy', but gradually he evolved towards the artcore side. In early '95, the term 'jungle' has already been outmoded by the music's onward and outward diffusion. That familiar matrix of influences, fusion/electro/Detroit, is pushing 'jungle' in all manner of astonishing directions – the cyber-jazz strangeness of Photek and Alex Reece, the cinematic hyper-soul of Hidden Agenda, the lambent aqua-funk serenity of LTJ Bukem and his cronies. On *Black Secret Technology*, Gerald daubs in all these different shades of the state-of-artcore palette. But his stuff is still too weird to get played at Speed, Bukem's Thursday-night salon for the drum and bass scene's inner circle of cognoscenti.

118

*

The critic Andrew Ross recently asked where (given US rap's current reliance on seventies funk, its old skool nostalgia) had hip hop's 'rage for the future' gone? The answer is: Britain, where phuturism is alive 'n' KICKIN'. From Tricky and Portishead to 4 Hero and Droppin' Science, Britain's first generation of B-boys have come of age. And the striking difference about trip hop and art-core jungle vis-a-vis US rap is that race is not the crucial determinant of belonging. Instead, what unites the massive is a shared attitude towards technology, an impatience to reach the future, signposted in track titles like 4 Horsemen of the Apocalypse's 'We Are the Future', Noise Factory's 'Futuroid', Red One's 'The Futurist'.

From the orgasmotronic rapture of 'Energy' to the cyborg paranoia of 'Gloktrak', Gerald's new LP is virtually an essay (non-verbal, bar the odd sample) about the bliss and the danger of techno-fetishism. The title, *Black Secret Technology*, expresses this ambivalence perfectly. Gerald heard the phrase on a TV talk-show about government mind-control via the media, where some kind of witch-woman used the word 'black' to denote malign sorcery. But Gerald has redeployed the word to evoke the science fiction fantasies of black pop's maverick tradition – Sun Ra as Saturn-born ambassador for the Omniverse, Hendrix landing his kinky machine, George Clinton's Mothership taking the Afronauts to a lost homeland on the other side of the galaxy, Afrika Bambaataa's fetish for Kraftwerk and Nubian science, Juan Atkins and Derrick May's cybertronic mindscapes.

At this fraught fin de millennium moment, technology appears as instrument both of domination and of resistance; machines can both castrate and superhumanise you. Gerald belongs to a subculture based around abusing technology (jungle's all about doing things with machines unintended by the manufacturer) rather than being abused by it. And it all goes back to his childhood.

'I got a tank for Christmas and it played a tune, and I just had to know how it worked. I took a knife but I couldn't get these mad screws to open. So I heated the knife on the oven and sliced through the plastic, and ripped the tape recorder out. I just *had* to know!'

Gerald still has that small boy's confidence about technology. As with a lot of post-rave producers, there's something vaguely auto-erotic to his techno-fetishism. When I ask him if he ever feels like a cyborg, in so far as his machines are extensions of his body that give him superhuman powers, he frankly admits that working in his studio, 'it's like your own world and you become like the god'.

Like a lot of artcore producers, Gerald's eager to extend his dominion from the aural to the visual; he's hungry for the new frontier of virtual reality. He dreams of a machine that 'could convert sound into visuals. You'd feed a sound in and the computer would turn it into an image on a screen. Then you'd manipulate that vision and turn it back into sound. There's still scope for new things using sound. But hooking into the visual would make it even more interesting. Especially for kids nowadays, who're into computer games.'

On the album, 'Cybergen' is all about an 'imaginary drug that's basically virtual reality. The vocal goes "it takes you up, down, anywhere you want to go." It's a drug where you're in total control of the experience: if you wanted a steel globe floating about, then going purple, you'd have it. Then the vocal says, "it's too late to turn back now", and that's making the point that it's no use saying we can't cope with this technology, that it's going to ruin society. 'Cos the technology's already here. You either cope with it or you're lost. Kids today are already totally hooked into it. Kids today are frightening! I grew up with records, and now I know how to manipulate records. When today's kids grow up, they'll know how to manipulate the visual side of it.'

So do you think people will lose interest in music?

'Yeah, sound will just become a small part of it. I can't imagine a kid today just sitting down and listening to an album. It's progression, innit?'

Feeling like a fogey, I quibble: isn't part of music's magic the way it makes you come up with your own mind's-eye imagery? Gerald's chirpy response is that with CD-ROMs you'll soon have the power to create your own graphics. But, I counter feebly, who actually has the energy for all this interactive self-expression?

'Not people who grew up in our era. But kids today, given ten years, they'll be on it.'

People from 'our era', even those who are getting online, feel a deep anxiety about the digital revolution. The sense of being outstripped by technology's exponential development has even penetrated the subconscious: once, schizophrenics imagined loss of control in terms of demons and incubi, but now they rant about microchips implanted behind their eyes or satellites irradiating them with a brainwashing beam. But Gerald is gung-ho about technology's empowering potential. He takes a boyish delight in the sheer 'deviousness' of the ever-escalating, techno-mediated struggle between Control and Anarchy.

'There are always ways around it. Say if someone was scanning into this room with a directional microphone and listening to us, we could scan them back and find out their exact location. Your phone can be bugged, but you can get devices that scramble the signal. When we were at school, we used to fiddle fruit machines. They always came back with some new trick to stop us, but we always got round it. We'd find ways to get credits on Space Invaders machines. It was, like, ghetto technology!'

Melody Maker, 1995

MINIMAL TECHNO: Gas and the Germanic Visions of Wolfgang Voigt

It starts with a fanfare, dilated into a canopy of sombre sonorousness, a slowly unfurling cloud-bank of sound like the distant lowing of massed Alpine horns. Listening, you feel like you're on a high mountain path, looking down on mist draping the lower slopes. When the bass-drum pulse finally kicks in, it's like your heart starting up again after being stopped dead with awe.

This is the titleless fifth track of *Königsforst*, part of a remarkable tetralogy of techno albums released in the late nineties under the name Gas, by the prolific producer Wolfgang Voigt. Although critically acclaimed at the time for those releases and his work using alter egos such as Mike Ink and M:I:5, Voigt is best known today as co-founder of Kompakt, the Cologne-based label that's contributed more than any other to Germany's dominance of electronic dance music in the 2000s. Voigt's decision to reissue the four Gas albums on Kompakt (they originally came out on Frankfurt's Mille Plateaux label) as a deluxe box set titled *Nah und Fern*, in parallel with the publication via Raster-Noton of a book of photographic work (an integral, if not widely known, element of the Gas project) that also includes a CD of unreleased music, is an intriguing gesture. It's a statement of belief in the artistic durability of (some) electronic music, at a time when the sheer volume of output and high turnover of micro-fads in post-rave music contributes to a sense of 'growing ephemerality' (Voigt's words). The monumentality of the box set – a chest for sounds worth treasuring – claims for techno what is a routine occurrence (and unexamined assumption) within rock: this music will stand the test of time. The Gas work passes posterity's entrance exam. Alongside the records released contemporaneously by Berlin's twinned labels Basic Channel and Chain Reaction, these albums represent the towering achievement of German electronic music in the second half of the nineties.

The core of the Gas series resides in 1997's *Zauberberg* and 1998's *Königsforst*. Although partly bidden by Voigt's overt framing of the project through the album titles and the colour-treated cover pictures (*Königsforst*'s sunlight dappling through the leaf canopy, *Zauberberg*'s sombre throng of conifer trunks, both derived from the photographic stockpile that composes the accompanying book), the music does irresistibly conjure mind's-eye imagery of rugged natural grandeur: the deep forest's rustling shadows, Alpine vistas of altitude and remoteness. Named after woodlands near Cologne, *Königsforst* actually gives off more of an Alpine aura – sensations of panoramic splendour and rare air – than does *Zauberberg* (which translates as 'magic mountain'). On *Zauberberg*, the untitled fifth track's tenebrous shimmers and lustrous darkness make me picture a regiment of dwarves marching through Tolkien's Mirkwood.

In interviews at the time, Voigt talked of his desire 'to bring the German forest into the disco'. Gas was the first publically released product of a fictitious 'lab project' called Blei, which involved Voigt putting Austro-German classical music (Wagner, Berg, Schoenberg), brass bands, *Volksmusik* and the schlocky middle-of-the-road pop known as *Schlager* 'under the microscope' in order to find a sort of audio-cultural

124

DNA. The Gas sound is literally spliced together out of small samples from classical records, which Voigt subjected to processes of 'zoom, loop and alienation'. The music's provenance is instantly audible from the rainfall-like hiss of aged vinyl, the discernibly orchestral sonorities of the grave cellos and tingling violins. There's a marvellous irony to the fact that one of the signal triumphs of techno, that most future-fixated genre, is sourced almost entirely in music from the latter decades of the nineteenth century, when late-Romantic composition scaled its summit of portentous majesty before swerving into the angst-wracked realm of twelve-tone and serialism.

Voigt received some criticism at the time from German music journalists, who, hyper-conscious of a shady side to the national cult of mountains and forest, worried that Gas was somehow the missing link between Eno's ambient classic *On Land* and 'blood and soil'. Oversensitive as this may seem (surely that kind of craggy and verdant natural grandeur has a primordial appeal that cuts across cultures? Then again, perhaps 'primordialism' itself *is* the problem . . .), it's understandable perhaps given that in German left-wing circles anything that seems to flirt with nationalism will necessarily invite close scrutiny. (This was also not *that* long after the reunification of West and East Germany, when all these issues were particularly raw.)

It is also undeniable that historically Germany has had a peculiar *thing* for the Alps and the *Wald* (their term for uncultivated forest land, of which there remains an unusually large amount for an industrialised European nation). *Zauberberg*'s title nods to Thomas Mann, but 'magic mountain' has resonances that run through Goethe, Wagner, Strauss and Nietzsche, to name just a few. Prone to sickliness, Nietzsche was literally inspired by the exhilarating air of Switzerland. He described his ideal reader as a hardy soul 'accustomed to living on mountain tops' and possessed of 'loftiness of soul'. You could see Nietzsche's philosophical ideal of 'self-surpassing' as a kind of spiritual alpinism, while his hermit-prophet Zara-thustra spends ten years of solitude in the mountains before descending with wisdom for humanity. Richard Strauss in turn composed stirring works like *An Alpine Symphony* (which depicts a day-long climb to a mountain's peak) and *Also Sprach Zarathustra*, whose 'mountain sunrise' sequence is well known to us as the bombastic main theme of *2001, A Space Odyssey*.

'Zauberberg' is also a hair's breadth from *Der heilige Berg* (*The Holy Mountain*), the title of Arnold Fanck's 1926 movie and one of the most famous 'mountain films' (a genre unique to between-the-wars Germany and whose biggest female star was the young Leni Riefenstahl). Socialist critics in 1920s Germany accused the genre's cult of rugged athleticism and Alpine purity of being 'blatant propaganda for a lofty humanity and eternal blondeness', with the film historian Siegfried Kracauer subsequently concluding that their 'overblown heroism and glorification of the German Alps as a supernatural force' (the words here are Riefenstahl biographer Jürgen Trimborn's paraphrase) prepared the climate for Nazism. Riefenstahl's later, allegedly apolitical work, *Tiefland* (Lowlands), which was begun during the Second World War but only released in 1954, was based on an obscure opera that contrasted decadent lowland dwellers with pure-of-spirit mountain folk: an opposi-tion between 'civilisation' (seen as Franco-Mediterranean) and 'culture' (Germano-Nordic) briefly espoused by Thomas Mann himself during the First World War.

As for the forest, there is an association between woodland and German national identity that goes back to the Romans' failure to conquer the *Wald*-dwelling pagan tribes, and reverberates on through German Romanticism, the Brothers Grimm, painters like Caspar David Friedrich and Anselm

Kiefer, and even the Green movement. Although Voigt was tapping into all of this as part of his long-term desire to make a 'genuinely German form of pop music', his primary associations were personal: childhood family vacations to the Alps, hallucinogen-enhanced teenage adventures in Königsforst, which he describes as 'Hansel and Gretel on acid' but also as a womb-like 'spiritual refuge'.

Contrasting the amorphous immensity of Gas – and similar 'heroin house' (as critic Kevin Martin termed the style) tracks released on Basic Channel and Chain Reaction – with today's German electronic music, you can see a revealing shift in the meaning of 'minimal'. In the mid-nineties, the word was suggestive of austerity and meditational spirituality. Even though the scene was rampantly druggy, underneath the hedonism there was a sense of quest, a reaching out to a transcendent beyond, a vastness conjured through music built to overwhelm. Gas took that impulse and connected it back to Romanticism, to an idea of the sublime as outside society and essentially barbarian.

Today's electronic culture is secular and agnostic; 'minimal' connotes the elegance of exquisitely dainty details. Known initially as microhouse but now more commonly and confusingly called 'minimal' – and sometimes cutely abbreviated to mnml – contemporary German electronica drifts around in the area between house, techno, trance, disco and the more glitchy-twitchy zones of experimental electronics. Where minimal techno used to be based around reduction (Voigt's 'high art of leaving out'), today it is often quite busy, riddled with fussy nuances. Minimal signifies more what is avoided out of tastefulness: the crassly anthemic hooks of cheesy mainstream club music. Modern minimal is designed to reward the close attention of the connoisseur ear, attuned to slight fluctuations of texture and rhythm but also historically informed enough to appreciate the borrowings and citations from earlier phases in dance music's rich tapestry.

'Connoisseur' is key, because contemporary minimal presents itself as gourmet audio for the discerning aural palate. Alongside its German counterparts such as Get Physical, Kompakt pioneered the art of positioning the record label as a quality brand. Of course, there has long been a cult of particular labels within techno. But what's changed is how electronic music as a whole situates itself in relationship with the mainstream. In the nineties, the subculture saw itself as both a vanguard and an underground; techno rhetoric then was full of paramilitary imagery and appeals to 'belief'. And operations like Basic Channel or Underground Resistance *did* seem shrouded in mystery in a way that today's labels, including Kompakt, couldn't recreate even if they wanted to; digital culture's over-bright omnipresence of knowledge has chased away the shadows (just as the digital audio workstations that took over at the close of the nineties enabled the obsessively finessed productions that today cluster under the misnomer 'minimal'). The *mise en scène* for the music has changed too. Minimal techno from the 1990s brings to mind a cavernous space – a spartan hangar or hall (in Germany, the ultimate perhaps being E-Werk's abandoned power plant). 'Minimal' today is mostly experienced in designer bars with comfortable seating and expensive prices.

For electronic music today, the model is no longer the underground (in opposition to mass culture) but the boutique (a niche market running in parallel with the mainstream but at a slight elevation). But as I write this, I realise that I'm reconstituting that dubious binary between culture and civilisation: nineties techno representing a cluster of values (heroic pioneers and explorers, the great outdoors) with an unmistakably virile cast, while early-twenty-first-century electronica suggests an equally gender-coded opposite (audio-decor, metrosexuality, postmodern pastiche). Vanguard itself is a term of military origin, of course.

It all seems an aeon ago, the belief in rave as a movement and the idea of being a soldier for the techno 'cause' – irrecoverable, even slightly silly. Gas was arguably the swan song of that impulse. Beneath Voigt's shimmering clouds of glory, there's often a submerged martial feel to the rhythm, a trudging resoluteness. The sound, perhaps, of an army marching home to disband.

Frieze, 2008

IDM: Boards of Canada

Once upon a time there was a London vintage clothing boutique that lured customers inside with the slogan, 'Don't follow fashion, buy something that's already out-of-date!' Some musicians opt for a similar strategy: avoiding the timely, they aim to achieve the timeless.

That's what Boards of Canada were going for when they recorded *Music Has the Right to Children* in the late 1990s. At that time, the reigning aesthetic in electronic music was crisply digital, frenetically hyper-rhythmic, and futuristic. But the Scottish duo quietly and firmly abstained from these norms and conventions. Michael Sandison and his differently surnamed brother Marcus Eoin came up with something completely different: a hazy sound of smeared synth-tones and soft-focus, analogue-decayed production, carried by patient, sleepwalking beats, and aching with nostalgia.

'What I still like about the album relates to everything it doesn't do, in the context of the world of music it came into,' says Sandison today. This time-out-of-joint quality is all the more fitting because *Music Has the Right to Children* is about the uncanniness of memory, the way we are each haunted by ghosts from a private image-bank as well as from the collective unconscious of shared public culture. It's not so much that this persistence of the past inside the present is the subject

131

of *Music Has the Right to Children* as that it's the substance
out of which Boards of Canada weave their music, its spectral
warp-and-weft.

In the late nineties, looking back was the last thing on the
collective mind of electronic dance music. From drum and
bass to trance, from gabber to minimal techno, the music
promised the sound of tomorrow, today. Each scene saw itself
as a vanguard – dancing to these beats, you were in some
sense already *in* the future. Drawing heavily from cyberpunk
fiction, dystopian movies and scientific terminology, the track
titles, the artist names, the sampled soundbites and the record
designs relied almost uniformly on futuristic imagery. Which
could get pretty corny and kitschy at times – just think of the
garish hyperreal colours and baroquely biomorphic shapes in
The Future Sound of London's artwork circa *Lifeforms* and
Dead Cities.

True, there was a countercurrent at work in a corner of IDM
(Intelligent Dance Music), what you could call idyllictronica:
the spangly music-box chimes and ice-cream van melodies of
Mouse on Mars, certain Aphex Twin tracks that evoked childhood innocence and halcyon memories. Boards of Canada had
something in common with this tendency, but crucially they
bent it to the sinister – as with the front cover of *Music Has
the Right to Children*, a faded photograph of a family of seven
on vacation, their faces eerily bleached into featureless blanks.

The album came out in April 1998, a joint release by scene-
leading Warp Records and the rising second-wave IDM label
Skam. Although *Music Has the Right to Children* has the
feeling of a debut, a bold entrance statement, Sandison and
Eoin – aged twenty-seven and twenty-six when the album was
released – had already accumulated a fairly substantial, if low-
profile, discography across the previous three years, including
an album and a barely released cassette on their own imprint

Music70, and the *Hi Scores* EP for Skam. Although BoC's sound sat fairly unobtrusively amid the Autechre-indebted crunchy beats and pensive melodies of the Skam roster, there were glimmers of a distinctive identity discernible to the sharp-eared: a certain elegiac, autumnal quality to the synth-tones.

While BoC were honing their sound, the IDM community was scrambling to catch up with the rhythmic innovations of jungle, which had come as an ambush out of the lumpen left-field. The dominant sound in late-nineties IDM was a controlled paroxysm of percussion, with micro-edited breakbeats densely layered and texturised with digital signal processing. Practically all the big names were chopping breaks and assembling baroque architectures of contorted polyrhythm: Aphex Twin with his *Richard D. James Album* and the AFX EP *Hangable Auto Bulb*, Luke Vibert in both his Plug and Wagon Christ identities, µ-Ziq with *Lunatic Harness*, and Squarepusher with a ballistic barrage of releases that included *Hard Normal Daddy* and *Big Loada* in 1997 alone. People nicknamed this style 'drill and bass', but 'droll and bass' would have fitted even better: the mood was antic and whimsical, with artists like Aphex favouring daft samples and an almost slapstick, cartoon-crazy feel.

Boards of Canada stood aside from all this pell-mell puerility. Where jungle and its not-so-early adopters in IDM's first division were reversing conventional musical priorities by turning the drums and the bass into the focal foreground, BoC reversed that reversal and restated the primacy of melody and mood. In early interviews, Sandison and Eoin stressed their disinterest in going along with the jungle programme, which they regarded as a fashion trend. For Boards of Canada, rhythms were 'just a vehicle for carrying strange and beautiful melodies'. And that was the first thing that struck you listening to *Music Has the Right to Children* – how songs like 'Roygbiv' featured gorgeously elongated melody lines stretching over many bars, whereas most electronic music of the era tended to involve concise melody-riffs and brief, flickering vamps.

'I always felt rhythm is the part of music that dates it, for better or worse,' says Sandison today. 'It gives away the era; it's the replaceable part in cover versions. But people get attached to a chord progression, or a figure of notes, because those are timeless. We have a subtractive way of putting our music together. So a lot of what we were doing with *Music Has the Right* was actually the process of removal; discarding the things that other people would do that annoyed us, until the skeletal remains didn't annoy us anymore. And this pushed the whole sound into a kind of apparition of the music that was not quite all there.'

It's not that there aren't some imposing beats on *Music Has the Right*. In fact, there's a surprising amount of hip hop in the mix, a sort of sedated boom-bap feel at times. Featuring scratching and a looped break, 'An Eagle in Your Mind' is like a GIF of faded footage of old skool B-boy crew West Street Mob spinning on their backs and knees to their 1983 track 'Electric Boogie'. Other tracks, like 'Rue the Whirl', with its clattery drum rolls, similarly conjure a bygone Bronx, but relocate it incongruously to rural Scotland. Overall, though, the beats on Boards of Canada tracks create a dreamy sensation of suspension from time rather than a surge forward through it.

The other thing that separated *Music Has the Right to Children* from contemporaneous releases by apparent peers like Autechre and Two Lone Swordsmen was the record's overall sound design, which broke with the clean, clear, clinical aura of the era. Instead, BoC used a mixture of analogue and digital techniques to give their music a wavering, mottled quality redolent of formats like film, vinyl and magnetic tape that are susceptible to decay and distortion with the passage of time.

Listening to tracks like 'Wildlife Analysis' or 'The Color of the Fire', you can't help but think of yellowing photographs in the family album, blotchy and washed-out Super 8 films, or the drop-out-addled sound of favourite cassettes left too long on the car dashboard.

In interviews around *Music Has the Right*, BoC talked about how they barely listened to – or even liked – contemporary electronic music, citing instead such seemingly unlikely synth forebears as Devo and Tomita, and gushing about the acoustic lushness of Joni Mitchell. The brothers talked of applying 'a process of corruption' to their melodies, the vocals they sampled, and pretty much every texture in their music.

'Arriving at that sound was a really gradual thing with us,' says Eoin now. 'We'd been recording in various forms of the band as teens through much of the eighties, and already had a big collection of our own old crappy recordings that we were really fond of. Then, around 1987 or 1988, we were beginning to experiment with collage tapes of demos we'd deliberately destroyed, to give the impression of chewed-up library tapes that had been found in a field somewhere. That was the seed for the whole project. In those days, everyone used to have drawers full of unique cassettes with old snippets from radio and TV; it's kind of a lost thing now, sadly. To me, it's fascinating and precious to find some lost recordings in a cupboard, so part of it was an idea to create new music that really felt like an old familiar thing.'

The origins of the Boards of Canada sound go back as far as 1981, when the brothers engaged in rudimentary experiments with tape editing. 'We used to chop up shortwave radio recordings on an ancient portable recorder and make tunes out of them by punching-in and layering tracks in a crude way,' they told the Scottish electronic music website EHX in early 1998, in what appears to be BoC's very first interview.

These schoolboy stabs at *musique concrète* suggest a proximity with the UK's industrial scene, the tape collages and ambient dronescapes spun by Nurse with Wound and Zoviet France from the early eighties onwards. But by the early 1990s, Boards of Canada were closer to a proper band, with guitar, bass, live drums and the occasional vocal. They weren't the sort of band that rocked out on stage, though, but nearer to what they described as 'experimental atmospheric rock' outfits such as Cocteau Twins and My Bloody Valentine, dedicated to exploring guitar textures and the studio's sound-painting possibilities. Like Kevin Shields on *Loveless*, BoC experimented with sampling their own guitars. A shoegaze inheritance lingers right through to *Music Has the Right* tracks like 'Smokes Quantity', a gaseous quality that recalls MBV at their most indistinct and tonally warped.

Where most of the first wave of British IDM artists started out making banging techno and shrieking acid for the hardcore ravefloor, Boards of Canada's trajectory was more like Seefeel, a guitar band who passed through post-rock into abstract electronica, or Ultramarine, who evolved out of the second-wave industrial outfit A Primary Industry. 'Our angle coming into electronic music was more from experimental alternative stuff,' recalls Eoin. 'All these artists had some sort of agenda. But when dance music took over in the nineties it just seemed really disposable to us. We've never had much interest in techno or dance music.' In the interviews around *Music Has the Right*, the brothers candidly indicated that making people move was not a priority: 'If you can dance to one of our tracks, well and good, but it's not what we're aiming at.'

Boards of Canada were making music for the head and the heart, then, not the body. But rather than IDM, their true bearings came from psychedelia, that earlier music for 'heads'. From their earliest EPs through to their most recent release,

2013's *Tomorrow's Harvest*, their work is shot through with psychedelia's abiding obsessions: nature, childhood, higher (or simply other) states of consciousness, and the allure of a tribal mode of communal living. Like Donovan's and the Incredible String Band's attempts at living communally in remote and unspoiled regions of Scotland and Wales during the late sixties, Boards of Canada made their music amid the glens and cairns of the Pentland Hills outside Edinburgh as part of a collective of artistic and spiritual kinsfolk. Around the time of recording *Music Has the Right to Children*, they lived right beside a wildlife sanctuary.

The group's name came from the National Film Board of Canada, whose nature documentaries and educational animations they remembered from school days. The brothers found inspiration not just in the subject matter of these programmes but in their 'grainy and wobbly' look, and from the music: electronic underscores and themes largely made by the Quebecois composer Alain Clavier. Some of the shorter electronic interludes and codas on *Music Has the Right* could almost be direct sonic grafts from the synthesiser audio logo that starts each National Film Board of Canada documentary.

When I was nine years old, back in the early seventies, my ambition in life was to be a naturalist: Canada seemed like paradise, a barely populated expanse of forest and prairie teeming with unique wildlife and birds. To my child-mind, wholly uninterested in urban thrills and temptations, it seemed like you could never get – forgive me – bored of Canada. As youngsters, Sandison and Eoin were lucky enough to live in the prairie province of Alberta for a few years, when their parents worked in the construction industry there. 'My memory of Calgary is a picture of boxy 1970s office blocks dumped in the middle of nowhere against a permanent sunset,' Sandison told *NME* in 2002. The family photo on the front of *Music Has the Right* was actually taken at Banff Springs, a picturesque vista in Alberta's stretch of the Rocky Mountains.

The album contains a profusion of allusions to nature, and some actual sounds taken from the great outdoors. There are bird cries, sometimes sourced indirectly from records (the seagulls on 'Happy Cycling' come from Vangelis's *La Fête sauvage*) and sometimes documented by the brothers. While making 'Rue the Whirl', the window to the studio got left open unintentionally; during the playback of a prototype version, Sandison and Eoin realised the birdsong enhanced the music, and it was incorporated into the final track. 'An Eagle in Your Mind' features no actual eagles, alas, but instead there is a voice-over from an otter documentary, using terms like 'holts' and 'spraints' that would have thrilled the nine-year-old me. 'Chinook', a non-album B-side of this era, takes its name from a wind that wafts through the Pacific Northwest and into the Canadian Prairies.

Another hippie-era obsession detectable on *Music Has the Right* is what Canadians now call the First Nations: Native American tribal peoples like the Cree. 'Kaini Industries' borrows its title from a company set up to create employment for inhabitants of Alberta's Blood Reserve, while 'Pete Standing Alone' shares its name with a young Blackfoot who appears in National Film Board of Canada documentaries like *Circle of the Sun*. From late-sixties types like Jim Morrison, through goths like Southern Death Cult, to rave-era anarcho-mystics like Spiral Tribe, Native American folkways have had a romantic allure, representing a pre-capitalist way of life at once more grounded and more spiritual in its non-exploitative coexistence with the natural world. BoC themselves have often struck an anti-urban and neo-tribal note in their interviews, talking of how their idea of a good night out is not going clubbing in the pumping heart of the city, but convening a gathering of a few dozen friends 'somewhere in the hills' around 'a huge bonfire'.

But the biggest psychedelia-flashback element to *Music Has the Right* is its cult of childhood. A high proportion of the pre-teen voices that litter the album come from *Sesame Street*: 'The Color of the Fire' features a little kid adorably sounding out the phrase 'I love you', while 'Aquarius' is laced with glorious giggles and the refrain 'Yeah, that's right!' from a pair of children. Framing the whole album, there's that mysterious title itself. On the one hand, 'music has the right to children' seems to propose an ideal listener or listening state for this music: impressionable, receptive, open to the in-rush of experience. That interpretation is strengthened by the duo's own description of the title as 'a statement of our intention to affect the audience using sound'.

But *Music Has the Right to Children* could be taken differently: not so much about listeners coming 'under the influence', and more about Boards of Canada as a generative force, inspiring other musicians. And BoC have indeed been genre-ative, creating a style of music in their own image. For better or worse, they've spawned a legion of soundalikes within the IDM field (such as Tycho, to name just one). And they've scattered their sonic seed far and wide beyond strictly electronic confines, audible in groups as far apart as Black Moth Super Rainbow and Radiohead (Thom Yorke referenced BoC frequently during the *Kid A/Amnesiac* era).

Although BoC's use of filtering and phasing effects occasionally sounds like an actual acid-rock flashback, for the most part they are in the business of reinventing psychedelia: misusing technology to simulate or stimulate hallucinatory or 'non-sane' states of mind. Speaking about 'Nlogax', a track on their 1996 EP *Hi Scores*, Sandison and Eoin have described its effects as 'like your brain is starting to malfunction in the middle of the tune'. They've talked about aiming to induce a sort of wide-asleep trance state: 'It's like when you glaze over when you're listening to something, but you're still there at the same time.'

Glazed and diffused is pretty much how I felt when I first fell deep for, and deep into, *Music Has the Right to Children*. The album had bypassed me initially: as a jungle fanatic, my metabolism was wired to the frantic futurism of breakbeat science. But something drew me back several months later – perhaps testimonials from others, or a gathering sense of its reputation. And that time around, *Music Has the Right* took over my life for a good while. The wistful ripples of milky synth in 'Roygbiv' felt like a twinkle in time, a cinematic dissolve into my private past. Like fast-moving clouds casting shadows against a hillside, the melody-loop of 'Rue the Whirl' shuddered with a sense of the sublime, the awful unknowable majesty of the world.

Like many others, I found that *Music Has the Right to Children* had an extraordinary power to trigger memories. Partly this was a side effect of the wavering off-pitch synths, redolent of the music on TV programmes from my seventies childhood. But in a far more profound, fundamental and deeply mysterious way, Boards of Canada seemed to be tapping into those deepest recesses of personal memory. Blending intimacy and otherness, the music put you back in touch with parts of yourself you'd lost. That was the group's gift to the listener.

Reaching for some kind of parallel or precursor, I could only think of David Byrne and Brian Eno's *My Life in the Bush of Ghosts*, with its use of speech snippets as one-off singularities (as opposed to the looped vocal samples that tend to figure in dance music and hip hop). But where *Bush of Ghosts*, with its Arabic singers and born-again preachers, worked through an exoticism of geography and cultural distance, *Music Has the Right* involved an exoticism of time. The memories it triggered

140

for me were actually rather mundane: I pictured municipal spaces like parks and recreation grounds, classrooms and school science labs, back gardens or rainy afternoons indoors watching kids' TV. They carried no particular emotional charge, but they were numinous with significance, akin to the way dream images can linger long into your waking hours, without ever revealing anything as legible as a meaning. *Music Has the Right*, in fact, was like a dream you could turn on at will.

As much as Boards of Canada harked back to *Bush of Ghosts*, they also harked forward to Ghost Box, the British label whose ectoplasmic sound and elegiac sensibility have come to define the twenty-first-century genre known as hauntology. Perhaps 'memoradelia', an alternative genre tag briefly floated by the critic Patrick McNally, is a better umbrella term for the audio traits and cultural preoccupations that BoC share with Ghost Box artists like the Focus Group, Belbury Poly and the Advisory Circle, along with their kindred spirits Moon Wiring Club and Mordant Music. Among the many common concerns, a nostalgic fascination for television stands out as the major connection. During the 1970s especially, children's TV programming in the UK featured a peculiar preponderance of ghost stories, tales of the uncanny and apocalyptic scenarios (like *The Changes*, in which the populace rises up and destroys all technology). In between this creepy fare, young eyes were regularly assaulted by Public Information Films, a genre of short British programmes made for TV broadcast and ostensibly designed to educate and advise, but which often seemed to be scripted and directed by child-hating sadists whose true goal was to increase nightmares and bed-wetting. Featuring the macabre voice-over tones of actor Donald Pleasence, 'Dark and Lonely Water', for instance, warned of the dangers of ponds and other bodies of water, while 'Apaches' showed in grisly detail what might befall a bunch of kids messing about in a farmyard.

141

The unsettling content of all this vintage kids-oriented TV seeped into the brains of Sandison and Eoin at a young and vulnerable age. But what seems to have lingered even more insidiously in the memory of Boards of Canada, and the hauntologists that came after them, is the music. For many Brit kids, the sound effects and incidental motifs made for these programmes by outfits like the BBC Radiophonic Workshop were their first exposure to abstract electronic sounds. Speaking in 1998, Sandison claimed that these theme tunes and soundtracks were 'a stronger influence than modern music, or any other music that we listened to back then. Like it or not, they're the tunes that keep going around in our heads.'

Another hauntology theme that Boards of Canada anticipated is the notion of the lost future. Again, this tends to be identified most with the seventies and that decade's queasy ambivalence about runaway technological change: on the one hand, there was still a lingering post-WW2 optimism abroad, but it was increasingly contaminated with paranoid anxiety about ecological catastrophe and the rise of a surveillance state. 'Looking back at TV and film from that decade, a lot of what you see was pretty dark,' says Sandison. By the early nineties, when Boards of Canada were finding their identity, 'all the sounds and pictures from back then seemed like a kind of partially remembered nightmare. For us, it was a great source of inspiration. We couldn't understand why it hadn't occurred to anyone else to do it; it was a really obvious, natural thing to use.'

Another seventies-in-vibe obsession of the brothers is what they call 'strange science', that zone where the boundary between reason and superstition gets muddy: bodies of renegade knowledge and 'independent research' such as parapsychology, Erich von Däniken's best-selling books about 'ancient astronauts', New Age with its beliefs and techniques concern-

142

ing healing vibrations and energy flows, and many other forms of quasi-scientific magic and mysticism. 'I do actually believe that there are powers in music that are almost supernatural,' Eoin once argued. 'I think you actually manipulate people with music, and that is definitely what we are trying to do.'

Part of that manipulation of the listener goes beyond the sound itself and involves the framing of the music. Boards of Canada's work is intricately brocaded with arcane references and encrypted allusions. They have cultivated cultishness. For a measure of their success, just check a Boards of Canada fan site, where you'll find a feast of annotations and speculations: competing attempts to decode the meaning of titles, to locate the sources of samples, to decipher the half-buried fragments of speech.

'There is a story behind every title we use,' the brothers revealed in their first interview. It's as if they were setting out the terms for future engagement with their work. Yet, as Sandison admitted in a later interview, most of those carefully placed meanings necessarily remained elusive and impenetrable. 'If we were to explain all the tracks and their meanings . . . I think it would ruin them for a lot of people. It's more like viewing something through the bottom of a murky glass, and that's the beauty of it.'

For Boards of Canada, this deliberately hermetic aesthetic is designed to induct the listener into a deeper mode of engagement, and to conjure a sense that something more is going on than just sound for sound's sake. 'If it's not about something, it feels unfinished,' Sandison says now. 'Even as instrumental artists, you don't have to neglect having a message or agenda just because of the absence of a vocalist. The kinds of bands we like have something going on that is way beyond just the music itself. I appreciate all that world-building, especially if the artist is doing something separate from the main flow.'

143

With *Music Has the Right*, BoC did build their own world, set apart from the wider currents of late-nineties electronica. After such an achievement, it would be unreasonable to expect the brothers to unfurl a wholly new sound and vision on each subsequent album. As their discography unfolded over the ensuing twenty years, the brothers first intensified their approach with *In a Beautiful Place out in the Country* and *Geogaddi*, then inflected it with the shoegaze-tinged *The Campfire Headphase*, and finally simply reiterated it with *Tomorrow's Harvest*. But then the idea of Boards of Canada 'progressing' or 'evolving' goes against their very essence. Their intent with *Music Has the Right to Children* was to create a haunted haven outside the onward flow of Time. Why wouldn't they want to live there forever?

Pitchfork, 2018

GRIME: We Run the Roads

Grime emerged from London's pirate radio underground. Its immediate precursor was 2-step (aka UK garage), which at the turn of the millennium broke into the UK pop mainstream in a massive way. 2-step had been shaped by the 'feminine pressure' for sing-along melodies and wind-your-waist grooviness. Grime arose as a backlash against this crossover sound, a violent swing in the scene's inner gender-pendulum from yin to yang. Out went 2-step's high-pitched diva vocals, sensual swing and sexed-up amorousness; in came gruff rapping, stiff electro-influenced beats and raucous aggression.

MCs have been part of the pirate radio tradition for at least fifteen years, going back through garage and jungle to the early days of hardcore rave. By the end of the nineties, however, the MCs were moving beyond their customary restricted role as party 'hosts' and sidekicks to the DJ. Instead of gimmicky vocal licks and praise-the-selector exhortations, they began to rap actual verses: initially, extended takes on traditional boasts about their own mic skills, but soon getting into narrative, complicated metaphors and rhyme schemes, vicious dissing of rivals, and even introspective soliloquies. The MC's rise swiftly eclipsed the DJ, hitherto the most prominent figure on rave flyers or the main designated artist on record releases. The turning point came in 2001, when MCs shunted selectors out of the spotlight. So Solid Crew broke into the pop charts, and the underground seethed with similar collectives modelled on the clan/dynasty structures that prevail in American hip hop and Jamaican dancehall.

Emerging from the transitional sound known as 'garage rap', grime really defined itself as a distinct genre when the first tracks appeared that were designed purely as 'MC tools' – riddims for rappers to ride. These grimestrumentals were largely sourced in the electro diaspora – post-Sleng Teng dancehall ragga, Miami bass, New Orleans bounce, Dirty South crunk and 'street rap' producers like Swizz Beatz. Like these genres, grime doesn't go in much for sampling but prefers synths, typically with cheap 'n' nasty timbres that vaguely evoke the eighties and often seem to be influenced by pulp-movie video soundtracks, videogame musik, and even mobile phone ringtones. But in grime's textured beats and complex programming you can also hear the imprint of the jungle that most of these late-teens/early-twenties producers grew up on, alongside folk-memory traces of gabber and techno. Sometimes, listening, you might imagine you can hear uncanny echoes of postpunk-era electro-primitivists such as The Normal, D.A.F., Cabaret Voltaire or the calligraphic exquisiteness of Japan, Thomas Leer and The Residents.

Inherited from the period when 2-step ruled the Top 10, but also inspired by enviously watching the living-large of American rap superstars, grime feels a powerful drive to invade the mainstream and get 'paid in full'. Pirate radio, a broadcast medium with a potentially vast audience, encourages this grandiosity. One peculiar byproduct of grime's ambition is the scene's craze for DVD releases, like *Risky Roadz* and *Lord of the Mic*, containing documentary material with live footage. It's as if the scene is DIY-ing the sort of TV coverage it feels

146

it deserves but isn't getting. Yet while some of the top MCs
are being groomed for stardom by major-label-owned boutique
labels, the day-to-day reality of grime is grafting to get by in a
narrowcast culture. Selling 500 copies of a track is considered
a good result. The way grime operates – small-run vinyl-only
pressings and mixtapes, often sold directly to specialist stores
– has a surprising amount in common with micro-cultures like
noise, free folk, improv and extreme metal. Like these genres,
grime is what musician-theorist Chris Cutler would call an
'engaged' culture, with a high ratio of performers to consumers. These aspiring MCs, DJs and producers have a deeper
understanding of what constitutes skill and innovation in their
scene. Grime even has an improv element with its freestyles
and MC battles. There's a glorious ephemerality to the way
MCs riff off-the-cuff lyrics during pirate sessions, although fans
have always tape-recorded the shows and some are now getting
archived on the web.

Unlike globally dispersed micro-cultures such as noise and
extreme metal, grime is geographically concentrated. It's
popular across London and has outposts in other multiracial UK
cities, but its absolute heartland consists of a few square miles
in that part of East London not served by the Tube. In truth,
it's a parochial scene, obsessed with a sense of place, riven by
internecine conflicts and territorial rivalries (the intense com-
petitiveness being one reason grime's so creative). Still, despite
this insularity, grime has never been easier for 'outsiders' to
investigate, thanks to 1Xtra (the BBC's digital radio station
for UK 'urban' music), the trend for pirates like Rinse FM to go
online as well as broadcast terrestrially, mail-order via companies like Rhythm Division and Independence, and the swarm of
blogs covering the scene.

SO SOLID CREW
DILEMMA
So Solid (1999)

OXIDE & NEUTRINO
BOUND 4 DA RELOAD (CASUALTY)
EastWest (2000)

So Solid are famous as the first MC crew to cross over big-time – they hit No. 1 with '21 Seconds' – and infamous for their frequent brushes with the law. In grime terms, though, their single most influential track is this instrumental, which replaced 2-step's sultry swing with an electro-derived coldness and rigour. This new starkness was a timely move given that 2-step had reached the inevitable 'over-ripe' phase that afflicts all dance genres, its beats becoming cluttered and fussy. With its hard-angled drum machine snares and single-note sustained bass-drone veering upward in pitch, 'Dilemma' rediscovered the Kraftwerk principle: inflexibility can sometimes be funkier than suppleness. So solid, indeed: 'Dilemma' is like a huge block of ice in the middle of the dancefloor, a real vibe-chiller.

So Solid affiliates DJ Oxide and MC Neutrino also scored a No. 1 UK hit with 'Bound 4 da Reload'. Initially a pirate radio anthem through 1999, 'Reload' created a massive rift in the garage scene: older types loathed it; young 'uns loved it. Today's grime heads would probably disown their teenage favourite as a mere novelty track. Which it certainly was, from the *Casualty* TV theme sample to the 'can everyone stop getting shot?' soundbite from *Lock, Stock and Two Smoking Barrels*. Gimmicks aside, Oxide's production is *heavy*, from the ice-stab pizzicato violins ('strings of death', perhaps, given the track's allusions to the

148

rising blood-tide of violence on London's streets) to the doom-boom of sub-bass to the morgue-chilly echo swathing much of the record. Probably equally repellent to 2-step fans was the nagging, nasal insistence of Neutrino's rapping, which is remorselessly unmelodic but horribly catchy. Instantly demoting 2-step from 'the sound of now' to its current nostalgia-night status as 'old skool', 'Reload' has strong claims to being the first grime tune.

PAY AS U GO CARTEL
KNOW WE
Solid City (2001)

WILEY AND ROLL DEEP
TERRIBLE
Solid City (2001)

Circulating on dubplate as early as 1999, 'Know We' was in constant pirate rotation by the time of its 2001 release, alongside chip-off-the-same-block track 'Terrible'. Both are back-to-basics affairs: simple programmed beats, in each case adorned with the solitary hook of a violin flourish, functioning purely as a vehicle for the MCs. Another striking shared characteristic is the use of the first-person plural. Each MC bigs up himself when it's his turn on the mic, but at the chorus individualism is subsumed in a collective thrust for prestige. 'Now we're going on *terrible*' promise/threaten Roll Deep, and they don't mean they're about to give a weak performance. 'Roll deep' itself meaning marauding around town as a mob. But there's a hint of precariousness to Pay As U Go's assertions of universal renown. The sense of grandeur is latent; they're not stars *yet*. What does come through loud and clear on both tracks is the hunger. 'Terrible' starts with a Puff

Daddy soundbite: 'sometimes I don't think you motherfuckers understand where I'm coming from, where I'm trying to *get to*'. Both the PAUG and Roll Deep tracks were produced by a young prodigy named Wiley, whose catchphrase back then was 'They call me William/I'm gonna make a million'. Roll Deep are grime's NWA (its ranks have included such luminaries as Dizzee Rascal, Riko, Flowdan, Trim and Danny Weed), with Wiley as its Dr Dre. If he's yet to make that first million, this human dynamo must surely have released close to that number of tracks these last four years.

GENIUS CRU

COURSE BRUV

Kronik (2001)

The gangsta rap comparison isn't an idle one. PAUG and Roll Deep pioneered criminal-minded lyrics. Taking them literally isn't always advisable, as the imagery of 'slewing' and 'merking' is often purely metaphorical, signifying the destruction of rival MCs in verbal combat, the maiming of egos rather than bodies. Still, the genre wasn't always so relentlessly hostile. Just before the grimy era, 'garage rap' outfits like Heartless Crew and Genius Cru exuded playful bonhomie. The follow-up to their No. 12 pop hit 'Boom Selection', Genius's 'Course Bruv' talks about spreading 'nuff love' in the club and stresses that they 'still don't wanna hurt nobody'. The chorus even celebrates the rave-era ritual of sharing your soft drinks with complete strangers, the 'course bruv' being Genius's gracious acquiescence to 'can I have a sip of that?' Producer Capone weaves an effervescent merry-go-round groove of chiming bass-melody and giddy looped strings, while the MCs hypnotise with the sheer bubbling fluidity of their chat. The verses are deliberately preposterous playa wish-fulfilment: 'Number one breadwinner', Keflon claims he's 'invested in many shares, many

many stocks', while Fizzy purports to date 'celeb chicks', 'ballerinas' and even have 'hot chicks as my household cleaners'.

PLATINUM 45 featuring MORE FIRE
OI!
Go Beat (2002)

Pirate radio culture evolves in small increments, month by month. The onset of one genre or sub-flava overlaps with the twilight of its predecessor. There are rarely clean breaks. Still, every so often a track comes along that yells 'IT'S THE NEW STYLE!!!!' in your face. 'Oi!' was one of them. Drawing on the most anti-pop, street vanguard elements in black music history – ragga's twitch 'n' lurch, electro's (f)rigidity, jump-up jungle's bruising bass-blows – producer Platinum 45 created a most unlikely No. 7 hit. Factor in the barely decipherable jabber of More Fire's Lethal B, Ozzie B and Neeko, and the result was one of the most abrasively alien *Top of the Pops* appearances ever. The tune's pogo-like hard-bounce bass and uncouth Cockney-goes-ragga chants mean that 'Oi!' has more in common with Cockney Rejects-style punk than you'd imagine. 'Oi!', then – grime's biggest hit to date, before the genre even had a name.

MUSICAL MOB
PULSE X (VIP Mix)
Inspired Sounds Records (2002)

Widely regarded at the time as UK garage's absolute nadir, 'Pulse X' is actually a pivotal track: the scene's first purpose-built MC tool. Locating a new rhythm at the exact intersection of electro and gabber, 'Pulse' is virtually unlistenable – those dead-eyed claps, those numbly concussive kicks – on its own. But in combination with a great MC, the skeletal riddim becomes an instant and massive intravenous jolt of pure adrenalin. It's not just the headbanging energy, though; it's the track's very structure that is radical. 'Pulse X' was the first eight-bar tune, so-called because the rhythm switches every eight bars, thereby enabling MCs to take turns to drop sixteen bars of rhymes using both beat-patterns. Far from being UK garage's death-rattle, 'Pulse X' rescued the scene, rudderless and demoralised after 2-step's pop bubble burst. The sheer phallic rigour of 'Pulse X' gave the scene a spine, a forward direction.

DIZZEE RASCAL
I LUV U/VEXED
XL (2003)

Circulating as a white label from summer 2002 onwards, 'I Luv U' turned London pirate culture around as much as 'Pulse X'. Legendarily creating the track in a single afternoon during a school music class, Dizzee took the same sort of sounds Musical Mob used – gabber-like distorted kick drums, shearing-metal claps – and turned them into actual music. Add a teenage MC genius desperate to announce himself to the world, and you have grime's 'Anarchy in the U.K.' The punk parallel applies because of the harsh Englishness of Dizzee's vocal timbre and the lovelessness of the lyric, which depicts the pitfalls of the, er, dating game from the p.o.v. of too-much-too-young sixteen-year-olds whose hearts have been calloused into premature cynicism. Dizzee's snotty derision is almost eclipsed by the comeback from female MC Jeanine Jacques, who throws 'that girl's some bitch yunno' back in his face with the equally corrosive 'that boy's some prick yunno'. The original white featured the 'Luv U' instrumental, but tossed away on the XL re-release's B-side is the classic 'Vexed': Dizzee's stressed delivery makes you picture steam coming out of his ears and the music – beats like ice floes cracking, shrill synth-tingles – renders instantly obsolete the entire previous half-decade of retro-electro.

WILEY

ESKIMO

Wiley Kat Recordings (2002)

ICE RINK

Wiley Kat Recordings (2003)

Ex-Pay As U Go but at this point still Rolling Deep, Wiley invented an entire mini-genre of low-key, emaciated instrumentals: asymmetrically structured grooves based around sidewinder B-lines that 'Slinky downstairs' (as DJ Paul Kennedy put it), and glinting, fragmentary melodies. From his legion of imitators, these tended to be strictly MC-funktional beats, but in Wiley's case, more often than not the tracks are highly listenable stand-alone aesthetic objects even without rhyming. The first in an ongoing series of ice-themed tunes ('Igloo', 'Frostbite', 'Snowkat', et al), 'Eskimo' was the blueprint for this dinky-yet-creepy micro-genre (which Wiley dubbed 'Eskibeat'). 'Ice Rink' took the concept of MC tool to the next level. Instead of just being sold as an instrumental for MCs to use, it was released in some eight versions featuring different MCs. Spread across two 12-inches, 'Ice Rink' constituted a de facto grime equivalent to dancehall reggae's one-riddim albums. Dizzee's turn is the stand-out, his scrawny voice oozing the impudence of someone at the top of his game, as he invites all haters to plant their lips upon his posterior: 'kiss from the left to the right/kiss 'til my black bum-cheeks turn white'. Wiley's palsy of door-slam kicks and mercury-splash blips jostles with Dizzee for your attention.

JAMMER

WEED MAN

Hot Sound (2003)

JAMMER featuring D DOUBLE E

BIRDS IN THE SKY

Hot Sound (2003)

The year 2003 saw a slew of eight-bar instrumentals suffused
with fake Far East exoticism. As incongruous as a pagoda plopped
smack dab in the centre of Bow, 'Weed Man' is the supreme example of 'sinogrime', *Hyperdub* webzine's term for this micro-genre.
Produced by Nasty Crew's Jammer, the track is dedicated to 'all
the marijuana smokers' and appropriately the tempo is torpid to a
trip hop-like degree. The loping, sprained rhythm flashes back to
Sylvian–Sakamoto's 'Bamboo Music' while the ceremonial bassline
and breathy flute conjure mind's-eye imagery of Zen gardens and
temples. But where Wiley's similar excursions eastwards were
fuelled by record-buying trips to world music record store Sterns,
Jammer mostly likely derived his notion of Oriental mystery from
videogame music and martial arts movie soundtracks. 'Birds in
the Sky' has a similarly medieval atmosphere but, apart from the
plucked twang of some kind of stringed East Asian instrument,
is less obviously an ethnological forgery. The solo debut of one of
grime's greatest MCs, D Double E, 'Birds' has a brooding meditational aura. The lyric pivots around the bizarre trope of a verbal
drive-by, the MC firing off word-bullets that are also 'like birds in
the sky/hit one of your bredren's in the eye'. Double muses on his
motivations – 'why?/cos I'm an evil guy' – then emits his signature
vocal licks, the pain-pleasure groan of 'oooh-oooh' and the mouth-
mangled 'it's me, me', which sounds more like 'mwui-mwui'.

154

RIKO AND TARGET
CHOSEN ONE
Aim High (2004)

RUFF SQWAD
LETHAL INJECTION
White Label (2004)

Former Pay As U Go stalwart and man behind the ace *Aim High* compilations, Target here creates one of grime's most stirringly cinematic epics, placing a heart-tugging orchestral refrain amid a strange, decentred drum track whose flurries of claps and kicks seem to trip over themselves. This groove's sensation of impeded yet steadfast forward motion totally fits the lyric's theme of deter-mination and destiny. In his smoky, patois-tinged baritone, Riko (another PAUG alumnus) counsels calmness and composure to all those struggling, whether they're aspiring MCs striving to make it or regular folk trying to make it through everyday strife: 'Use your head to battle through/cos you are the chosen one'. The synth swells favoured by Ruff Sqwad also have a cinematic grandeur, like gangsta Vangelis. 'Lethal Injection', though, is one of their more minimal efforts, consisting of a wibbly keyboard line, the boom of a heavily echoed kick drum, and the Sqwad's rapid-fire jabber, swathed in a susurrating shroud of reverb and background chat. Not a tear-jerker like 'Chosen One', but incredibly atmospheric.

TERROR DANJAH
INDUSTRY STANDARD EP
Aftershock (2003)

VARIOUS ARTISTS

PAY BACK EP (THE REMIX)

Aftershock (2003)

Judging by *Industry Standard*, you could justly describe Terror
Danjah as one of the most accomplished electronic musicians of
the twenty-first century. On tracks like 'Juggling' and 'Sneak
Attack', the intricate syncopation, texturised beats, spatialised
production and 'abstracty sounds' (Danjah's own phrase) make
this 'headphone grime' – not something that could be claimed
for too many operators on the scene. Yet all this finesse is
marshalled in service of a fanatically doomy and monolithic
mood, Gothic in the original barbarian-invader meaning. The
atmosphere of domineering darkness is distilled in Danjah's
audio-logo, a demonic cackle that resembles some jeering, leering
cyborg death-dwarf, which appears in all of his productions and
remixes. 'Creep Crawler', the first tune on *Industry Standard*,
and its sister track 'Frontline (Creepy Crawler Mix)', which kicks
off *Pay Back*, are Danjah's sound at its most pungently oppressive. 'Creep Crawler' begins with the producer smirking aloud
('heh-heh, they're gonna hate me *now*'), then a bone-crusher
beat stomps everything in its path, while ominous horn-blasts
pummel in the lower midrange and synths wince like the onset
of migraine. From its opening something-wicked-this-way-comes
note-sequence onwards, Big E.D.'s original 'Frontline' was hair-
raising already. Danjah's remix of his acolyte's monster tune
essentially merges it with 'Creep Crawler', deploying the same
astringent synth-dissonance and trademark bass-blare fanfares
(filtered to create a weird sensation of suppressed bombast) but
to even more intimidating and shudder-inducing effect.

MARK ONE VERSUS PLASTICMAN

HARD GRAFT 1/HARD GRAFT 2

Contagious (2003)

LOEFAH

BOMBAY SQUAD

(on *Grime 2*, Rephlex Compilation, 2004)

If you hadn't already guessed from the name, grime inverts values. Dutty, stinkin', even disgustin' – all are positive attributes in grime parlance. So when I say 'Hard Graft' is utterly *dismal*, you'll know this is the thumbs-up. Grime often represents itself as gutter music. Mark One and Plasticman go further, or deeper, with this track, and seem to plunge into the sewage system. Full of clanking beats, septic gurglings, eerie echoes and scuttling percussion, 'Hard Graft' makes you imagine pipes, storm drains, dank chambers.

Mark One, Plasticman and their cohorts constitute not so much a subgenre of grime as a side-genre, running adjacent to the scene proper. The sound is techy, MC-free and more danceable than grime. Although a number of black producers are involved, you could fairly describe this style's sonic coding as whiter than grime, and situate it on a Euro continuum running through Belgian industrial techno (Meng Syndicate, 80 Aum) through the cold technoid end of rave (Nebula II) to No U Turn's techstep and Photek-style neurofunk (the beats on 'Hard Graft' sometimes recall his 'Ni Ten Ichi Ryu'). The proximity of the name Plastic-man to the Richie Hawtin alias Plastikman seems telling.

People are starting to call this new style 'dubstep', and, as that name suggests, the black component to this sound comes from Jamaica: roots reggae's swaying rhythm, deep bass and spatial-ised production effects. Loefah's clanking skank connects to a

157

lineage of industrial-but-rootical UK music: On U Sound, bleep
'n' bass (Ability II's 'Pressure', say), The Orb, Techno-Animal.
'Bombay Squad' is built around what feels like a half-finished,
or partially erased, groove: massive echo-laden snare-cracks,
a liquid pitter of tablas situated in a corner of the mix and . . .
that's it, apart from the dark river of sub-bass that propels the
track forward. The intertextual traces of the title 'Bombay Squad'
include Public Enemy's producers the Bomb Squad and 2 Bad
Mice's rave anthem 'Bombscare', but actually allude to the track's
sole colouration, the plaintive ululation of a Bollywood diva.

JAMMER featuring KANO
BOYS LOVE GIRLS
Hot Sound (2003)

WONDER featuring KANO
WHAT HAVE YOU DONE
New Era (2004)

TERROR DANJAH featuring KANO and SADIE
SO SURE
Aftershock (2004)

The backing tracks are fabulous – Jammer's frenetic snare-roll
clatter, Wonder's tonally harrowed synths, Danjah's aching ripples
of idyllic electronics – but it's the MC who really shines. With some
grime rhymesters, the flow resembles an involuntary discharge
(D Double E being the ultimate exponent of MCing as automatic
poetry). But even at his most hectic, as on 'Boys Love Girls', Kano
always sounds in complete control. All poise and deliberation, Kano

158

invariably sounds like he's weighing up the angles, calculating his moves, calibrating which outcomes serve his interests. That's blatant on 'Boys' and 'What Have You Done', both cold-hearted takes on modern romance that depict sex in transactional terms, a ledger of positives and minuses, credits and debits: a war of the genders in which keeping your feelings checked and maintaining distance is strategically crucial. But it comes through even in the gorgeous ballad 'So Sure', on which Kano blurs the border between loverman and soldier drawing up plans for conquest: 'ain't got time to be one of them guys just watching you and wasting time/next time I'm clocking you I'm stopping you to make you mine'. As much as the acutely observed lyrical details, it's the timbre of Kano's voice that's enthralling: slick yet grainy, like varnished wood, and knotty with halting cadences that convince you he's thinking these thoughts aloud for the very first time.

DAVINCHE

DIRTY CANVAS EP

Paperchase Recordings (2004)

ESSENTIALS

HEADQUARTERS

White Label (2004)

'So Sure' is an example of the burgeoning subgenre R&G (rhythm and grime), which is basically a transparent attempt to lure the ladies back onto the floor, after they'd been turned off by the testosterone-heavy vibe of tracks more suitable for moshing than sexy dancing. As the name R&G suggests, the mini-genre replicates 2-step's original move of copping American R&B's luxurious arrangements and diva-melisma. Alongside Terror Danjah,

Davinche pioneered R&G with tunes like 'Leave Me Alone'. Too often these attempts at Brit-Beyoncé fall short, owing to a lack of grounding in songcraft and the studio art of mic'ing vocalists, and end up sounding slightly thin and shabby. So I prefer Davinche's instrumental efforts like the *Dirty Canvas* EP series. The quasi-soundtrack orchestration of 'Stinger' – flurrying strings, decaying tones from a softly struck gong – is designed to swathe any MC who rhymes over it with an aura of slightly harried majesty.

Grime is synonymous with East London, but other parts of the city are starting to get a look-in. Essentials, Davinche's crew, operate out of South. This powerful sense of territoriality is integral to the concept of 'Headquarters', which draws on the talents of a veritable battalion of MCs, some guests and some from Essentials' own barracks. At each chorus, a drill sergeant barks questions at the MC who's stepping up for his mic turn: 'state your name, soldier', 'state your location' (usually 'East' or 'South', sometimes a specific postal district), 'who you reppin'' (usually a crew, like Essentials, N.A.S.T.Y, Aftershock, but sometimes just 'myself'). Then the sergeant orders each recruit to get down and 'give me sixteen' – not press-ups, but sixteen bars of rhymes. The amazing production seals the conceptual deal, the chorus being accompanied by cello-like instrumentation that's been digitally contorted into an unearthly wraith-like whinny, or a cyberwolf howling at the moon.

LETHAL B featuring FUMIN, D DOUBLE E, NAPPA, JAMAKABI, NEEKO, FLOWDAN, OZZI B, FORCER, DEMON & HOT SHOT

POW (FORWARD)

Relentless (2004)

Following a failed mainstream-bid album, More Fire looked all washed up in 2003, but Lethal B rebuilt their street rep from the ground up. In 2004, 'Pow', Lethal plus ten guest MCs spitting over producer Dexplicit's 'Forward' riddim, became the scene's biggest anthem. The track ultimately barged its way to the outskirts of the Top 10, achieving grime's highest chart placing since . . . well, 'Oi!' The riddim is basic verging on crude, a madly gyrating loop that resembles an out-of-control carousel. 'Pow!!!', Lethal's chorus chant, evokes the fisticuffs of comic book superheroes. Matching the track's rowdy vibe (it was reputedly banned in some clubs for inciting mayhem on the floor), the squadron of top MCs lay on the ultraviolence, the cartoon flavour of which can be gleaned from Demon's immortal warning: 'you don't wanna bring some beef/Bring some beef you'll lose some teeth'.

JAMMER featuring WILEY, D DOUBLE E, KANO & DURRTY GOODZ

DESTRUCTION REMIX

White Label (2004)

D DOUBLE E & P-JAM

ANGER MANAGEMENT

Dice Recordings (2004)

Like 'Pow', 'Destruction' is a rollercoaster of pugilistic noise and lyrical aggro, but Jammer's production is marginally more sophisticated, slicing 'n' dicing brassy fanfares (probably from blacksploitation movies) and filtering them to create a sort of surging-yet-leashed effect, like the track is simmering with pent-up rage. The four scene-leading MCs rise to the occasion, from Wiley's riffed variations on 'I know Trouble but Trouble says he don't know you', to Kano's quaintly anglicised gangsta

161

boast 'from lamp post to lamp post, we run the road'. But the star performance comes from D Double E. Seemingly battling multiple speech impediments, he expectorates glottal gouts of raw verbiage. As so often, there's that characteristic sense of involuntary utterance, like it's him who's being spoken through. 'Spitting' is too decorous a word for his rhyme style; retching is closer. Witness Double's astonishing first six bars on 'Destruction', a gargoyle-like gibber closer to hieroglyphics than language, and seemingly emanating from the same infrahuman zone Iggy Pop plumbed on 'Loose' and 'TV Eye'. On Double's first solo single since 'Birds in the Sky', rising producer P-Jam's snaking wooze of gaseous malevolence sparks one of the MC's most Tourettic performances. Barely tethered to the beat's bar scheme, Double seems to be wading waist-deep through sonic sludge. He boasts of 'sucking up MCs like a hoover', an image possibly cued by the 'Mentasm'-like miasma unloosed by P-Jam.

TRIM

BOOGIEMAN

Aftershock (2004)

BRUZA

NOT CONVINCED

Aftershock (2005)

Like most producers in most dance genres, grime beat-makers typically invent a striking sound, then wear it out with endless market-milking iterations. Terror Danjah has often approached that danger zone, but on 'Boogieman' he shows how much scope for inventive arrangement remains in the 'Creep Crawler' template. You can hear the cartoon-comical

162

wooh-wooh ghostly touches best on the instrumental version, 'Haunted' (on Aftershock's *Roadsweeper* EP). 'Boogieman' itself is a showcase for rising star Trim, here honing his persona of scoffing imperturbability: 'I'm not scared of the boogieman/I *scare* the boogieman'.

On 'Not Convinced', Danjah drafts a whole new template that reveals the producer's roots in drum and bass (the track's futuristic tingles vaguely recall Foul Play's 'Being with You' remix). Again, though, the MC makes it hard to focus on the riddim. More than anyone apart from not-grime-really Mike Skinner, Bruza incorporates British intonation and idiom into a totally effective style of rapping, in which the not-flow of stilted English cadences becomes a *new* flow. It sounds 'brutal and British', as Bruza puts it. As his name suggests, the MC has also perfected a hard-man persona that feels authentically English rather than a gangsta fantasy based on Compton or Kingston. He exudes a laconic, steely menace redolent of bouncers. 'Not Convinced' extrapolates from this not-easily-impressed persona to create a typology of character in which the world is divided into the serious and the silly, the latter lacking the substance and conviction to give their words authority. Bruza addresses, and dresses down, a wannabe MC, a kid pretending to be a man: 'I'm not convinced/Since you've been spitting/I haven't believed one word/Not one inch/Not even a millimeter/To me you sound like a silly speaker/Silly features in your style/You spit silly/And you spit like how kids be'.

KANO featuring D DOUBLE E & DEMON
RELOAD IT

(697, on debut album, due autumn 2005)

Circling back to 'Bound 4 da Reload', this track celebrates the pirate radio and rave tradition of the DJ rewind, when the crowd hollers (or home-listening audience text-messages) its demand for the selector to wheel and come again. Until grime, the trigger for rewinds would be a killer sampled vocal lick, thrilling bass-drop or even just a mad breakbeat. Nowadays, the MC being king, the crowd clamours to hear their favourite rhymes. 'This is what it means when DJs reload it/That sixteen was *mean* and he knows it,' explains Kano, before listing the other top-dog MCs who get nuff rewinds (two of them, Double and Demon, guest on the track). 'I get a reload purely for the flow,' Kano preens, and you can see why as he glides with lethal panache between quick-time rapping and a leisurely, drawn-out gait that seems to drag on the beat to slow it down. The track itself, co-produced by Kano and Diplo, is all shimmery excitement, pivoting around a spangly filtered riff that ascends and descends the same four notes, driven by a funky rampage of live-sounding drums, and punctuated by horn samples, Beni G's scratching, and orgasmic girl-moans. The old skool breakbeat-like energy suggests an attempt to sell the notion of grime as British hip hop, yet if transatlantic crossover is the intent, that's subverted by the lyric, its theme being as localised and grime-reflexive as imaginable. 'Reload It' encapsulates the conflicted impulses that fuel this scene: undergroundist insularity versus an extrovert hunger to engage with, and conquer, the whole wide world.

Originally published as 'THE PRIMER: GRIME',
The Wire, 2005

DUBSTEP: Burial

The title of Burial's second album rings out like an accusation. 'Untrue' is a slightly old-fashioned way of describing someone – a lover, usually – who's unfaithful. It could also be a simple assertion that something is a lie. But you might also say that 'untruth' is a quintessential attribute of music itself. The word captures something about the insubstantiality of sound, its quality of dream or mirage: the way it conjures up tantalising visions of a more perfect existence, out of reach and unattainable. Music can be a place where we hide from the harshness of the world as it really is.

Rarely interviewed, Burial has only once offered an explanation for the title *Untrue*, and a partial one. 'It's like when someone's not acting like themselves,' he told Australian critic Anwen Crawford in 2007. 'They're off-key, something's wrong, an atmosphere has entered the room.'

Titles are very important things in instrumental electronic music – surprisingly perhaps, given that the music is otherwise non-verbal. An inspired track or album title lightly guides the listener through the abstract sensations and emotions stirred up by the music. Burial is a maestro of titles. Some are jarringly concrete ('Dog Shelter', 'In McDonalds'), others are enigmatic ('Etched Headplate'), or poetic ('Shell of Light'). But perhaps his greatest feat of nomenclature is his own alias.

165

The name Burial pays homage to the reggae roots of dubstep, the genre to which he's loosely affiliated, and the sound-system tradition that informs UK rave culture. When rival systems compete in a sound-clash, they save their most devastating dubplate – sometimes called the 'burial tune' – for the final stage of battle. That term migrated into the rave lexicon: the biggest anthem of 1994, jungle's breakout year in the UK, was Leviticus's 'Burial', while Gant's 'Sound Bwoy Burial' was an early UK garage classic. These layered ancestral echoes, rippling back across the decades – from the murky clubs and rowdy pirate radio stations of 1990s London all the way to Kingston, Jamaica, in the 1970s – are something that Burial consciously honours with the name he chose to hide behind.

But the name Burial sets in motion another set of associations, plugging into the sombre side of postpunk. The moniker brings to my mind the cover of Joy Division's *Closer*: a photograph, taken in an Italian cemetery, of a sculpted tableau of a dead man who could be Christ surrounded by mourners. That image was personally selected by the band's singer, Ian Curtis, a few months before he committed suicide, as if he already knew he would end his life and become a rock martyr.

Reading about how Burial liked to test his tunes by driving around South London in the dead of night, to see if they had the quality of 'distance' he sought, always reminded me of the tales of Joy Division producer Martin Hannett making similar psycho-geographic jaunts through the post-industrial zones of Manchester in the late seventies, listening to contemporaries like PiL and Pere Ubu in his car. Both Hannett and Burial share an obsession with using reverb and near-subliminal sound effects, often taken from the real world, to conjure an atmosphere of eerie space.

Beyond the sonic resemblances and a shared aura of desolation, there are other parallels between Burial and Joy Division.

Both released startling, out-of-nowhere debuts that introduced a revelatory sound that felt visual, making your ears gaze into the distance. Both followed those up with immaculate sequels that completed and perfected the initial statement. Neither released a third studio album – although in Burial's case, that remains a (seemingly faint) possibility.

The postpunk connection helps to explain why Burial is the one dubstep artist that people who don't follow dubstep, or even electronic dance music, have latched onto. His albums have been embraced by music fans whose preferred listening might be the Cure (a group whose early and gloomiest music Burial is said to adore) or Radiohead. It makes sense to slot Burial in that pale lineage of 'young men, the weight on their shoulders', to quote an Ian Curtis lyric – to see him as another of those sad-eyed 'missing boys' who left 'some signs' and is 'now a legend', to quote the Durutti Column's tribute to the dead Curtis, 'The Missing Boy'.

For people respond to Burial's work in a way that is different to anybody else in dance music – different even from the cult reverence for Aphex Twin. Fans testify in a much more alternative-rock way about how his tunes 'saved my life'. The sound of Burial has touched people, opened them up to difficult emotions, hurt them in valuable ways.

As well as the reggae-to-rave and postpunk traditions, there's a third zone of contemporary music with which Burial has an affinity: hauntology, that largely British genre of eerie electronics fixated on ideas of decaying memory and lost futures. You can hear it in Burial's love of spooky atmospheres, disquieting sound effects, the hiss and crackle of vinyl – all hallmarks of artists like the Caretaker, who has released a series of foggy, elegiac works across nearly two decades. Even the way Burial talks about his music aligns closely with Ghost Box, the UK label that's home to spectral audio exponents

167

like the Focus Group and Belbury Poly. The short-lived spate of interviews he did around *Untrue* teem with references to uncanny presences, subliminal hums, moments when you glance at the face of a friend or family member and catch something alien in their expression. Burial even enthused about his childhood love of the ghost stories of M.R. James, one of those gentlemen supernatural horror writers who are touchstones for the UK hauntologists.

Interviewed by the late British critic Mark Fisher, Burial spoke of creepy epiphanies he'd experienced walking through deserted night-time areas of London: 'Sometimes you get that feeling like a ghost touched your heart, like someone walks with you.' Song titles like 'Archangel' and 'Feral Witchchild' suggest superstitious thinking, or at least an openness to the idea that there are supernatural dimensions, other realms that leak through into our reality in the form of visions or unsettling sensations.

An early champion of Burial, Fisher provided an enduringly compelling interpretation of his work. Writing first in his blog, k-punk, and later in *The Wire*, Fisher pegged Burial's self-titled 2006 debut album as 'an elegy for the hardcore continuum': a misty-eyed memorial to the British subculture of pirate radio and warehouse raves that coalesced at the end of the eighties, evolved through mutant nineties styles like jungle and 2-step garage, then splintered into twenty-first-century offshoots like grime and dubstep. Listening to Burial, Fisher wrote, felt 'like walking into the abandoned spaces once carnivalised by raves and finding them returned to depopulated dereliction. Muted air horns flare like the ghosts of raves past.'

This idea that the debut was less an album of contemporary dance music than an album about the glories of UK dance music's past was bolstered by soundbites like the one in 'Gutted'. Sampled from Jim Jarmusch's 1999 movie *Ghost*

Dog: The Way of the Samurai, the voice of Forest Whitaker murmurs: 'Me and him, we're from different, ancient tribes . . . now we're both almost extinct . . . sometimes you gotta stick with the ancient ways . . . old school ways.' On *Untrue*, the closing track 'Raver' reprises the idea with its vocal licks about 'dream life' and a long-gone world that was 'easy'. During rave's early-nineties peak, a multitude of tracks featured the word 'dream', often with an undertone suggesting that participants in the movement knew deep down that it was all just a dream, that utopia built on a chemical could only be a flimsy and transitory construction. This could offer another shade of meaning to 'untrue': rave as the dream that died, or worse, the dream that lied. Indeed, the phrase 'dream life' in 'Raver' could be heard as 'dream-lie'.

What Burial related through samples and moody orchestrations, Mike Skinner had earlier conveyed with words on 'Weak Become Heroes' on *Original Pirate Material*, his 2002 debut album as The Streets. The song describes the flashback of a former raver, abruptly set adrift on blissed memories of love and unity on the dancefloor, until he's snapped back to the dreary streets of a hostile and hopeless twenty-first-century England: 'grey concrete and deadbeats . . . no surprises no treats . . . My life's been up and down since I walked from that crowd.'

'Weak', in Skinner's song, means not just personally frail but politically powerless. The weak became heroes when they became a mass, uniting around the unwritten manifesto in the music: someday there'll be a better way, but in the meantime let's shelter for a while in this dreamspace. But the collective energy triggered by MDMA never got beyond the level of a pre-political potential; the moment dissipated.

In his *Untrue*-era interviews, Burial often refers to 'unity', music's power to dissolve divisions. Talking about the rave era's classic anthems, he told *FACT* magazine, 'It sounds stupid, but it's like they were trying to unite the whole UK, but they failed. So when I listen back to them I get kind of sad.' Too young to participate directly during rave's nineties prime, Burial got a second-hand dose of the vibe via the vinyl 12-inches and mixtapes that his older brother played him along with the stories he brought home of his raving exploits. Like those who came of age in the seventies feeling like they'd missed the great sixties adventure, Burial feasted on the recorded relics and fetishised the legend. Rave, for Burial, is almost like an implanted memory, *Blade Runner*-style.

Behind the ghost of rave haunting Burial's music lurks another spectre: socialism. The concept of hauntology was originally coined by the philosopher Jacques Derrida in 1993 to evoke how, even after the fall of communism and the triumph of globalised free market capitalism, the contemporary world remained haunted by that movement's originating ideals: social justice, equality, a kinder world free of exploitation and deprivation.

These ideological battles played out in late-twentieth-century Britain in ways that formed the background to Burial's music and shaped his bleak vision of modern urban life. Tony Blair's New Labour party co-opted D:Ream's 1993 pop-rave anthem 'Things Can Only Get Better' as the theme for its successful 1997 election campaign, which ended eighteen years of Conservative Party rule. But it was only by abandoning Labour's longstanding commitment to public stewardship of the economy and by distancing itself from the unions that Blair was able to get his hands on power.

The thirteen years of New Labour rule that ensued – the period in which Burial came of age and created his two albums – were essentially the extension of Margaret Thatcher's post-socialist vision for Britain, deep into the twenty-first century.

Workers increasingly submitted to 'flexible' employment (no guaranteed number of hours per week, last-minute notifications) that left employees in a permanent state of anxious uncertainty. Welfare became a punitive system designed to push people into the job market. Compulsory 'jobseeker' training sessions aimed to instill qualities like positivity, relentlessly pounding into the unemployed the idea that failure was the result of an individual deficiency of initiative rather than larger economic forces. And after Labour's introduction of tuition fees for students, many graduates found themselves burdened with debt and confronting an employment landscape of endless internships or the non-career-track jobs of the 'gig economy'.

To a large degree, the Thatcher project was to make Britain more like America in its attitudes to work and enterprise, the role of the state and the very concept of 'public'. That project continued under Blair. The end result is a stark feeling of being on your own in this life; your fate is in your own hands. 'It's easy to fall away and fuck up, and for many people there's no safety net,' Burial told *The Wire* in 2007. As dissected in Fisher's book *Capitalist Realism: Is There No Alternative?*, the result of this new precariousness has been pandemic levels of mental illness, rising suicide rates, and widespread dependence on anti-depression and anti-anxiety meds.

Where dance music is generally about abandon, Burial's music is about abandonment. Listening to his work, I'm sometimes reminded of nothing so much as The Beatles' 'Eleanor Rigby' – one long lament for 'all the lonely people' adrift in the modern city. Again, just look at the titles: 'Loner', 'Broken Home', 'Rough Sleeper', 'Homeless', 'Fostercare'. With 'Dog Shelter', Burial even has empathy to spare for all the lonely canines. (As it happens, around the time of making *Untrue*, he was actually mourning the death of a beloved dog.)

171

When his songs aren't about feeling bereft and forsaken, the titles point to emotional damage, or its corollary, the capacity of damaged people to lash out and perpetuate the cycle: 'Wounder', 'Gutted', 'U Hurt Me', 'Young Death'. It's like Burial's antennae are tuned into the frequencies of pain emanating from the metropolis, all the human flotsam and jetsam who have bailed out from abusive family situations or cycled downwards through self-destructive behaviours.

On 7 July 2005, a series of co-ordinated terrorist attacks killed and maimed a diverse mixture of Londoners setting off for work on an overstretched public transportation system. The fact that it was an assault on public spaces where the city's mongrel population mingle seemed to have particularly affected Burial. His own travel plans disrupted by the chaos on that day, he headed on foot from South London into the city centre, and then back again, during which time he listened intermittently to a mixtape of jungle and dubstep tunes he'd compiled. The city felt 'like it had been hurt', he told journalist Martin Clark later that year. 'All the dubstep and jungle shit became like comfort music: the sorrow just came out of it. I felt the music deeper from that point on.'

The trauma of 7/7 shaped Burial's conception of what his own music could become. 'A Burial album would sound deep and hypnotic at the start,' he told Clark in late 2005, a good six months before the debut's release. 'Just like someone picking themselves up, fixing up, getting by. The middle of the album would be proper underground, more rolled out, and then the end would be club tunes, like, "He made it out of there" . . . But the whole thing would be sad. I can't help it. London feels sad to me, but there's uplift in there.'

The 'uplift' comes from the way that the city creates epiphanies of grandeur, through the scope it offers for heroic aloneness and apartness. Burial's *Untrue* track 'In McDonalds' could be an updated audio translation of Edward Hopper's *Nighthawks* painting. Like Hopper's brightly lit diner surrounded by dark deserted streets, the fast-food eatery is a haven for the weary and cash-poor. And *Untrue*'s cover drawing could be a Burial self-portrait in the Hopper mode: moody in a hoodie, eyes and mouth downturned, lost in his own thoughts as a cup of coffee steams into the café's cold air.

The most famous of Burial's locales of loneliness, though, is the 'Night Bus', as immortalised on the debut album. Every city in the world has night buses, but there is a specific London resonance to this mode of transport. Until quite recently, when the London Tube finally went to twenty-four-hour service, the double-decker night bus was the only option for clubbers who couldn't afford a taxi. Since these cash-strapped youth typically lived in the low-rent, furthest-out zones of the city, this meant that the after-rave experience involved a long journey home. A comedown from the collective high, the bus returned ravers to privatised isolation, but offered the consolation prize of a twinkling, kinetic view of the city. The beat-free, strings-swept tingle of 'Night Bus' captures the poignancy of 'the afterglow' – Burial's term for the relationship between his music and rave culture.

Seeing the cityscape from an elevated perspective is integral to the *mise en scène* of Burial's cinematic sound. The cover of the debut album told us how to hear this music: it's an aerial view of the South London borough of Wandsworth, symbolising 'a pirate signal above London, just floating in the air', Burial has said. In the interview with Clark, Burial described how he made his tunes in a room whose window overlooked a prison, its grounds and a stretch of South London motorway that sloped down to the River Thames, with the entire vista often shrouded in wintry mist. 'Southern Comfort', his first classic tune, has a rolling fog-bank sound and a majestic sense of looking down from above.

That aura of altitude in Burial's music, along with the feeling of pained empathy in tracks like 'Broken Home', is surely what made me flash on the movie *Wings of Desire* when I reviewed his debut in 2006. Wim Wenders's 1987 film is a mood piece about the kindness of guardian angels who invisibly soothe suffering humans. On *Untrue*, this latent idea became explicit with the album's first song, 'Archangel'. 'My new tunes are about . . . wanting an angel watching over you, when there's nowhere to go and all you can do is sit in McDonald's late at night, not answering your phone,' Burial told *The Wire*.

Beyond the overt religiosity of titles like 'Prayer' and 'Prophecy', there's a feeling in Burial's music of reaching out in the darkness to higher powers. When collective dreaming – whether via progressive political projects or music movements like punk or rave – fades from the scene, people look to other sources of strength: traditional organised religions but also pulp spirituality, quasi-magical techniques of positive thinking, and other feel-good salves.

The spiritual yearning in Burial's music stems partly from the influence of Todd Edwards, an American garage producer whose impact in the UK far surpasses his modest profile in his homeland. A devout Christian whose tracks bear titles like 'Light of the Son', 'Saved My Life (Todd's Revelation)' and even 'Isaiah 41:13', Edwards developed a production style that he dubbed 'the sample choir': chopping up soulful vocals into miniscule snippets, then weaving them into a rapturously rejoicing tapestry of gasps and blurts. Edwards's innovations contributed to the rise of 'vocal science', a term originally coined by UK dance pundit Anindya Bhattacharyya, which involves techniques of micro-editing vocal samples into new melodic and rhythmic patterns. This had been a fixture of UK rave music from the start, but Edwards's virtuosity pushed it to the next level. His tracks 'Never Far from You' and 'Push

174

the Love' were massive hits on the UK garage scene in the late 1990s, and vocal science became a hallmark of the 2-step garage sound, which is the primary template on which Burial's music is based.

Burial's own use of vocal science harked back to both rave's ecstatic pyrotechnics and 2-step's sultry amorousness. But the mood now tilted to the sombre. Circa *Untrue*, Burial talked about being 'obsessed' with making his music 'glow a bit more' compared with the first album: 'having these little clips of vocals, and tiny moments of warmth for a split-second, and then it would go'. He compared the vocals to 'embers', 'little glowing bits' that fade out quickly, leaving an 'eerie and empty' darkness.

Vocal science derives its frisson from the juxtaposition of something intimate and bodily – the human voice – with cold-blooded technicality. Chopping and resequencing a vocal performance into a new shape is like vivisection and Frankenstein-style recombination. 'I cut up *a capellas* and made different sentences, even if they didn't make sense but they summed up what I was feeling,' Burial told *The Wire*. The remark shows how his artistry involves literally speaking through the voices of others, but it also points to the spooki-ness of sampling in general, and vocal science in particular. Really, it's closer to sorcery than science: taking a performer's deeply personal inmost possession, and making that voice sing melodies and transmit feelings at your command.

Perhaps that's why Burial often locates the sampled vocals in his tracks in an uncanny realm, comparing them at various points to the sound of 'a banshee, a strange, wounded animal cry', 'something not human I've got chained up in the yard' and a 'forbidden siren', at once a reference to the sirens of classical legend, bird-women whose seductive tones lured sailors to shipwreck – and a nod to a PlayStation game.

175

Burial manipulates phrases like 'holding you', 'if I trust you' and 'tell me I belong' like an expert glassblower, distending them into glistening bubbles of decontextualised passion. The transparency of specific meaning is gone but the translucence of pure emotion glows even more intensely.

Just as Todd Edwards's sample choir is overtly angelic and thus genderless, Burial is drawn to the way that vocal science can etherealise the source, rendering it androgynous. 'I wanted to make something that was kind of half-boy, half-girl' is how he described *Untrue* to Anwen Crawford. Later, Burial would articulate this implicit genderfluid politics with the track 'Come Down to Us', on 2013's *Rival Dealer* EP, which features sound-bites about self-acceptance and sexual blurriness, including words from a speech by the trans filmmaker Lana Wachowski delivered when receiving the Human Rights Campaign Visibility Award.

You could make a case for Burial's music as radically androgynous: open-hearted, aching with empathy, unafraid of prettiness or heart-tugging emotion. *Untrue* was in fact conceived as a sort of 'pop' move, its emphasis on vocals differentiating it from the emaciated brutalism of dubstep, which, if it featured vocals at all, usually went for gruff roots reggae samples. Prior to embarking on *Untrue*, Burial had actually produced a whole album's worth of material in a darker, technically intricate style of hyper-masculine moodiness. 'All the tunes sounded like some kind of weapon that was being taken apart and put back together again,' he told *The Wire*. But he scrapped that album in its entirety, discouraged by the fact that his mother hadn't liked any of the tunes he'd played her, and started again in a totally new direction based around ecstatic vocal samples. (Liberated by the impulsive decision to jettison all that hard work, Burial knocked out *Untrue* in just a couple of weeks.)

176

It's hard to imagine anybody else in dubstep – Coki or Skream, Pinch or Plasticman – reacting so drastically to a negative maternal verdict, but then, as Burial told *The Wire*, 'I was brought up most by my mum, I'm my mum's son. I look like her. I am her.' Of *Untrue*, he offered, 'Blokes might be, like, "What the fuck is this?" But hopefully their girlfriends will like it.'

Here Burial placed himself firmly on one side of a divide running through UK rave culture, whose evolution has involved a pendulum-like shift back and forth between two poles that I like to characterise as 'feminine pressure' versus 'masculine armour'. The latter is a lineage that is militaristic, scientific and apocalyptic in vibe – a vein of dark, stark tracks that runs from Metalheadz and techstep to the most mechanistic and bass-bombastic dubstep. The feminine pressure strand embraces vocal melody, song structure (albeit fractured), film-score orchestrations and a bursting emotionalism: its high points include early rave, the ambient and jazzy directions in drum and bass, the breakaway style known as happy hardcore and the entire UK garage phase, but especially 2-step.

Burial's loping grooves and skippy woodblock snares have much more in common with UK garage than with the clanking lurch of dubstep. The roots of his style are tracks like Groove Chronicles' 2-step classic 'Stone Cold', which layered sultry slices of Aaliyah's yearning vocal from 'One in a Million' over languidly swinging drums and a moody bass-drone. But instead of the feverish sexuality in 2-step, Burial picks up on the neediness and the longing.

Released by Hyperdub on 5 November 2007, *Untrue* was showered with critical praise. Named Album of the Year in major publications, it would go on to be nominated for the UK's Mercury Prize in 2008. In the meantime, *Untrue*'s impact on the

UK dance scene had started to come through in the form of a self-conscious turn towards emotionality: not the primary-colour, explosive emotions of old skool rave, but subtle shades of intro-spective melancholy. Producers like James Blake, Jamie Woon and Darkstar went even further than Burial, incorporating their own vocals into the music and writing actual songs. Some callous wag dubbed this mixed blessing of a trend 'blubstep' (OK, it was me) as producer after producer announced that their greatest ambition was to make people cry on the dancefloor.

Burial's influence was also evident in the work of UK dance producers like Andy Stott and Raime. The latter's label, Black-est Ever Black, deepened the occult links between postpunk and post-dubstep that Burial had hinted at, exploring the unlikely dancefloor potential of eighties goth and industrial sounds. The xx offered another version of this connection, their music fusing Burial's doleful moodiness with the spare intimacy of postpunk's Young Marble Giants. On his solo track 'Gosh', that band's Jamie xx participated in another persistent trend that owes something to Burial: a strain of retro-rave in which bygone styles like hardcore and jungle are created as faded facsimiles, at once precise in every period detail yet hazy like the memories in an aged raver's brain. You could detect faint, far-flung traces of the Burial aesthetic in the ambient amorphousness of cloud rap, while a quasi-genre of cinemati-cally melancholy, inwardly focused music sourced from diverse points in the modern music landscape was dubbed 'Night Bus' in clear homage to the maker of the track of the same name.

In another sense, you could say that Burial certainly was early to tap into – if not invent – an emotional tenor that characterises our era and which Mark Fisher dubbed 'the secret sadness of the twenty-first century'. The peg for this coinage was James Blake's 2013 album *Overgrown*, but the listless mood of vague gloom was something you could track all across the spectrum, a hollow-souled emptiness lurking within the seemingly triumphant hedonism of Drake, Kanye West, Future, The Weeknd and Travis Scott.

Burial himself has not attempted to follow up *Untrue*. Instead, he's broken out with a sporadic scatter of smaller statements. Some of his EPs have been almost as long as an old-fashioned vinyl LP but consisted of just three tracks: extended pieces, full of shifts, switches and subsections that, as Pitchfork's Mark Richardson wrote, 'feel like miniature albums' in their own right.

No real direction has been discernible in his post-*Untrue* music. Some of the tracks are an extension and consummation of *Untrue*: 'Stolen Dog', for instance, is a widescreen ache of anguish woven from piteous moans and strangled mewls, gorgeously evoking the misery of the dog wrenched from home and family, the grief of the original owner, perhaps even the desperation of the thief. Elsewhere there were unexpected flavours of trance-pop, as on 'Ashtray Wasp' and 'Come Down to Us' – a disconcerting proximity to the world of Calvin Harris. Other tracks seemed deliberately, almost perversely, unpolished, or vandalised on a whim by their creator after completion. 'Rough Sleeper' and 'Truant' resembled radios drifting between stations.

A gathering formlessness makes itself felt in Burial's music as we approach the present: tracks that crumble away suddenly, like a sandcastle reclaimed by the surf, or halt as if suddenly vacated by the will to continue. This year's 'Beachfires' and 'Subtemple' are rhythmless chasms of droning ambience and found sounds that have more in common with experimental industrial outfits like Zoviet France than anything in the UK rave tradition.

These featureless expanses of sound parallel the steadfast erasure of Burial's public profile since *Untrue*. To my knowl-

179

edge, since the spate of interviews around that album, he has not spoken to the press. Most likely his withdrawal is a reaction to the forced exposure of his real-world identity in 2008. He went public with his name and face that year, but only as a pre-emptive measure to undercut mainstream newspaper journalists bent on sleuthing out the truth.

Burial's initial intent was always to stay true to the radical anonymity and facelessness of rave culture and underground techno. Like some of us, he grew up fascinated by the enigmatic and outlandish artist names – LTJ Bukem, Rufige Kru, 2 Bad Mice, Dr S Gachet – that offered no clues to the colour or class of these shadowy operators, no hint of where they came from, or even how many people were involved.

'I want to be unknown,' Burial declared in the 2007 *Wire* interview. 'Most of the tunes I like, I never knew what the people who made them looked like, anyway. It draws you in. You could believe in it more . . . I just want to be in a symbol . . . the name of a tune.' After a brief dalliance with attention circa *Untrue*, Burial has done his best to go back to being an anonymous enigma. Not an actual human mired in the mundane, but a spirit observing London from on high.

Pitchfork, 2017

MAXIMAL NATION: Rustie and the Rise of Digital Maximalism

Read the reviews for Scottish producer Rustie's *Glass Swords*, one of 2011's great albums, and there's this word that keeps on recurring. *Dummy*'s Chal Ravens hails its 'no-genres-barred maximalism', *The Wire*'s Mark Fisher situates the album in an electronic dance counter-tradition of 'maximalism' and 'managed overload', and Pitchfork's own Jess Harvell refers approvingly to the record's 'maximalist zeal'. 'Maximalism' is vague and capacious enough to contain a whole bunch of ideas and associations, but the general slant of these verdicts is that there are a hell of a lot of inputs here, in terms of influences and sources, and a hell of a lot of outputs, in terms of density, scale, structural convolution and sheer majesty.

Shove 'digital' in front of 'maximalism' and you've got a phrase that captures what has emerged as the dominant current in electronic music over the last year or two. Like all trends, digital maximalism achieves self-definition through contrast with what came before. Until quite recently, electronic dance music, by and large, had always been under the sway of minimalist aesthetics. The key words – as praise terms for fans and critics, and ideals for producers and DJs – were 'deep', 'dark', 'stripped-down'. Oh, you can find exceptions: Basement

Jaxx's Prince-like largesse, 808 State's garish fusion-techno, the endlessly morphing complexities of the Future Sound of London. But overall, deep/dark/stark ruled. Especially in the 1990s – just think of that decade's most feted electronic artists: Richie Hawtin, Robert 'Minimal Nation' Hood, Jeff Mills, Photek, Basic Channel, Green Velvet, Gas and many more. But minimalism's thrall extended a long way into the twenty-first century too: German microhouse and minimal, grime (think Wiley's skeletal Eski rhythms), the angularity and severity of DFA-style postpunk-influenced dance-rock, electroclash and, above all, dubstep.

Reversing all these priorities, *Glass Swords* swaps deep/ dark/stark for flat/bright/busy. This music has no interest in 'atmosphere' – it's about dazzle so fierce it chases away all the shadows. And rather than aiming for a hypnotic trance induced by subtly inflected monotony, tunes like 'Globes' and 'Cry Flames' are eye-poppingly awake. The mood is up, preposterously euphoric but genuinely awesome: not so much striking a balance between sublime and ridiculous as merging them until they're indistinguishable.

Compared with the analogue hardware that underpinned early house and techno, the digital software used by the vast majority of dance producers today has an inherent tendency towards maximalism. In an article for *Loops*, Matthew Ingram wrote about how digital audio workstations like Ableton Live and FL Studio encourage 'interminable layering' and how the graphic interface insidiously inculcates a view of music as 'a giant sandwich of vertically arranged elements stacked upon one another'. Meanwhile, the software's scope for tweaking the parameters of any given sonic event opens up a potential 'bad infinity' abyss of fiddly fine-tuning. When digital software meshes with the minimalist aesthetic you get what Ingram calls 'audio trickle': a finicky focus on sound design, intricate

182

fluctuations in rhythm, and other minutiae that will be awfully familiar to anyone who has followed minimal or post-dubstep during the last decade. But now that same digital technology is getting deployed to opposite purposes: rococo-florid riffs, eruptions of digitally enhanced virtuosity, skyscraping solos and other 'maxutiae', all daubed from a palette of fluorescent primary colours. Audio trickle has given way to audio torrent – the frothing extravagance of fountain gardens in the Versailles style.

If *Glass Swords* represents the triumph of more-is-*more*, the path to victory was paved by Rustie's buddy Hudson Mohawke (with 2009's *Butter*). Other key figures in the rise of maximalism include Flying Lotus and Thundercat (whose 2011 album *The Golden Age of Apocalypse* was FlyLo produced). Then there are the varied and distinct shades of progtronica represented by Nicolas Jaar, Amon Tobin and Dam Mantle; the more stadium-rocky bombast of Joker; such banging-yet-convoluted Nightslugs producers as Mosca and Jam City; and the chuck-it-all-in-a-blender splatterstep of Skrillex and Bassnectar. (The latter describes his music as 'omni-tempo maximalism . . . an amalgamation of every sound I've ever heard', which sounds potentially catastrophic.)

Finally, there was the return of Justice, who – along with Digitalism and Jackson and His Computerband – pioneered an early form of digi-max overload with the 2D blare of 2007's †. Described all too accurately by the duo as 'a progressive rock record played by guys that don't know how to play', this year's *Audio, Video, Disco* was an ELO-meets-ELP farrago of clumsy crescendos and wannabe-epic fanfares, flashy rifferama and shrill male vocals that get you picturing crotch-hugging spandex. All of prog's oppressive bombast, in other words, but none of its redeeming complexity, fleetness and occasional sublimity.

Daft Punk are obviously Justice's forebears, and reviewers have rightly pinpointed 2001's *Discovery* as a prime antecedent

183

for *Glass Swords* – in particular the guitar solos on 'Digital Love' and 'Aerodynamic' – and Rustie's album is indeed plastered with gushing geysers of super-slick scalar prowess. But where *Discovery*'s daring was to fold seventies soft rock and pomp pop (Supertramp, 10cc, ELO) and eighties metal (Van Halen) into dance music, *Glass Swords* ventures further still into the forbidden zones of rock's past. Rustie's idol is Eddie Van Halen's own favourite guitarist, Allan Holdsworth, a solo artist and Soft Machine veteran renowned for his ultra-fluid legato style. Rustie admires his 'clean, soft, smooth' sound, which Holdsworth once described as shaved ('I start with a hairy sound, give it a shave, and see what's left'). In the 1980s the gadget-happy Yorkshireman would become controversial in the technical-magazine-reading community for embracing the SynthAxe, a fretted MIDI-controller that triggers an array of electronic synthesisers; Rustie himself sometimes uses a more recently invented MIDI-guitar that has pads as well as strings.

Fusion has been a hallowed reference point for electronic dance music since pretty much forever, emulated and sampled by everyone from Massive Attack circa *Blue Lines* to artcore drum and bass headz, along with Detroit techno mavens and countless deep house and broken beats producers. But veneration for the seventies as a lost golden age of musicality and 'vibe' was always filtered through a tight-pegged tastefulness. Fusion, for electronic producers, meant jazz-funk far more than jazz-rock: Roy Ayers as opposed to, say, Mahavishnu Orchestra. Fusion was drawn on as a textural palette (Rhodes piano, soft-glowing guitar tone, succulent analogue-synth splashes, a dash of flute) and it's been admired for qualities like lightness of touch, loose-yet-tight grooviness and an overall atmosphere of stoned mystic profundity. But the side of fusion involving grandstanding solos, overblown conceptual conceits and extreme duration (nineteen-minute tracks!) has been given a very wide berth. Basically, fusion-infatuated electronica always held back from slipping on the bellbottoms and going all the way.

Until now. *Glass Swords* constructs an alternate history for electronic dance music that bypasses the minimalism of Kraftwerk and Moroder altogether. It's a snazzy thread that veers towards a forgotten gaggle of British ex-fusioneers who embraced sequencers, MIDI and Fairlights (Man Jumping, Landscape), and then reaches back all the way to the gaudy electronic colour schemes of Yellow Magic Orchestra and Weather Report. Rustie's a fan of the latter's 1976 *Black Market*, but the key Weather Report platter in this alternative family tree is 1978's *Mr. Gone* – filled with disco flirtations and synth-heavy sounds, it earned a one-star review from a deploring *DownBeat*.

Alongside the Moogy wonderlands of seventies prog and fusion, you can hear swanky eighties synth-funk tones throughout *Glass Swords*, plus sped-up helium-diva vocals from early rave and arpeggiated melody-riffs that suggest trance if it had been invented by Bootsy Collins. There are analogue surrogates in Rustie's library of 'soft-synths' (digital simulations of vintage keyboards that dwell inside the computer's audio workstation software), but he has no special hang-up about analogue fatness or warmth and is equally fond of the digital synths of the late eighties/early nineties for their nostalgic associations with movie soundtracks of the era. The overall effect of pulling from all these different phases in the evolution of electronic music technology is a fiesta of retro-futures: as if flashing back simultaneously to all the moments when a bunch of new machines changed the sound of music could somehow redeliver that original shock of the now. But there's no melancholy for a 'lost future', just delirious reiteration, thrilling overkill.

Another effect of this post-historical electronic overload is a super-intensified sense of artificiality and plastic-ness.

Glass Swords's sound-world is utterly denatured. Sometimes it recalls the 'superflat' aesthetic of Takashi Murakami: fine art inspired by anime, manga and other forms of Japanese pop culture, often with overtones of sexual fetishism and grotesquerie. Hence 'Inside Pikachu's Cunt', the title of a track Rustie contributed to a Warp compilation. At other times the glistening, globular textures of *Glass Swords* recall airbrush art, that seventies Los Angeles school of lip gloss pin-ups and palm trees kitsch, and its twenty-first-century successor, hyper-realism, which uses digital technology to create images more crisply high-definition than the naked human eye can perceive by itself.

Glass Swords is superhuman too, a spectacle of flexed virtuosity that's been bionically enhanced using digital's bag of tricks. Most of the nu-progtronica producers don't really have the chops in the traditional muso sense, but they do have the 'cut-and-pastes': the twenty-first-century skills of editing, and effecting. For instance, most of the leads on *Glass Swords* emerged through jamming on synths, then the best takes were pieced together, cleaned up, and in some cases sped up to intensify the wow-factor. But a couple of tracks on the album feature honest-to-goodness electric guitar solos: before he got into DJing, Rustie played guitar between the ages of ten and fifteen and got pretty proficient. Stephen 'Thundercat' Bruner's *The Golden Age of Apocalypse* – a record positively unctuous with Jaco Pastorius/Stanley Clarke bass-noodle – is another 2011 marker for the skills-thrill aesthetic, though it's the result of a more literal digital maximalism: the handiwork of Bruner's nimble fingers. It also seems significant that Rustie's ally Hudson Mohawke not only is a fan of Holdsworth-era progger Jean-Luc Ponty but started out as a champion deckti-cian in turntablism, that performance-oriented, show-offy offshoot of hip hop.

Like *Butter* and Hudson Mohawke's *Satin Panthers* EP from this year, *Glass Swords* isn't dance music so much as rock music achieved electronically. The intent is blatantly signposted through the album's artwork and logo, designed by Jonathan Zawada according to Rustie's 'Roger Dean meets Zelda' guidelines. As well as the seventies heyday, Rustie follows through to what the proggers did in the eighties, which in most cases involved glossing up and crossing over. *Glass Swords* is full of the gated drum sounds pioneered by Phil Collins (a member of Brit fusion outfit Brand X as well as prog gods Genesis). Rustie has dabbled in drumming as well as guitar playing, so he knows how to program patterns and fills that sound 'rock'. There's simulated slap bass in there, too.

This deliberately dated universe of twangy twiddle and denatured digital crispness received an unlikely new recruit this year in the form of James Ferraro, the 'hypnagogic pop' cult figure hitherto known for the no-fi haze of albums like *Last American Hero*. This was no preparation for this year's *Far Side Virtual*, Ferraro's attempt to compose a 'symphonic music' whose basic cellular vocabulary comprises ringtones, computer start-up chimes and the ultra-brief refrains that serve as audio-logos for TV production companies at the end of programmes. Made quickly by soundtrack composers toiling solo in their home-studio sweatshops, this audio filler sounds cheap and nasty precisely because it relies on digital simulations of acoustic instruments like horns, piano, strings (the sonic equivalent of fake wood panelling). Ferraro's heightened deployment of this ersatz palette – so close to 'the real thing', yet falling fatally short – creates a creepy feeling of unlife that is similar to animatronics.

Although *Far Side Virtual*'s reference points in its song titles and soundbites – Google, Starbucks, Macs, iPods, Pixar, Gordon Ramsay, *Sex and the City* – are twenty-first century, sonically

187

the album seems to hark back to the early nineties: the same clunkiness and thin-bodied textures characteristic of early digital synths and short-memory samplers that has recently attracted Daniel Lopatin of Oneohtrix Point Never. Ferraro and Lopatin are godfathers of an emerging genre of retrofuturist Muzak called vaporwave. Like Lopatin's sound-art project 'The Martinellis Bring Home a Desire System' (based on a 1994 infomercial for Macintosh Performa), *Far Side Virtual* seems to undertake an archaeology of the recent past, conjuring the onset of the internet revolution and nineties optimism about information technology. But that recent past could equally be a case of 'the long present' in so far as the digiculture ideology of convenience/instant access/maximisation of options now permeates everyday life and is arguably where faint residues of utopianism persist in an otherwise gloomy and anxious culture. As Adam Harper wrote of *Far Side Virtual*, 'Each track is bristling with the maximalist promise of a world of possibilities waiting behind the screen for your double-click.' That word again: maximalist.

I got quite a long way into this piece before discovering that the term 'digital maximalism' was already claimed by a writer operating completely outside the context of music criticism: William Powers, the author of *Hamlet's BlackBerry: Building a Good Life in the Digital Age*. Powers coined 'digital maximalism' to describe the contemporary creed that the maximisation of connectivity is both essential and life-enhancing. *Hamlet's BlackBerry* is just one of a growing genre of book-length critiques of modern lifestyles deemed overly organised around screens and smartphones. The common note sounded by all these books is that maximising connectivity can max out your nervous system, leaving you in a brittle state of hectic numbness, overwhelmed by options, increasingly incapable of focused concentration or fully immersed enjoyment.

Some reviews of *Glass Swords* have connected these two kinds of digital maximalism, musical and lifestyle. One of the very first writers to single out Rustie as an emerging talent made this link in a Pitchfork column a couple of years ago: Martin Clark suggested that Rustie's overloading of 'the midrange with bleeps and riffs heading in disparate directions' served as 'a metaphor for living in intense digital excess'. Rustie politely demurs from this kind of reading of his music, noting sagely that people have been hand-wringing about the shrivelling of attention spans for decades, and pointing out that 'I'm not plugged in all the time – I'm too busy making music!'

Still, there's no doubt that something about *Glass Swords* and its ilk seems to speak to our current moment. The super-sharp sheen and crisp separation, the compressed-and-EQ'd in-your-face dazzle of the sound parallel the endless upgrades in audio-video entertainment, from high-definition flatscreen TV to CGI-saturated movies and 3D cinema to the ever more real-seeming unreality of games.

Digital maximalism doesn't just affect the vividness and hyperactivity of the music, it also expands the range of sources it draws on. Which is why you can find similar properties of post-everything omnivorousness, structural convolution and texture-saturated overload in such disparate, often outright non-electronic entities as Grimes, Battles, Sun Araw, Dâm-Funk, Florence and the Machine (and 'my incorrigible maximalism', as Ms Welch put it) and Gang Gang Dance. The latter's latest album *Eye Contact* starts with the maximalist maxim: 'I can hear everything. It's everything time.' A proposition that sounds very 2011 but is also very seventies, echoing not just the ambition of prog and fusion, but their hubris too.

Grimes, aka twenty-three-year-old musician Claire Boucher, talks of her music as 'post-internet . . . The music of my child-

189

hood was really diverse because I had access to everything, so the music I make is sort of schizophrenic. Basically, I'm really impressionable and have no sense of consistency in anything I do.' Digital technology makes the artistic self at once hollow (buffeted by torrential, every-which-way flows of influence) and omnipotent (capable of moulding sound and melding styles at will). Having access to so many resources and being able to manipulate them so extensively lends itself to a certain grandiosity. Grimes talks of being a maker of worlds and envisions her discography unfolding with Tolkienesque endlessness: 'I want to make a tome – access every genre of music, and also create new genres with them. I want to have, like, thirty albums.' Her forthcoming LP is titled *Visions* and draws on everything from Enya to Aphex Twin, New Jack Swing to New Age, K-pop to glitch.

Books like *Hamlet's BlackBerry* express a yearning to rewind the clock to pre-internet days. Although they sensibly imagine creating special cordoned-off zones of immersion in the here-and-now, they are part of the same spectrum of net-discontent that includes more extreme fantasies of total withdrawal: all those testimonials from email addicts who've gone cold turkey and are attempting to see if it is even possible to live offline.

The alternative to such dreams of seclusion and info-sensory deprivation is to plunge deeper into digitalism, learn to surf (or 'Surph' as Rustie has it) the data-tsunami. One musical expression of this is Flying Lotus's sound on *Cosmogramma* and *Pattern + Grid World* EP: a fissile fusion of genres and idioms, as many as eighty layers in a single track. Derived from 'cosmogram', a word for geometric maps devised in ancient cultures that depict the known universe, *Cosmogramma* is where the astral aspirations of seventies fusion merge with the superpowers of digital technology and the infinite reach of the internet. Like Grimes, the ambition levels with FlyLo are soaring and grandiose: 'Just building a universe is the most inspiring thing to me – this is my opportunity to present a world to somebody!' he exulted in a Resident Advisor interview. 'I feel we're in a time now where people can handle whatever you can throw at them as long as there's something they recognise that they can hold on to, so why not just really fucking go there? Why not just have all these things from our past as well as all of the newest technology from today in one, and just really come up with the craziest shit we can? . . . With as much access as we have to all this stuff, to our musical history, our world history, we definitely can be killing shit way crazier . . . We have the technology!'

That FlyLo quote conveys the master-of-the-universe feeling these digital audio programs provide musicians who achieve fluency in them. You become at once a composer free to interminably tweak your score and a conductor able to repeatedly reconfigure your orchestra and run through endless variations of interpretation. That said, my own fleeting acquaintance with digital audio workstations (dabbling on my brother's Ableton) left me wondering how users manage to even start a track, let alone finish one. The combination of computer (infinite flexibility) and internet (infinite resources of raw material and 'inspiration') seems far more likely to cause complete artistic paralysis: the impulse of fusion collapsing into confusion, the musical equivalent of a gone-too-far collage. A lot of music today walks a line between collecting and hoarding; as Mark Richardson put it in his *Resonant Frequency* column, music-as-Tumblr – the barely annotated heap of all that's caught your ear.

Of course, people have been fretting about information overload for decades, even centuries. As Nicolas Carr points out in *The Shallows: What the Internet Is Doing to Our Brains*, only fifty years after Gutenberg there were folks griping about how there were too many books in print for people to assimilate and digest. Pere Ubu coined the term 'datapanik' in the 1970s, while the too-muchness and hyper-acceleration of modern existence inspired the 1982 movie *Koyaanisqatsi*. Godfrey Reggio's film is meant to be a sobering portrait of a sick society: the title is a Hopi Indian word for 'Life out of Balance'. But the sped-up time-lapse images of bustling streets and subways, in combination with Philip Glass's rippling and soaringly choral soundtrack, make *Koyaanisqatsi* a real rush. Despite its intent, you might just walk away from it feeling like Jonathan Richman, 'in love with the modern world'.

That's the emotion that Rustie's *Glass Swords* instills: giddy buoyancy, the euphoria of gliding frictionlessly across the data-scape. 'Ultra Thizz', one of the stand-out tracks, gets its name from the hyphy scene's slang for MDMA. The sound of the word echoes fizz and jizz, effervescence and ejaculation. It's perfect onomatopoeia for an album that's like a pornucopia of instant-access bliss.

Pitchfork, 2011

SYNTHS AND SENSIBILITY: A New Wave of Female Electronic Musicians

Suddenly it seems there are a lot more women twiddling those knobs than ever before.

Synthesiser music always had something of a masculine aura. A folk-memory hangover, perhaps, from the 1970s when people could mail-order build-your-own-synth kits via the back pages of magazines like *Practical Electronics*. But the abiding stereotype of the electronic musician is a science geek more comfortable with circuitry than emotion.

Recently this stereotype has started to erode with a spate of synth-empowered women who operate in the independent-label underground and have received increasing attention and praise from music magazines during the past year. Foremost among them are Laurel Halo, Maria Minerva, Stellar OM Source, Grimes and Sleep-Over. Others of note include Julia Holter, Nite Jewel, Geneva Jacuzzi, Holly Herndon, Kaitlyn Aurelia Smith and Katie Gately. New artists seem to pop up by the month, but it's still too early to say if the major labels will see Björk-like potential in any of them.

'It's undeniably happening,' said Stefanie Franciotti of Sleep-Over when asked about the female electronica trend. Franciotti, whose music ranges from ethereal nouveau-goth to ominous instrumentals reminiscent of John Carpenter's soundtrack work, couldn't say exactly why it was happening right now. But she noted that while 'synthesisers can seem inaccessible and complicated', they are also 'very tactile' instruments.

The music made by these young women varies widely in mood and method, from Laurel Halo's intricately textured techno to Maria Minerva's hazy lo-fi synthpop and Stellar OM Source's trippy mindscapes. They come from places as far apart as Antwerp, Belgium, and Austin, Texas. But they have plenty in common besides their sex, their penchant for synths and the inventiveness of their music.

Almost all of them are solo artists. Most deploy their own voices prominently, either to add an element of humanity, intimacy or pop appeal, or, conversely, to use the voice as a supremely flexible instrument capable of generating sounds as otherworldly and disorienting as anything made by machines. Most drape their work in lofty erudition drawn from fields like philosophy, experimental science fiction and mysticism. And most have a relationship with electronic dance music but approach it at a slightly askew angle, resulting in sounds that hover somewhere between the nightclub dancefloor and headphone-oriented listening.

Another element they share is a rapid rise from obscurity. Last year Laurel Halo, who is based in Brooklyn, was giving away her first record, *King Felix*, on the internet, but now she is recording for highly regarded labels like Hippos in Tanks and receiving acclaim from webzines and publications like *Fact* and the *Guardian*. Originally from Estonia and living in London, Maria Minerva made her debut in February 2011 with *Tallinn at Dawn*, a cassette/download-only release for the Los Angeles label Not Not Fun. Her profile has risen with her first full-length album, *Cabaret Cixous*, released in August.

Electronic dance music is enjoying a remarkable resurgence in America, but it's unlikely that the sounds of this female synth wave will be bursting out of the speaker stacks at EDM mega-raves like Electric Daisy Carnival. While they draw on dance music's history, particularly genres like 1980s house and 1990s techno, musicians like Laurel Halo and Maria Minerva have virtually nothing in common with the brash, blaring rock-tronica of today's crowd-pleasing DJ-producers like Skrillex.

They don't release their records through techno labels either, but via indie-rock underground labels like Not Not Fun and Olde English Spelling Bee. That realm, which puts a premium on eccentricity and sensitivity, has long been a more encouraging space for quirky female artists.

Mainstream dance music, by comparison, is 'much more macho', said Laurel Halo. It's true that the high proportion of women on dancefloors is not matched by their presence in DJ booths or behind mixing boards. Things have improved somewhat since the nineties, with female producers like Cooly G and Ikonika garnering critical plaudits, but overall female involvement in dance tracks is still too often limited to the role of vocalist.

The new female synth musicians use their voices too, but they also make the music over which they sing. Maria Minerva, whose real name is Maria Juur, and Claire Boucher of Grimes see themselves as producers rather than musicians. Both would like to become pop producers in the mould of Timbaland. 'I'd like to be the engineer figure behind the pop star, choosing their songs and their clothes,' Boucher said. As ambitions go, it's as revealing as it is empowering, pointing to the fact that production and studio sound engineering remain male-dominated fields.

This gender disparity probably has something to do with the enduring association of audio technology, like turntables and mixers or synthesisers and sequencers, with masculinity. 'It's not that you can compare computers and synths to trucks and cars, but it does still have that aura,' said Christelle Gualdi, who performs as Stellar OM Source. 'When I'm setting up my equipment on a stage to play live, every five minutes a guy will come up and ask, "Are you sure you don't need any help?"' Gualdi said that she just turns it back on the man, smiling big and offering to answer any technical queries he might have.

If you were to ask most people about electronic music, most likely you'd hear names like Stockhausen or Kraftwerk. Men, in other words. But there is an extensive history of involvement in experimental electronic music by women. In Britain, the BBC Radiophonic Workshop was co-founded by Daphne Oram, while its most famous composer, Delia Derbyshire, was just one of several female recruits to the state-owned broadcaster's experimental sound unit. In the United States, Pauline Oliveros and Bebe Baron pioneered the use of tape editing and electronic oscillators from the 1950s onwards, while subsequent decades saw important work done by composers like Laurie Spiegel, Ruth White, Daria Semegen, Alice Shields, Pril Smiley, Éliane Radigue, Beatriz Ferreyra and many more.

Most of these female composers were attached to university studios like the Columbia–Princeton Electronic Music Center. Although the approach and intent of these contemporary female synth musicians is substantially different from their ancestors', some of the modern counterparts also have academic training.

Laurel Halo attended the School of Music at the University of Michigan. But her discovery of electronic music came when, at sixteen, she attended the Detroit Electronic Music Festival, an annual event celebrating the city's claim to be techno's birthplace.

'I went with some orchestra friends, and we danced for two days straight,' she recalled. 'I had not really experienced live music outside the classical realm, so hearing these rhythms and sounds through a gigantic PA system, with the sub-bass massaging your entire body – it was an ear-opening experience.'

Unlike Halo and Gualdi, who also studied music, Maria Minerva and Grimes are self-taught musicians. But there is an academic influence to their music: both belong to a new breed of conceptualist musicians (male and female) who are well versed in critical theory.

Minerva is working on a master's in art and theory at Goldsmiths College in London, and her recordings teem with allusions to philosophy and critical theory. The title of her recent album, *Cabaret Cixous*, nods to the French feminist writer Hélène Cixous, while the track 'Spiral' actually samples a speech by the American theorist Avital Ronell protesting the way that academia has constrained her creativity and sensuality. Influenced by Cixous's notion of a fragmentary and free-flowing female poetics that she called 'écriture féminine', Minerva said her music expresses the alienated restlessness of modern women who inhabit a Wi-Fi world that combines connectivity and isolation. Minerva's *electronica féminine* is about 'this next-level irrationalism, not to do with primal instincts but the urban, neurotic modern woman who needs to escape and drifts around'. She adds, 'a lot of the songs are about being uncomfortable as a young woman in the world. I'm exploring the idea of the "female loser", which is new territory for pop. My records sound pretty crazy at times. Neurotic and scary.'

In conventional terms, it's the vocals that lend a feminine element to this new electronica. Minerva is influenced by her teenage love of diva-fronted house music and the Pet Shop Boys. She coats her high breathy voice in reverb, adding blurriness to the deliberately 'smudgy' production. The Grimes album *Halfaxa* and Sleep-Over's *Forever* often recall the ecstatic plainchant of eighties goth vocalists like Elizabeth Fraser and

Lisa Gerrard. Laurel Halo's fluttery vocals have been likened to Kate Bush and Enya.

Laurel Halo said she was impelled to merge electronic music with song craft and lyrics out of a desire to 'inject a little feeling back into it'. Grimes, on the other hand, sees the voice as a vehicle for the alien and transcendent. Often that involves technological processing. On 'Hallways', *Halfaxa*'s stand-out track, she used the pitch-correction technology Auto-Tune to alter her vocal melody, shifting it up and down randomly in leaps of three or four notes. Using the result as what studio engineers call a 'guide vocal', she then re-sang the new pattern in order to 'put the emotion back into it'. Grimes says that she feels 'that there are so many possibilities with the human voice that haven't been explored'.

Disorienting strangeness and spaciousness are qualities that electronic musicians have often pursued, including Louis and Bebe Barron's soundtrack for the sci-fi classic *Forbidden Planet* and Morton Subotnick's 1967 LP *Silver Apples of the Moon*. Halo draws inspiration from 'the sheer inhumanity and impossibility of science' as well as the mystical paranoia of the novelist Philip K. Dick, while Gualdi, a former architect, reveres the fantastical blueprints for unbuildable cities drawn up by outfits like Archigram and Superstudio.

'I am still blown away by those utopian visions,' she said, adding that she sees a connection between the optimistic futurism of 1970s popular science and the cosmic synth epics composed by groups like Tangerine Dream. Her own first dabblings with electronics came when she helped her musician father create the soundtrack to an exhibition called Musique et Espace.

Halo brought up a direct parallel between space exploration and electronic sound equipment. 'When you're playing a synth, you can't help but have this voyager mentality,' she said. 'It feels like a control panel.' Perhaps it's this combination of discovery and autonomy that accounts for the rise of the new female synthesists. Capable of generating a big and texturally rich sound without the need for band mates or compromise, synthesisers enable them to make solo trips into the unknown.

New York Times, 2011,
published under the title 'Breaking the Synth Barrier'

XENOMANIA: Loving the Alien in the Internet's Ever Widening World of Sound

My book *Retromania* is partly an investigation of the ways in which the internet has transformed twenty-first-century listening habits and music-making. Imagine the media as a hydraulic system: broadband has dramatically expanded the pipes and channels through which cultural data, including music, passes. The result has been a monstrous increase in the volume and range of music that the average listener can access. Before file-sharing, a music fan's ability to explore the wide world of sound was restricted: the cost of buying records inhibited one's willingness to risk checking out unfamiliar sounds, and curiosity was constrained further by the vagaries of distribution and media exposure. All those analogue-era deterrents and blockages have been swept aside by the torrential every-which-way data flows of Web 2.0. The internet is a gigantic archive, a collectively assembled and chaotic audio-video library that contains every form of popular (and unpopular) culture imaginable. Thanks to 'whole album' blogs and YouTube, there is no financial disincentive to trying out stuff, and precious little exertion required beyond the expenditure of one's time and attention. Infinite choice + infinitesimal cost = nomadic eclecticism as the default mode for today's music fan.

Retromania is primarily concerned with digital technology's effect on our sense of time: because the entire past of pop music is splayed out as this instant-access archive, older styles of music feel as 'present' as contemporary music, and this has the knock-on effect of encouraging music-makers to mix and match influences from all across the historical spectrum. But the internet's effect on space has been just as profound. A new generation of listeners and musicians is emerging whose consciousness is post-geographical as well as post-historical. There's a thirst for fresh musical stimuli that slips easily past geographical borders and cultural boundaries. At once satisfied and stoked further by album-sharing blogs, deposits of esoteric and outlandish treasure on YouTube, and a new breed of pan-global crate-digger record label, this appetite for the alien could be called xenomania, a play on the term 'xenophobia' and its less well-known sister-word 'xenophilia'.

Xenomania and retromania are both forms of exoticism. The difference is that xenomania is about geographical remoteness, whereas retromania is about distance in time (as in L.P. Hartley's famous maxim, 'The past is a foreign country: they do things differently there'). Sometimes the two fascinations converge: while one contingent of Western hipsters are fever-ishly tracking contemporary sounds from far-flung corners of the globe, another bunch are investigating the musical *pasts* of all these non-Western countries.

The first kind of xenomania comes out of dance culture, in the form of early-adopter beat-geeks who compete to find exciting new rhythms from all over the world. I say 'new' but often the dance subcultures in question have actually been in existence for decades; it's just that Western DJs and produc-ers have only just discovered them. The first of these 'global ghetto grooves' to become trendy was *funk carioca*, which was spawned in the slums of Brazil. Next came *kwaito* house and *gqom* (South Africa), which was soon followed by *kuduro* (Angola), *cumbia* (originally from Colombia but spreading in mutated forms through Peru, Chile and Argentina), *desi* (the worldwide Indian diaspora), *coupé-décalé* (Ivory Coast) and more. Recently there's been a smatter of hipster chatter about the Egyptian dance music that gets played at Cairo street weddings. There's also bubblin', an example of a related but slightly different phenomenon: a musical hybrid that hatched in the West but in the bosom of an immigrant community. The story goes that bubblin' sprang into existence when immigrants from the Dutch Antilles to the Netherlands responded with unexpected fervour to a Den Haag DJ who accidentally accelerated a dancehall track (or, in some accounts, a reggaeton track) by playing it at 45 rpm. Bubblin' has subsequently gone on to spawn another hybrid dance sound called moombahton whose genesis is even more tangled and confusingly post-geographical.

Whether they're spawned in European cities like Lisbon and London, or in the ghettos of the southern hemisphere, what all these exotic dance genres share is impurity: they are the creole children of a sound-clash between folk forms and Western styles like hip hop, house and techno. Ethnic vibes (traditional instrumental textures such as accordions, unusual polyrhythms) mesh with American/European staples like the booming 808 bassline or the house synth-vamp. Rowdy chanted MC vocals influenced by gangsta rap and dancehall are offset by cheesily tuneful choruses invariably given the cheap gloss of Auto-Tune. Inspired by the circa-2005 fad for *funk carioca*, the writer Matthew Ingram coined the playful term 'shanty house' to pinpoint both the common sonic traits these styles share and how they are rooted in social conditions that are sadly similar all over the world. Made quick and cheap using pirated software, laced with unlicensed samples from mainstream pop songs, this is party-hard music for ruffneck youth from the inner-city areas that scare the bourgeoisie ('favelas', they call them in Brazil, which is roughly equivalent to 'projects' in America, 'estates' in the UK and 'garrisons' in Jamaica). Despite growing up amid poverty, when these kids go out to dance they dress 'rich'. Style-wise they're fluent in the international language of bling: gold jewellery, flashy man-made fabrics, name-brand sneakers. Often there's a link between this music and gangs: the lyrics tend to celebrate the fast-money lifestyle of criminality, when they're not addressing perennial topics like the female rump and the urgent necessity of shaking it. The Angolan version of shanty house, *kuduro* actually translates as 'hard ass', although whether that means 'tight buttocks' or 'tough guy' I've yet been unable to establish.

All these global ghetto sounds have much in common with the bass-heavy street beats of America (local hip hop offshoots such as hyphy, Baltimore breaks, jerk, bounce), the UK (grime, bassline, funky, donk) and the Caribbean (dancehall, soca, reggaeton). And all face condescension and sometimes repression in their native context: feared by the political and cultural establishments for their underclass uncouthness and links to a shady nightlife underworld, they are typically scorned by more liberal-minded progressives and sophisticates too, who regard the music as formulaic trash and object to the aggression, sexism and hyper-materialism of the lyrics.

Divorced from the local context and its class antagonisms, it's these very qualities of gritty menace and rude-boy raucousness that appeal to Western hipsters. That and the jagged inventiveness of the beats, which are often wilder and weirder than the self-consciously arty experimentalists of left-field dance music. The earliest of the early-adopting beat-geeks were DJs like Diplo (M.I.A.'s producer partner early on and someone wont to boast about how his quest for rare beats took him to

Latin American urban danger zones where no other 'gringo' dared go) and DJ/rupture (responsible for globe-roaming mix-CDs like *Gold Teeth Thief* and the blogs Mudd Up and Dutty Artz). Lately they've been joined by figures like Mosca, who emerged from the UK's dubstep scene but as a DJ draws for super-obscure styles like Guadeloupe's gwoka.

Recently the interest in non-Western sounds has moved beyond pure dance forms to include plaintively melodic music that is roughly equivalent to mainstream pop, perhaps even the local MOR equivalents of Celine Dion for all anyone really knows. Sublime Frequencies, the Seattle-based label founded by Alan Bishop of the trippy-tribal band Sun City Girls, has released a series of CDs documenting the ultra-sweet pop fare of countries like Java, Sumatra, Algeria, Burma, Palestine, Thailand and Niger. Some, like *Radio Myanmar*, were taped directly off the radio, while others draw from cassettes picked up in street markets. In nearby Portland, the Sublime Frequencies-style audio-tourism concept was taken to the next level by Chris Kirkley and his label Sahelsounds. His two *Music from Saharan Cellphones* compilations (initially distributed for free on the internet) gather up songs by artists from Nigeria, Algeria, Niger, Morocco, Mali, Ivory Coast and the Sahel region of Mauritania that circulate promiscuously throughout North Africa when cellphone users transfer and trade them in MP3 form. As Pitchfork's Mark Richardson noted, part of the appeal of *Saharan Cellphones* in particular and nu-exotica in general is that the music seems 'rare'. Unlike most Western pop and unpop, where even the most obscure artist is exhaustively documented and annotated by fans on the web, the performers on the *Saharan Cellphone* comps remain shrouded in mystique, with some artists and songs only partially identified. So it *feels* like a throwback to the analogue era, even though the way the music is distributed (both in its original Saharan context

and in the trend-chasing blog world) is totally digital. For the
exotic beat-freaks and the global street pop enthusiasts alike,
something of the thrill of the hunt has been restored; it's just
that the safari now takes you through the deeper recesses
of YouTube or the hinterlands of the web, rather than to an
out-of-the-way record store or street market.

Other explorers are heading not just far afield, but far back
into the past as well. In recent years there has been a surge
in the number of reissue labels and music blogs that specialise
in ethnological field recordings and in non-Western music from
the sixties and seventies (i.e., prior to the original 'world music'
phenomenon of the eighties that led to major labels signing
artists like King Sunny Adé and Youssou N'Dour). This retro-
exotica boom often draws on field recordings of tribal chants
and gamelan orchestras that back in the day were released in
the West by ethnomusicology specialist labels like Ocora and
UNESCO Collection. But increasingly people are digging much
deeper. Witness the rise of a new breed of A&R archaeolo-
gist who ventures abroad to scoop up the battered vinyl and
worn cassettes of music only ever released in its native land.
Whenever possible these are then licensed for Western 'reissue'
(strictly speaking that should be 'issue', since it was never
available outside its homeland in the first place).

Prime movers in this ethno-retro field include labels like
Finders Keepers, Honest Jon's, Soundway Records, Strut,
Dust-to-Digital and Now-Again (an offshoot of the crate-digger
hip hop label Stone's Throw). There's also Numero Group,
who generally put out American music but have a series of
releases called *Cult Cargo* that looks at the impact of US soul
and funk on the indigenous music cultures in other countries,
particularly those in the Caribbean. Key blogs include Awesome Tapes from Africa, Brain Goreng, Holy Warbles, Ghost
Capital and Anywhere Else but Here Today (some of whom

are branching out into reissuing themselves). These labels and blogs pursue every imaginable kind of vintage exotica, from field recordings made with hand-held microphones by roving anthropologists in the fifties and sixties, to pop and showbiz (every nation seems to have a domestic equivalent to what Americans call schlock or schmaltz, what the Germans call *Schlager*) to hipper sounds (everything from Indonesian hard rock to Turkish psychedelia to South African disco). Some go *really* far back in time, disinterring from dusty warehouses the 78 rpm shellac platters recorded by companies like EMI to supply the local populations back when they were still under the sway of British imperialism.

Because the music was usually recorded quickly in a rudimentary studio, because it's a strictly analogue affair with none of the digital gloss and computer trickery of global-ghetto-groove styles like *kuduro*, these older styles of non-Western music seem 'purer'. But when you look into them more closely, it turns out that is just an illusion caused by the passage of time. Most of the stuff that gets reissued by the crate-digger labels is not traditional folk music handed down generation to generation. More often than not, it's an already-hybrid style contaminated by Western pop: many of the troupes collected on the celebrated *Ethiopiques* series were heavily influenced by the flamboyant frenzy of James Brown's seventies funk, while the Indonesian hard rock and progressive rock bands on Now-Again's marvellous *Those Shocking, Shaking Days* compilation followed the template laid down by their British and American arena-touring models as closely as possible. Indeed, the pro-Western regime running Indonesia actively promoted the spread of rock music in parallel with their solicitation of investment from Western companies. As with the rap-and-rave-influenced global-ghetto styles, there can sometimes be an unsettling sense that the attraction of this music is that it provides a distorted mirror image of Western pop: in other words, a slightly askew, exotic-but-ultimately-familiar version of things we already love.

What's going to be really intriguing as this decade unfolds is tracking the impact on music-making in the hip West as xenomania and omnivorous cosmopolitanism spread and intensify. We've already heard flickers of it in the music of Vampire Weekend and The Dirty Projectors. On 2010's brilliant *A Sufi and a Killer*, Gonjasufi samples 1960s rembetiko, a Greek style of low-down music that often gets compared to the blues and that dates back to the end of the nineteenth century. Battles' less brilliant but always interesting *Gloss Drop* slickly fuses everything from techno to Tropicália, synthpop to soca. The band's Ian Williams recently observed to *The Wire* magazine that seventies progressive rock was shaped by what was available – classical music, jazz and rock – to hippies and progressive-minded musicians. 'With the internet, everybody's exposed to World Music now, and a much wider wealth of influence that comes from everywhere. The library that people are exposed to is much bigger now.'

A case in point is Ariel Pink, a retromaniac if ever there was, but who has recently been developing a chronic case of xenomania. His 2010 album *Before Today* featured the delightful fusion-flavoured instrumental 'Reminiscences', effectively a cover of an Ethiopian eighties golden oldie 'Liben Sitarochew' as sung by Yeshimebet Dubale and Kenede Mengesha. The retitling comes from the Ethiopian song-form *tizita*, 'the song of nostalgia and remembrances'. Pink actually came across the tune through visiting Los Angeles' 'Little Ethiopia', the Mercato area of the city where cassette tapes originally recorded secretly and distributed illegally under the Derg regime of the 1980s can still be picked up. But he could have just as easily stumbled across the song on the internet, via the Ethiopian

208

version of YouTube called Diretube. It's on YouTube that Pink encountered his latest crush, Soviet new wave music of the 1980s, a style associated with the youth subculture known as *Stilyagi.*

Of course, the phenomenon of musicians looking outside the West for inspiration is not particularly new. Rock stars like Paul Simon, Peter Gabriel and David Byrne embraced rhythms, melodies and instrumental textures from Africa, the Middle East and Latin America; Gabriel was involved in the founding of the UK world music festival WOMAD, while Byrne launched his own record label, Luaka Bop, as an outlet for music from South America, Asia and Africa. For his debut solo album *Duck Rock*, Malcolm McLaren traipsed around the world in search of earthy roots-music antidotes to glossed-up, synthetic eighties pop, in the process making bizarre collages of Soweto guitar pop, Bronx scratching 'n' rapping and Appalachian square-dancing. The trumpeter Jon Hassell coined the concept of Fourth World Music, the merger of Western hi-tech and ethnic music. He also influenced the landmark Brian Eno and David Byrne project *My Life in the Bush of Ghosts*, with its sampled voices from Folkways-style field recordings and Arabic pop.

But Hassell, Byrne and Eno were in many ways simply reiterating and developing 1970s notions of a 'One World Music' as pursued by artists like Miles Davis, Don Cherry, Traffic and Can. Can's Holger Czukay loved to tune into exotic transmissions via shortwave radio, sometimes working them into Can's live performances using a Dictaphone. Czukay's gorgeous 'Persian Love' (on his 1979 solo album *Movies*) was based around Iranian pop songs he recorded off shortwave. But here he was reprising a technique he'd first tried in 1969 with the *Canaxis* project, which involved creating tape loops out of Vietnamese traditional songs. Czukay probably got that idea

from Karlheinz Stockhausen, whom he'd studied under: specifically works like *Telemusik*, which combined electronic sounds
with ethnic music and forged strange hybrids (the chants of
Japanese monks merged with music from the Shipibo Indians
of Amazonian Peru), or *Hymnen*, based around national
anthems from all around the world. But you can go much
further back (to composers like Debussy who was inspired by
non-Western tonalities he encountered at the 1889 Paris World
Exhibition) or sideways into the mainstream (the sixties craze
for Indian raga that influenced The Byrds and The Beatles).
All that's really different now is that the internet makes it so
much easier to 'travel' far and wide in your listening, while
digital technology means it is easy to harvest found sound off
the web and to incorporate it seamlessly into your own music.

'I can hear everything,' proclaims a voice at the start of *Eye
Contact*, the latest album by ethnodelic New York outfit Gang
Gang Dance. 'It's everything time.' But just because you *can*
hear everything, it doesn't mean you should try to. It's not a
given that you'll be able to make good use of all that influx
of input. There are definite downsides to all this net-enabled
hyper-eclecticism. For listeners, the temptation is to pig out at
the world's greatest buffet, to heap your plate with a little of
everything, savouring nothing in depth, overloading the palate
with clashing cuisines and ultimately leaving you with indiges-
tion. Listening to too much decontextualised music can just
be numbing. For musicians, attempting to assimilate inputs
of such diverse provenance can lead to the audio equivalent of
fusion cuisine gone wrong: a cacophony of incompatible flavour
profiles. Intriguingly, *New York* magazine's classical music
critic Justin Davidson has observed this syndrome at work in
the world of up-and-coming young composers. 'For the YouTube
generation, technology . . . grants entrance to a virtually
infinite thrift store of influences,' he noted earlier this year.

But the ease of access depletes a crucial element of dedication and quest. 'A century ago, Bartók had to haul his gramophone through the mud of Moravia to learn about folk music. Now a curious kid in Brooklyn can track down an Azerbaijani song in seconds. Today's styles need not be born of deep experience; they form out of collisions that bypass history and geography.' On the macro level of genres rather than individual artists, it seems to be the case that the slowly gestated mongrel styles of the analogue era (reggae emerging as a form of rhythmically inverted New Orleans R&B, for instance) have more staying power and fruitfulness than the cut-and-paste hybrids of the digital age. There is a faddishness to the chase for exotic beats and ethnic obscurities that is exacerbated by the high-turnover cycles of the bloggified music scene.

A more generous interpretation of this trend could start by noting the proximity of xenophilia (fervour for the foreign) to neophilia (ardour for the new). The impulse to seek out the alien sounds that already exist on the planet (that may indeed have existed for decades) but are effectively new to you could be a displacement of the future-hunger, the quest for the unknown, that used to be the motor driving the vanguard sectors of Western pop. If our own rock and pop traditions seem stagnant and stalled, their forward motion obstructed by the sheer accumulation of glorious history, it could be that one way to escape the dead end is to step sideways. Get yourself outside the Western narrative altogether and explore all the elsewheres now accessible like never before.

MTV Iggy, 2011

FOOTWORK: Jlin's Martial Artform

Black Origami, the title of the new album by electronic warrior Jlin (real name Jerrilynn Patton), is a perfect analogy for her creative process. It always begins, she says, with nothing: no formula, no preconceptions, no sampled materials, just the blind urge to make. Origami, similarly, 'starts out as a blank sheet of paper', she says, 'which you bend and fold, and then you end up with this beautiful, complex thing'. Jlin's elegantly angular beat-constructions rather resemble origami's blend of geometric planes and exquisite delicacy. 'Taking simplicity and making it complex – I got that ideology from Coco Chanel,' she adds.

The album title is an extension of an earlier and equally apt analogy that Jlin made on her 2015 debut *Dark Energy*, with the track 'Black Ballet'. Just as the ballerina's movements look effortless and weightless, but the audience never sees the blood-soaked wraps around her feet or the stress damage to her spinal discs, likewise listeners are transported by the eerie levitational grace of Jlin's music but don't hear the hundreds of agonised hours of detail-work and fanatical focus embedded in each track.

Footwork, the Chicago genre of fractured machine-funk with which Jlin is generally associated, but which she's left far behind with *Black Origami*, is a functional style designed for dance battles: barebones beats built to spur competitors to new feats of gravity-defying grace, spiced with sliced 'n' diced samples. There are seemingly zero hand-played instrumental elements: instead of creating vamps and melody-riffs, keyboards are strictly for stretching a sample – a horn, a voice, a snippet of orchestration – across the octaves, then tapping out jittery hyperkinetic patterns, which effectively turns each source-sound into just another component of a giant drum kit. Although footwork evolved out of the ghetto house style known as juke, it actually sounds much more like a distant cousin of jungle, or a twenty-first-century extension of electro. Likewise the battles place footwork in the continuum of break dancing and body popping: dance as a gladiatorial display of prowess, as opposed to the communal ecstasy of the disco tradition, where you lose yourself in the crowd.

Jlin – who hails from Gary, Indiana, a forty-five-minute drive from Chicago – thinks 'fighting forms and dance are one and the same, just like music and math are the same. I feel that dance is based off of fighting steps, and I reference both back to the way an animal moves.' But where *Dark Energy* often made you think of martial arts or fight-dance styles like Brazilian *capoeira*, *Black Origami* has a different feel: more ceremonial and ritualistic. The listener might picture drum choirs, street pageants, the court music of imperial Japan. Partly that's down to the glittering array of exotic percussion textures that Jlin has added to her arsenal, clattery timbres that evoke ankle bells, shakers, Tibetan bells and 'storm drum'. The last of these was a gift from Avril Stormy Unger, a choreographer from Bangalore with whom Jlin has collaborated on performance pieces at the Unsound festival in Kraków and for a Boiler Room webcast transmitted live from India.

Working with figures like Unger reflects the extent to which Jlin has left behind not just footwork but club-oriented dance music altogether. Her collaborators on *Black Origami* are

nearly all from the avant-garde: electronic experimentalist
Holly Herndon, tape-loop composer William Basinski, French
gothtronica artist Fawkes. Jlin is also currently composing
a score for contemporary-dance superstar and choreographer
Wayne McGregor.

But if Jlin has moved beyond the combat-dance of footwork
tracks into an artier realm of album-length experimentation,
she has retained the battling spirit of the Chicago scene.
It's just that for her it's a more solitary struggle of creating
something ex nihilo. She likens the programming of each of
her tracks to 'a hard, dreadful birth, trying to push this thing
inside of you, getting it out'. Throughout her conversation,
there's a leitmotif of self-overcoming. Jlin talks about creating
from 'the most uncomfortable space'; 'when a person listens,
they're hearing my vulnerability'; 'every time I create, it's
scary'. 'I have no foundation whatsoever,' she adds. 'I'm starting from ground zero. Literally every time I sit in this chair
– it's a fight.'

Despite the gruelling nature of her process, Jlin says, 'when
it comes together, it's very fulfilling, because you know you
drew it from nothing'. But the feeling of triumph doesn't last
long. 'Maybe for an hour afterwards. But usually I'm like,
"what do I do next?"'

Some of Jlin's track titles seem freighted with political
intent or black power resonance. On *Dark Energy*, there was
'Guantanamo' and 'Mansa Musa', the latter named after a
fourteenth-century ruler of the Mali Empire in West Africa,
regarded by some historians as likely the richest man who
ever lived. On *Black Origami*, the title '1%' seems like a direct
reference to America's equality chasm, and this time there
are no fewer than two tracks in tribute to African potentates:
'Nandi' comes from the Zulu queen mother of the warrior-king
Shaka, while 'Hatshepsut' nods to a fifteenth-century BC female

215

pharaoh who ruled Egypt when it was the most advanced civilisation in the world.

But Jlin brushes off any attempts to connect her frequent talk of 'darkness' to real-world politics or apocalyptic fears that the world is heading into a new Dark Age. 'No, no, no,' she insists. 'This has solely to do with me.' At the same time, she says she doesn't really draw from her personal life, from real-world problems or emotional conflicts. Again, it all goes back to that mystical, almost Nietzschean struggle against the self's own limits. 'It's like jumping off a cliff – no cables, no bungee.'

Where do her tenacity and drive come from? Sometimes Patton's patter has a slight flavour of positive thinking (the true American religion) and other times you get the faintest whiff of New Age ('Kyanite', on *Black Origami*, shares its name with a crystal that reputedly neither accumulates nor retains negative energy, which apparently makes it excellent for 'metaphysical purposes'). Conversely, it's tempting to attribute it to the steel-town toughness of Gary, Indiana (where until fairly recently Jlin worked at a mill 'driving a 50,000-pound tractor, transporting steel from one department to another'), an atmosphere that has only got harsher and more desolate with the closing of mills and the further erosion of jobs through automation.

But I suspect the real source of Jlin's strength and will comes from her mother, who sounds like a formidable character and has played a key role in her daughter's musical evolution at various points. 'She's never babied me, ever,' says Jlin, recalling a turning point when she played her mom a track that relied on a sample (from Teena Marie's 'Portuguese Love'). 'I asked her what she thought of it, and my mom said she liked it, but then she asked me "What do *you* sound like?" That was the moment at which my approach changed and my sound changed.'

More recently, Jlin's mother helped her out by titling one of *Black Origami*'s best tunes, 'Nyakinyua Rise'. 'I was completely frustrated, I couldn't think of what I should call the track, so I asked her to listen and she said, "Ah, that's Nyakinyua Rise". See, Nyakinyua Rise! is the name of an organisation that my mom and a friend of hers in Kenya set up to provide solar lamps to kids over there, because when the sun goes down they can't see to do their homework.'

Wherever it comes from – the woman who raised her, the hard-bitten industrial town in which she grew up, the war-dance spirit of footwork, or some mystical inner-zone of her spirit – Jlin is a steely-minded perfectionist who believes that failure – pushing yourself further than you're capable of going – is the key to success. The last track on *Black Origami* is titled 'Challenge (to Be Continued)' and it relates to Jlin's belief in what she calls 'Infinity'.

'I don't think I'll ever be satisfied with my work. I don't *want* to be satisfied with my work. I don't believe in a concept like "the peak". To me that's an insult – who are you to say that someone's at the height of their career, or has reached the peak of their art? For myself, I believe in Infinity. Once we start, we just keep going up.'

Guardian, 2017

DAFT PUNK: 'Digital Love', *Random Access Memories* and the Failure of the Future

On 2001's *Discovery*, Daft Punk took their existing filter-disco house sound, as pioneered on tracks like 'Musique', and blended in a palette of textures and tones sourced in 1970s radio rock at its most overground, overproduced and over-lit. As the title hinted, the album staged a magical recovery of discovery: a flashback to pop's primal scene, your first encounters with otherworldly transmissions from Planet Pop beamed through the transistor radio or TV screen. Daft Punk wanted to tap back into that virgin state of pre-teen openness to everything, before you learn the rules of cool and uncool.

An exquisite mesh of irony and awe runs through the entire album, but nowhere more ecstatically than 'Digital Love', a fusion of disco, AOR, glam metal and new wave (the choppy guitar-riff breakdown practically forces you to dance in jumpy formation like you're in a Toni Basil video – something I did with my toddler son, Kieran, on countless occasions in the early 2000s). 'Digital Love' shimmers with a transcendent artificiality, a splendour of sound at once camp and sublime. The hazy glaze of the filter effect on the twirling main riff is like if plastic could rust. At the breakdown, Supertramp's keyboard sound is

219

duplicated with eerie exactness (or not so eerie, given that Daft Punk used the exact same Wurlitzer piano as the seventies soft rock group). Then there's the ridiculous majesty of that Van Halen-style guitar solo, frothing and bubbling over like a geyser of hot-pink liquid latex. Yet within all the deliciously knowing allusions, the heart of 'Digital Love' aches with unrequited longing: it's a rewrite of 'Jump' tilted to the tentative, whose last words implore 'why don't you play the game?'

The promo for 'Digital Love', like its precursor *Discovery* singles 'One More Time' and 'Aerodynamic', was hewn from Daft Punk's anime movie *Interstella 5555*, a project that captured an abiding truth about pop as well as forecasting its twenty-first-century destiny: pop's pulpy essence has far more to do with cartoons, comics and videogames than literature or the other high arts.

But then, in a startling development (yet one that now seems logical, perhaps even predestined), Daft Punk fell *out* of 'digital love'. Towards the end of the 2000s, the duo – Thomas Bangalter and Guy-Manuel de Homem-Christo – abandoned sampling and embarked upon an epic back-to-analogue quest that culminated in *Random Access Memories*.

It became the biggest pop event of 2013. 'Get Lucky', a Chic pastiche featuring Nile Rodgers on guitar, seemed to be on the radio hourly for an entire year. That single and the album cleaned up at the Grammys, winning six trophies, and Daft Punk jammed with Rodgers and Stevie Wonder on stage at the awards ceremony. Total triumph that capped a year of full-spectrum dominance of the airwaves and the discourse.

But if *Random Access Memories* defined 2013, it was actually through rejecting 2013 – the record rebelled against a radioscape of 'uniformity' that Daft Punk blamed on digital technologies like Pro Tools and Auto-Tune. Musically, the project was informed by a paradox specific to Daft Punk's own dilemma as artists who had done sample-based dance music in the late nineties and early 2000s, and taken that as far as they could. How to go forward? Daft Punk decided the only way was to go back. The sounds they'd helped to pioneer had become the Top 40 radio norm by the early 2010s. The future-rush that these digitally processed timbres transmitted to listeners in the 1990s, when they felt like a preview of the twenty-first century, had necessarily gone. Becoming omnipresent and everyday made these sounds mundane – at best, not futurism but NOW-ism.

So Daft Punk mounted a full-blown reversion to how records were made in the late seventies and early eighties: the pristine peak of analogue recording, when multitracking and overdubbing combined with the virtuoso playing of session musicians to create music of unparalleled sumptuousness and slickness. Their models were the disco-funk symphonies of Michael Jackson and Earth Wind and Fire; the soft rock and sophisto sounds of Fleetwood Mac, Steely Dan and the Eagles; late-period progressive rock and new wave at its most radio-friendly (The Cars, say). There was a cut-off point for this time-travel exercise: the mid-eighties moment when Fairlight samplers, sequenced rhythms, drum machines and MIDI became the new state of the art. Believing that there is a subtle but crucial difference between machine-implemented exactness and the kind of precision aspired to by high-calibre musicians, Daft Punk spurned the very equipment they'd become maestros at using, and instead called on the services of players like Omar Hakim, a veteran sticksman who'd drummed for David Bowie and Dire Straits among many others. 'It's an infinity of nuance, in the shuffles and the grooves,' Bangalter enthused. 'These things are impossible to create with machines.'

Random Access Memories is probably the most high-profile pop music embodiment of the uncanny temporality of the

221

twenty-first century, the syndromes that critics like Mark
Fisher and I have explored in our writings about hauntology
and retromania. The album self-consciously addresses these
themes, teeming with references to time, transience, the notion
of a lost future, and memory. The song 'Fragments of Time',
for instance, is about instant nostalgia, this sort of future
anterior syndrome when we experience rapture or epiphany,
then immediately project ahead to looking back at it. The title
Random Access Memories itself is a pun on computer memory
versus human memory.

Two of the hallmark impulses in modernism are the terror
of repeating something that another artist has already done,
and the terror of repeating yourself. For Daft Punk those two
impulses became at loggerheads: they didn't want to repeat
what they had done before (because in a context where their
influence is legion, they would no longer stand out), so they
were impelled to repeat styles of music that were superseded
over thirty years ago.

Geeta Dayal described Daft Punk's approach as sampling
taken to the next level: they reconstructed the sort of teams of
skilled musicians and sound engineers that made the very kind
of music that Daft Punk in the nineties loved to sample and
rework into contemporary dancefloor anthems. But I reckon
they went even further than that: it's as though they wished
to 'sample' the zeitgeist of the late seventies and early eighties.
They attempted to reconstruct the entire cultural matrix that
once produced albums like *Rumours* and *Off the Wall*. Not just
the analogue means of production, but the analogue sense of
temporality. In particular, the Event, the mass synchronised
experience of 'the whole world' tuning into some kind of
cultural artefact: movies like *Star Wars*, records like *Thriller*.
Hence the much-discussed *Random Access Memories* promo-
tional campaign with its teasing hints and initial reliance on

analogue-era techniques like billboards and television ads. There's a nostalgia here not just for the monoculture ('pop *is* the monoculture,' Thomas Bangalter insisted) but for monotemporality: a shared experience of time.

This feeling of mass synchrony is inseparable, I think, from concepts like progress and the future. That is made clear on *Random Access Memories* with the two key tracks, 'Giorgio by Moroder' and 'Contact'.

'Giorgio by Moroder' involves a towering figure of twentieth-century popular music looking back on his own looking forward. Producer of Donna Summer and pioneer of the electronic disco style known as Eurodisco, Moroder was interviewed at length by Daft Punk. Two small snippets appear on the track. The key segment concerns the making of 'I Feel Love', an international No. 1 hit in 1977, and notable for being the first all-electronic dance track.

Moroder speaks of the Donna Summer album on which 'I Feel Love' appeared, *I Remember Yesterday*, a sort of disco concept album about time and memory: 'I wanted to do an album with the sounds of the fifties, the sound of the sixties, of the seventies – and then have a sound of the future – and I thought, "Wait a second, I know the synthesiser – why don't I use a synthesiser, which *is* the sound of the future?" . . . I knew that could be a sound of the future, but I didn't realise how much the impact would be.'

And the rest, as they say, was history. The history of future pop. Eighties synthpop and Hi-NRG and house, nineties techno and trance – these and so many other things can be sourced back to this landmark breakthrough, 'I Feel Love'.

It's totally charming that Daft Punk pay tribute to their ancestor-hero with 'Giorgio by Moroder'. Interestingly, however, Daft Punk and Moroder don't collaborate musically. Instead they use his voice, the one thing he's not particularly famous

223

for. And the melancholy implication of the collaboration is that neither Daft Punk nor Moroder felt capable of making any kind of future music, together or separately. What Daft Punk do instead is to make an accurate reproduction of the electronic Eurodisco sound.

Nobody is going to rush out of the front door, like Brian Eno did with David Bowie, and tell their friends, 'I have heard the future of pop!' Rather, listening to 'Giorgio by Moroder', you might say, wistfully, 'Do you remember when music sounded like the future?'

'Contact' is the final track on *Random Access Memories*, and it aspires to be a grand finale. It starts with a sampled voice from a NASA transmission, the Apollo 17 mission, from December 1972. It's Eugene Cernan, the last astronaut to stand on the moon's surface. He's talking about 'a bright object, it's obviously rotating because it's flashing, it's way out in the distance'. After describing it in some detail, Cernan says, *'there's something out there'*.

Right there, you have encapsulated all the romance of the space race, the final frontier. There's that mystical inkling of something being out there that is our destiny as a species to find and make contact with. We must boldly go – it's our nature, our calling.

What Cernan actually said when he climbed the ladder back into the lunar module and bid adieu to the moon was this: 'As I take man's last step from the surface, back home for some time to come – but we believe not too long into the future – I'd like to just say what I believe history will record. That America's challenge of today has forged man's destiny of tomorrow.'

'Contact' itself is a thrilling track, the least dated-sounding on *Random Access Memories* (it could almost be a Chemical Brothers tune from the rocktronica golden age of 1997). A whooshing rush of sound is sustained, modulated and intensified for quite a long stretch of time. But then it sputters out anticlimactically, just like the space race did.

'Future' and 'Space' both signify the unknown, a virgin realm of wide-open possibility and adventure. In *Retromania*, I observed that the dominant model for artists and musicians in the 1960s was the astronaut, the explorer of new frontiers; today most musicians, and many artists and designers, are closer to archaeologists, excavating in the archives and curating the treasure they find. Space, in both the outer and inner senses, has been displaced by what we once called cyberspace. It's a quaint nineties term now, almost kitsch. But more important, it's an inaccurate term. Online isn't how Gibson imagined it in *Neuromancer*; it isn't spacious, there aren't distances you traverse on journeys of exploration. It's a zone of absolute proximity, where everything that is, and ever was, is crammed right next to everything else, separated only by a few taps on a keyboard and a mouse-click. Nonetheless, you could still say that our desire to 'go' and to go fast has imploded into the internet.

It's a generational shift of some enormity, and to bring out that aspect I'm going to make it personal and contrast myself and my son Kieran, who's now fourteen. That's the age I would have been when I was discovering the science fiction of writers like Fredrick Pohl and John Brunner. I grew up with S.F., with *Doctor Who* and its BBC Radiophonic Workshop electronic sound effects, while in the background was the still-pretty-exciting wake of the moon landings (Soyuz, the Viking unmanned mission to Mars in 1976) and a lot of articles and popular science books about astrophysics and black holes and so forth.

I have a strong sense that these things – outer space, the possibility of alien life, the inconceivable mysteries of space-time – have only the weakest grip on my son's imagination. When he reads, it's multivolume mega-narratives like *Game of Thrones* or *Harry Potter*. Mostly, though, he's all about sandbox games like Minecraft, social media, YouTube, apps. Everything computerised and internetty.

I navigate that realm proficiently enough, but I retain embedded cultural and neurological memories of analogue life. My son is a complete digital native, that's the real world to him, whereas IRL, I sense, feels flat and humdrum to him. He can't wait to get back to his laptop.

As well as a non-cathexis with the notion and the reality of space, my son doesn't really live with an idea of the future. By that I mean a cultural idea of the future. Obviously time is unfolding in a linear direction; he looks forward to things, he has vague thoughts about college and what he'll do when he's a grown-up. But there is no special excitement about the future with a capital F – little sense that it'll be better or even drastically different from the present.

Partly that stems, I would imagine, from not having a specific date to project towards like 1999 or 2000 or 2001. Those were dates that if you grew up in the twentieth century sent reverberations through you: just the sight of those numerals, the difference between '19' and '20'. Once you crossed the threshold between centuries, between millennia, you'd be living in some totally transformed world, or so it felt. But as yet we don't have a set of mental pictures or even vague expectations about 2050 or 2100.

Deep in our bones, we know that in 2050 businessmen will still wear ties and suits. That the top speed for vehicular transport will be within the current range. And the same goes for air travel too. There is an awful dawning suspicion that popular music might actually be rather similar in 2050 to how it is now.

The non-cathexis with space that I see in my son, and I suspect is shared by his generation, is something that particularly fascinates and perplexes me. It seems that everything that is happening, *all the action*, is inside – literally indoors, but also inside the non-space or post-space in which things like Minecraft take place.

So there are huge differences between father and son. But there's still a chip-off-the-old-block aspect at work, in so far as he's caught up in that same psychology of obsession, inseparably coupled with obsolescence. He burns through all the latest jumps forward in digital technology. He's all about the latest game, the newest app. His computer can never be fast enough for him. On the level of metabolism, then, we're pretty close. We're wired for the chase. My son lives within his own version of propulsive linearity. That lends his life an impatient speediness; he's often in a state of irritable excitation. But the 'new' as a category does seem, however, to be uncoupled from any sense of 'progress' in the cultural-artistic-political sense.

Megamix of a 2013 *New York Times* profile of Daft Punk, a speech delivered in Glasgow at the Tomorrow Never Knows symposium that same year, and a 2021 'In memoriam Daft Punk' piece for NPR focused on 'Digital Love' and *Discovery*

THE LIFE OF AUTO-TUNE:
How Pitch-Correction Revolutionised Twenty-First-Century Pop, from Afrobeats to Atlanta Trap

It happened exactly thirty-six seconds into the song – a glimpse of the shape of pop to come, a feel of the fabric of the future we now inhabit. The phrase 'I can't break through' turned crystalline, like the singer suddenly disappeared behind frosted glass. That sparkly special effect reappeared in the next verse, but this time a robotic warble wobbled, 'So sa-a-a-ad that you're leaving.'

The song, of course, was Cher's 'Believe', a worldwide smash on its October 1998 release. And what we were really 'leaving' was the twentieth century.

The pitch-correction technology Auto-Tune had been on the market for about a year before 'Believe' hit the charts, but its previous appearances had been discreet, as its makers, Antares Audio Technologies, intended. Alongside Roy Vedas's 'Fragments of Life', 'Believe' was the first record where the effect drew attention to itself: the glow-and-flutter of Cher's voice at key points in the song announced its own technological artifice – a blend of posthuman perfection and angelic transcendence ideal for the vague religiosity of the chorus, 'Do you believe in life after love?'

The song's producers, Mark Taylor and Brian Rawling, tried to keep secret the source of their magic trick, even coming up with a cover story that identified the machine as a brand of vocoder pedal, that robotic-sounding analogue-era effect widely used in disco and funk. But the truth seeped out. Soon overtly Auto-Tuned vocals were cropping up all over the sonic landscape, in R&B and dancehall, pop, house and even country.

Right from the start, it always felt like a gimmick, something forever on the brink of falling from public favour. But Auto-Tune proved to be the fad that just wouldn't fade. Its use is now more entrenched than ever. Despite all the premature expectations of its imminent demise, Auto-Tune's potential as a creative tool turned out to be wider and wilder than anybody could ever have dreamed back when 'Believe' topped the charts in twenty-three countries.

One measure of its triumph is Beyoncé and Jay-Z's 'Apeshit'. Here Queen Bey jumps on the trap bandwagon, tracing over verses written by Migos's Quavo and Offset through the crinkled sheen of over-cranked Auto-Tune. Some might take 'Apeshit' as yet another example of Beyoncé's Midas-touch mastery, but really it was a transparent attempt to compete on urban radio by adopting the prevailing template of commercial-yet-street rap. Jay-Z certainly doesn't sound overjoyed about being surrounded on all sides by the effect, having proclaimed the 'death of Auto-Tune' a decade ago.

What follows is the story of the *life* of Auto-Tune – its unexpected staying power, its global penetration, its freakily persistent power to thrill listeners. Few innovations in sound production have been simultaneously so reviled and so revolutionary. Epoch-defining or epoch-defacing, Auto-Tune is indisputably the sound of the twenty-first century so far. Its imprint is the date stamp that detractors claim will make recordings from this era sound dated. But it seems far more likely to become a trigger for fond nostalgia: how we'll remember these strange times we're living through.

'Where the future is still what it used to be'
Antares Audio Technology marketing slogan

Long before inventing Auto-Tune, the mathematician Dr Andy Hildebrand made his first fortune helping the oil giant Exxon find drilling sites. Using fabulously complex algorithms to interpret the data generated by sonar, his company located likely deposits of fuel deep underground. Alongside maths, though, Hildebrand's other passion was music; he's an accomplished flute player who funded his college tuition by teaching the instrument. In 1989, he left behind the lucrative field of 'reflection seismology' to launch Antares Audio Technology, despite not being entirely certain what exactly the company would be researching and developing.

The seed of the technology that would make Hildebrand famous came during a lunch with colleagues in the field: when he asked the assembled company what needed to be invented, someone jokingly suggested a machine that would enable her to sing in tune. The idea lodged in his brain. Hildebrand realised that the same maths that he'd used to map the geological subsurface could be applied to pitch-correction.

The expressed goal of Antares at that time was to fix discrepancies of pitch in order to make songs more effectively expressive. 'When voices or instruments are out of tune, the emotional qualities of the performance are lost,' the original patent asserted sweepingly – seemingly oblivious of great swathes of musical history, from jazz and blues to rock, reggae and rap, where 'wrong' has become a new right, where transgressions of tone and timbre and pitch have expressed the cloudy complexity of emotion in abrasively new ways. As

231

sound-studies scholar Owen Marshall has observed, for the manufacturers of Auto-Tune, bad singing interfered with the clear transmission of feeling. The device was designed to bring voices up to code, as it were – to communicate fluently within a supposedly universal Esperanto of emotion.

And that is exactly how Auto-Tune has worked in the preponderance of its usage: some speculate that it features in 99 per cent of today's pop music. Available as stand-alone hardware but more commonly used as a plug-in for digital audio workstations, Auto-Tune turned out – like so many new pieces of music technology – to have unexpected capacities. In addition to selecting the key of the performance, the user must also set the 'retune' speed, which governs the slowness or fastness with which a note identified as off-key gets pushed towards the correct pitch. Singers slide between notes, so for a natural feel – what Antares assumed producers would always be seeking – there needed to be a gradual (we're talking milliseconds here) transition. As Hildebrand recalled in one interview, 'When a song is slower, like a ballad, the notes are long, and the pitch needs to shift slowly. For faster songs, the notes are short, the pitch needs to be changed quickly. I built in a dial where you could adjust the speed from 1 (fastest) to 10 (slowest). Just for kicks, I put a "zero" setting, which changed the pitch the exact moment it received the signal.'

It was the fastest settings – and that instant switch 'zero' – that gave birth to the effect first heard on 'Believe' and which has subsequently flourished in myriad varieties of brittle, glittering distortion. Technically known as 'pitch quantisation' – a relative of rhythmic quantisation, which can regularise grooves or, conversely, make them more swinging – the 'classic' Auto-Tune effect smooths out the miniscule variations in pitch that occur in singing. At the speediest retune settings, the gradual transitions between notes that a flesh-and-blood vocalist makes

232

are eliminated. Instead, each and every note is pegged to an exact pitch, fluctuations are stripped out, and Auto-Tune forces instant jumps between notes. The result is that sound we know so well: an intimate stranger hailing from the uncanny valley between organic and synthetic, human and superhuman. A voice born of the body but becoming pure information.

Over the ensuing years, Antares have refined and expanded what Auto-Tune can do, while also creating a range of related voice-processing plug-ins. Most of the new features have been in line with the original intent: repairing flawed vocals in a way that sounds naturalistic and is relatively inconspicuous on recordings. Hence functions like 'Humanize', which preserves the 'small variations in pitch' in a sustained note, and 'Flex-Tune', which retains an element of human error. Some of Auto-Tune's sister products add 'warmth' to vocals, increase 'presence', intensify breathiness. The freaky-sounding Throat EVO maps the vocal tract as a physical structure, just like Hildebrand mapping the oil fields miles underground. This phantasmal throat can be elongated or otherwise modified (you can adjust the position and width of vocal cords, mouth and lips too), allowing the user to 'literally design your own new vocal sound', according to the Antares website.

But as the more overtly artificial uses of Auto-Tune became a craze that never ran out of steam, Antares soon stepped in with anti-naturalistic software like Mutator EVO. Described as an 'extreme voice designer', Mutator enables the user to sculpt a voice and either 'mangle' it 'into a variety of strange creatures' or 'alienize' it, shredding the vocal into tiny slivers, stretching or compressing the length of those snippets, playing them in reverse, and so forth – ultimately creating your own unique version of an alien language.

All of this is Antares supplying a demand that it had never originally imagined would exist. The real impetus came, as always, from below: performers, producers, engineers and, beyond them, the marketplace of popular desire. If the general populace had uniformly recoiled from the Cher effect, or from its recurrence a half-decade later as the T-Pain effect, if Lil Wayne and Kanye West had reacted like Jay-Z and spurned the effect rather than embraced it as a creative tool, it's unlikely that Antares would be catering to the appetite for vocal distortion and mutation.

The crucial shift with Auto-Tune came when artists started to use it as a real-time process, rather than as a fix-it-in-the-mix application after the event. Singing or rapping in the booth, listening to their own Auto-Tuned voice through headphones, they learned how to push the effect. Some engineers will record the vocal so that there is a 'raw' version to be fixed up later, but – increasingly in rap – there is no uncooked original to work from. The true voice, the definitive performance, is Auto-Tuned right from the start.

Rap of the 2010s is where that process has played out most glaringly and compellingly: MCs like Future, Chief Keef and Quavo are almost literally cyborgs, inseparable from the vocal prosthetics that serve as their bionic superpowers. But we can also hear the long-term influence of Auto-Tune on singing styles on Top 40 radio. Vocalists have learned to bend with the effect, exploiting the supersmooth sheen it lends to long sustained notes, and intuitively singing slightly flat because that triggers over-correction in Auto-Tune pleasingly.

Rihanna is the dominant singer of our era, in no small part because the Barbados grain of her voice interacts well with Auto-Tune's nasal tinge, making for a sort of fire-and-ice combination. Voice effects have been prominent in many of her biggest hits, from the 'eh-eh-eh-eh-eh' pitch descents in 'Umbrella' to the melodious twinkle-chime of the chorus in 'Diamonds'. Then there's Katy Perry, whose voice is so lacking in textural width that Auto-Tune turns it into a stiletto of stridency that – on songs like 'Firework' and 'Part of Me' – seems to pierce deep into the listener's ear canal.

Just like Hoover with the vacuum cleaner or Kleenex with tissues, Auto-Tune has become the stand-in for a whole range of pitch-correction and vocal-processing equipment. The best known of these rivals, Melodyne, is preferred by many recording studio professionals for the greater scope it offers for intricately altering vocals.

Before you even get into the technicalities of its process and user interface, the difference between the two devices comes over in the names. Auto-Tune sounds like a machine or a company providing a service (car repair, even!). But Melodyne could be the name of a girl or an Ancient Greek goddess; perhaps the brand name of a medicine or the street name of a psychoactive drug. Even the name of the company that makes Melodyne sounds slightly mystical and hippy-dippy: Celemony. Where Auto-Tune's Dr Hildebrand worked for the oil industry, Melodyne inventor Peter Neubäcker apprenticed with a maker of stringed instruments and combined a passion for hardcore maths and computing with a fascination for alchemy and astrology.

Launched on the music technology market in early 2001, Melodyne was always conceived as an apparatus for total design of vocal performances, working on not just pitch adjustment but modifications to timing and phrasing. The program captures the characteristics of a vocal or instrumental performance and displays them graphically, with each note appearing as what Celemony calls a 'blob'. Sound becomes Play-Doh to be sculpted or tinted by a huge range of effects. The blobs can be stretched or squished by dragging the cursor. Internal fluctuations within a blob can be smoothed out or added, creating,

235

say, vibrato that didn't exist in the original performance. As for timing, a note-blob can be separated more cleanly from a preceding or following blob – or, conversely, pushed closer – to create effects of syncopation, stress or sharper attack. The entire feel of a rapper's flow or a singer's phrasing can be radically re-articulated. Emotion itself becomes raw material to be edited.

'Keeping it real-ish' seems to be the presiding ethos of Melodyne, and certainly something that its users prize and see as the edge it has over Auto-Tune. 'My goal is natural-sounding vocals,' says Chris 'TEK' O'Ryan, an in-demand vocal producer whose clientele includes Justin Bieber, Katy Perry and Mary J. Blige. 'It's like a good CGI monster – you don't want it to look fake.' O'Ryan uses Auto-Tune in the recording studio as well, but only so that he and the artist don't get distracted by striving to achieve a pitch-perfect take and can concentrate on delivery, timing, groove and character. The real work, though, comes later, when he removes the Auto-Tune and sculpts the vocal 'by hand' using Melodyne. 'I'll add trills, I'll emphasise attacks or the scoop up to a moment in a performance,' O'Ryan says. At the extreme, the recording of the singer might take three or four hours, and then he'll spend two to four days working it over in Melodyne on his own.

This sounds like a highly significant contribution, and O'Ryan doesn't flinch when it's suggested that in a sense he's the co-creator of these vocal performances, a sort of invisible but vital element of what you hear on the radio or through Spotify. But he emphasises that 'I'm embellishing – hearing what they're doing in the booth and following their lead'. He also stresses that the end goal must not sound overworked. Indeed, one of the reasons why both Auto-Tune and Melodyne have become so indispensable in studios is that they allow performers and producers to concentrate on the expressive

and characterful qualities in a vocal, rather than get bent out
of shape pursuing a perfectly in-tune take. They are labour-
saving devices to a large degree, especially for big stars who
face so many other demands on their time.

Still, there's no doubt that there is something magical
verging on sorcerous about what Melodyne, Auto-Tune and
similar technologies enable. A shiver ran through me when I
watched one Melodyne tutorial on YouTube about 'advanced
comping' – Celemony's radical extension of long-established
studio techniques of compiling fragments from different vocal
takes into an uber-performance. Comping started back in the
analogue era, with producers painstakingly stitching the best
lines of singing from multiple renditions into a superior final
performance that never actually occurred as a single event. But
Melodyne can take the expressive qualities of one take (or frac-
tion thereof) by mapping its characteristics and pasting those
attributes into an alternative take that is preferable for other
reasons. As the Celemony tutorial puts it, the newly created
blob 'inherits the intonation' of the first but also the timing
of the second take. And that's just one example of Melodyne's
superpowers: it can also work with polyphonic material, shifting a note within, say, a guitar chord, and it can change the
timbre and harmonics of a voice to the point of altering its
apparent gender.

Chances are that any vocal you hear on the radio today is a
complex artefact that's been subjected to an overlapping array
of processes. Think of it as similar to the hair on a pop star's
head, which has probably been dyed, then cut and layered,
then plastered with grooming products, and possibly had extensions woven into it. The result might have a natural feel to it,
even a stylised disorder, but it is an intensely cultivated and
sculpted assemblage. The same goes for the singing we hear on
records. But because at some deep level we still respond to the

237

voice in terms of intimacy and honesty – as an outpouring of the naked self – we don't really like to think of it as being as doctored and denatured as a neon green wig.

In the same way that pop has seen the rise of specialist producers whose sole activity is capturing vocal performances and remodelling them in post-production, in hip hop today there are name engineers whose main job is working with rappers – figures like the late Seth Firkins, who worked with Future, and Alex Tumay, Young Thug's engineer. Here, though, the emphasis is on real-time synergy between the rapper and the technician, who drags-and-drops plug-ins and effects as the recording process unfolds. This edge-of-chaos approach recalls the way that legendary dub producers of the 1970s used to mix live, hunched over a mixing board and swathed in a cloud of weed smoke, moving sliders up or down and triggering reverb and other sound effects.

Oddly, the very first example of rapping through Auto-Tune seems to have occurred in 'Too Much of Heaven' by the Euro-pop group Eiffel 65, way back in 2000. But the love affair between hip hop and Hildebrand's invention really started with T-Pain, although he actually abandoned rapping for Auto-Tune-enhanced singing in the mid-2000s. For several years, he was the Zelig of rap&B, scoring a string of hits himself and popping up in songs by Flo Rida, Kanye West, Lil Wayne and Rick Ross, to name just a few. Rappers seemed to relate to him warmly, embracing him like their era's very own Roger Troutman, the talk-box-boosted lover man of 1980s funk band Zapp. When Snoop Dogg put out his own T-Pain-like single, 'Sexual Eruption', in 2007, the video explicitly harked back to Zapp circa 1986's 'Computer Love': that same combo of sterile futuristic slickness and slinky funk sexiness.

As if by associational drift, the first rappers to really make something artistic out of Auto-Tune seemed to pick up on the word 'pain' in T-Pain (as opposed to his generally upbeat music). Something about the sound of Auto-Tune melted these rappers' hard hearts and opened up the possibility for tenderness and vulnerability: Lil Wayne's gooey ballad 'How to Love', or his emo romp 'Knockout', or his sensitive (despite its title) 'Prostitute Flange' and its tidied-up remake, 'Prostitute 2', on which Wayne's asthmatic croaks sound like his larynx is coated with writhing fluorescent nodes. As for Kanye West's 2008 album *808s and Heartbreak*, T-Pain claimed not only to have influenced the rapper's resort to Auto-Tune but to have inspired the album title. In time, T-Pain would complain that *808s & Heartbreak* received the critical praise that his debut album, *Rappa Ternt Sanga*, should have got four years earlier. He also griped that Kanye didn't even use the effect properly, adding it on later rather than singing with the effect live in the studio.

Correctly done or not, West's first notable foray into Auto-Tune was a guest verse in Young Jeezy's 'Put On' in the summer of 2008 – very much a dry (or weepy-moist) run for *Heartbreak* in so far as he waxed maudlin about the loss of his adored mother and his own feelings of being lost in Fame's hall-of-mirrors maze. Then came the full-blown album, described by its creator as therapy for his 'lonely at the top' life – an artistically sublimated substitute for suicide, even. The album's sound, West declared at the time, was 'Auto-Tune meets distortion, with a bit of delay on it and a whole bunch of fucked-up life'. Auto-Tune enabled a shaky singer to move into an R&B zone not really heard on his earlier albums. But the abrasive Auto-Tune treatments that shaped the entire album – like the wracked shivers shot through 'how could you be so' in 'Heartless', the aural equivalent of a trembling lip or twitching eyelid – were also attempts to forge new sonic signifiers for age-old emotions of anguish and abandonment.

Arguably, there was an even more radical late-2000s album that collided vocal-mangling effects with themes of pop stardom as disorientation and ego-disintegration: Britney Spears's *Blackout*. Britney's careening-out-of-control career was re-presented to the public as porno-pop, a self-referential spectacle that implicated listeners in their own voyeurism and schadenfreude. Drastically pitch-tweaked to form an angular melody, the chorus of 'Piece of Me' invited listeners to hear it as 'you wanna piece of meat?' The rhythm tracks on 'Gimme More' and 'Freakshow' sounded like they were made out of gasps and shudders of pained ecstasy or ecstatic pain. (T-Pain popped up as co-writer and background vocalist on 'Hot as Ice'.) Britney's trademark husky croak survived on *Blackout*, but on later albums and hits like 2011's 'Till the World Ends', her vocals got less distinctive as pitch-correction took hold. She began to blend into a Top 40 landscape dominated by Auto-Tune as default universal, a glacé glisten coating every voice on the radio.

'Boom Boom Pow', Black Eyed Peas' smash single of 2009, was at once typical and exemplary as pop fare at the end of the first decade of the twenty-first century. Every vocal in the track is Auto-Tuned to the max. will.i.am could have been hymning Antares Audio when he boasted of having 'that future flow, that digital spit'. But the Peas were peddling a frozen futurity, ideas about how tomorrow will sound and look and dress established a decade earlier in Hype Williams's videos and in films like *The Matrix*. Perhaps earlier still: the 'Boom Boom Pow' promo was meant to be set a thousand years from today but really looked like a pastiche of ideas from 1982's *Tron*. Amid this bonanza of retro-future clichés, Auto-Tune felt less like the true sound of the new millennium and more like a marginal twist on the vocoder – by the late 2000s, a decidedly nostalgic sound.

In 2009, the first big backlash against the omnipresence of Auto-Tune kicked off. On 'D.O.A. (Death of Auto-Tune)', Jay-Z accused his hip hop contemporaries of going pop and soft: 'Y'all n****s singing too much/Get back to rap, you T-Pain-ing too much.' Defining himself as a bastion of pure lyricism, he declared a 'moment of silence' for Auto-Tune, a machine made obsolete through overuse. That same year, Death Cab for Cutie turned up to the Grammy Awards sporting blue ribbons that obliquely symbolised the eroded humanity of music-making, via jazz's blue notes. 'Over the last ten years we've seen a lot of good musicians being affected by this newfound digital manipulation of the human voice, and we feel enough is enough,' declared frontman Ben Gibbard. 'Let's really try to get music back to its roots of actual people singing and sounding like human beings.' Guitar-maker Paul Reed Smith upbraided Dr Hildebrand in person, accusing him of having 'completely destroyed Western music'. In May 2010, *Time* magazine listed Auto-Tune among the fifty worst inventions of the modern era, alongside subprime mortgages, DDT, Crocs, Olestra, pop-up ads and New Coke.

Even T-Pain spoke up, trying to pull off a tricky juggling act – claiming pioneer status and preeminence in the field while simultaneously criticising recent exponents for not knowing how to get the best results out of the technology. He claimed that he'd spent two years researching Auto-Tune and thinking about it – including actually meeting with Hildebrand – before he even attempted to use it. 'A lot of math went into that shit,' he said. 'It would take us a fucking billion minutes to explain to regular motherfuckers. But I really studied this shit . . . I know why it catches certain notes and why it doesn't catch certain notes.'

The backlash kept on coming. Despite having used Auto-Tune and other vocal treatments on ecstatic tunes like 'One More Time' and 'Digital Love' off 2001's *Discovery*, Daft Punk staged a back-to-analogue recantation with 2013's *Random Access Memories*. Even Lady Gaga, the nu-glam queen of all things plastic-fantastical, tried the 'this is the real me' switch with 2016's 'Perfect Illusion', which drastically reduced the Auto-Tune levels on her singing and saw her adopting a dressed-down, cut-off jeans and plain-T-shirt look for the video. 'I believe many of us are wondering why there are so many fake things around us,' Gaga said. 'How do we look through these images that we know are filtered and altered, and decipher what is reality and what is a perfect illusion? . . . This song is about raging against it and letting it go. It's about wanting people to re-establish that human connection.'

Much of this anti-Auto-Tune sentiment presented the idea that the technology is a dehumanising deception foisted upon the public. Attempting to deflect this angle of attack, Hildebrand once offered an analogy with a generally accepted form of everyday artifice, asking, 'My wife wears makeup, does that make her evil?' Perhaps because of Cher's involvement in Auto-Tune's debut on the world pop stage, critics have often connected pitch-correction and cosmetic surgery, comparing the effect to Botox, face peels, collagen injections and the rest. In the video for 'Believe', Cher actually *looks* how Auto-Tune *sounds*. The combination of three levels of enhancement – surgery, makeup and that old trick of bright lights that flatten the skin surface into a blank dazzle – means that her face and her voice seem to be made out of the same immaterial substance. If the 'Believe' promo were produced today, a fourth level of falsification would be routinely applied: digital post-production procedures like motion-retouching or colourising that operate at the level of pixels rather than pores, fundamentally altering the integrity of the image.

This is exactly the same business that Auto-Tune and Melodyne are in. The taste for these effects and the revul-

sion against them are part of the same syndrome, reflecting
a deeply conflicted confusion in our desires: simultaneously
craving the real and the true while continuing to be seduced
by digital's perfection and the facility and flexibility of use it
offers. That's why young hipsters buy overpriced vinyl for the
aura of authenticity and analogue warmth but in practice use
the download codes to listen to the music on an everyday level.

But has there ever really been such a thing as 'natural'
singing, at least since the invention of recording, microphones
and live amplification? Right at the primal roots of rock 'n' roll,
Elvis Presley's voice came clad in slapback echo. The Beatles
enthusiastically adopted artificial double-tracking, a process
invented by Abbey Road engineer Ken Townsend that thick-
ened vocals by placing a doubled recording slightly out of synch
with the identical original. John Lennon also loved to alter the
natural timbre of his voice by putting it through a variably
rotating Leslie speaker and by slowing down the tape speed of
his recorded singing.

Reverb, EQ, phasing, stacking vocals, comping the best takes
to create a superhuman pseudo-event that never happened as
a real-time performance – all of these increasingly standard
studio techniques tampered with the integrity of what reached
the listener's ears. And that's before we even get to the digital
era, with its vastly expanded palette of modifications. It could
be further argued that all recording is intrinsically artificial,
that the simple act of 'canning' the voice in a preserved form
to be reactivated at will in places and times remote from the
original site of performance goes against nature, or at least
breaks drastically with the thousands of years when human
beings had to be in the presence of music-makers to hear
the sounds they made. If you go back just a little way, you
invariably find that the very sounds or qualities that the likes
of Death Cab for Cutie prize as 'warm' or 'real' – like fuzz-tone

guitar, or Hammond organ – were considered newfangled contrivances and lamentable depletions of the human touch.

In a profound sense, there is nothing necessarily 'natural' about the unadorned and unamplified human voice. More often than not, singing involves the cultivation of technique to a point where you could almost conceive of styles as diverse as opera, scatting, yodelling and Tuvan throat singing as tantamount to introjected technology.

'Voice is the original instrument,' according to the avant-garde vocalist Joan La Barbara. Which is true, but it also suggests that the voice is just like a violin or a Moog synthesiser: an apparatus for sound-generation. This combination of intimacy and artificiality is one of the things that makes singing compelling and more than a little eerie: the singer squeezes breath from the moist, abject depths of their physical interior to create sound-shapes that seem transcendent and immaterial. Singing is self-overcoming, pushing against the limits of the body, forcing air into friction with the throat, tongue and lips in exquisitely controlled and contrived ways. That applies as much to the history of pop, for all its down-to-earth aspirations and vernacular aura. 'Falsetto', that staple of so much pop music, from doo-wop to disco to today's R&B, contains the idea of fakeness in its very name. The next logical step would then be to simply resort to external assistance. Which is why when you listen to the Beach Boys or the Four Seasons or Queen, you almost hear them reaching towards an Auto-Tune sound.

Another commonly heard accusation mounted against Auto-Tune is that it depersonalises, eradicating the individuality and character of voices. In their natural mode, vocal cords don't produce a clear signal: there's 'noise' mixed in there, the grit and grain that are a physical residue of the process of speaking or singing. This is the very aspect of the voice – its carnal thickness – that differentiates one from another. Digital

244

transmission can interfere with that anyway, especially at the lower bandwidths – it's why, say, if you call your mum on her mobile from your mobile, she can sound unlike herself to an unsettling degree. But pitch-correction technology really messes with the voice as substance and signature. Given that this embodied quality, as opposed to the learned dramatic arts of singing expressively, is a big part of why one voice turns us on and another leaves us cold, surely anything that diminishes it is a reduction?

Maybe, and yet it is still possible to identify our favourite singers or rappers through the depersonalising medium of pitch-correction – and to form a bond with new performers. In fact, you could argue that Auto-Tune, by becoming an industry standard, creates even more premium on the other elements that make up vocal appeal – phrasing, personality – as well as extra-musical aspects like image and biography.

Take the example of Kesha. She found ways to use Auto-Tune and other voice-production tricks to dramatise herself on the radio as a sort of human cartoon. It's hard now to listen to her early hits without hearing them as documents of abuse, in light of her ongoing legal battles with producer Dr Luke, but 2009's breakout smash single 'TiK ToK' is a case study in how to push personality through a depersonalising technology: the deliciously impish gurgle that wracks the line 'I ain't comin' back', the word 'tipsy' slowing down like someone about to pass out, the screwed deceleration of the line 'shut us down' when the police pull the plug on the party. The sheer gimmickry of these effects suited Kesha's image as a trashed 'n' trashy party girl, mirroring her love of glitter as a form of cheap glamour.

These and other examples also lay waste to the related argument that pitch-correction is a deskilling innovation that allows the talent-free – performers who can't sing in tune without help – to make it. Actually, it refocused what talent in pop is. The history of popular music is full of super-professional session singers and backing vocalists who could sing pitch-perfect at the drop of a mic, but, for whatever reason, never made it as frontline stars – they lacked a certain characterful quality to the voice or just couldn't command the spotlight. Auto-Tune means that these attributes – less to do with training or technique than personality or presence – become even more important. Hitting the right notes has never been that important when it comes to having a hit.

Related to the complaints about falseness and impersonality is the accusation that Auto-Tune, especially in its overtly robotic-sounding uses, lacks soul. But you could argue the absolute reverse: that the sound of Auto-Tune is hyper-soul, a melodrama of micro-engineered melisma. Sometimes when I listen to Top 40 radio, I think, 'This doesn't sound like how emotion feels.' But it's not because it is less than human. It's because it's superhuman, the average song crammed with so many peaks and tremors. You could talk of an 'emotional compression' equivalent to the maximalist audio compression that engineers and music fans complain about – a feelings equivalent to the loudness war, with Auto-Tune and Melodyne enlisted to supercharge the tremulousness levels, while the teams of writers involved in any given pop single squeeze in as many uplifting pre-chorus moments and soaring ecstasies as possible. The end result is like froyo: already clotted with artificial flavours, then covered in gaudy toppings.

Writing about the rise of sequencers, programmed rhythm, sample-loops and MIDI, the academic Andrew Goodwin argued that 'we have grown used to connecting machines and funkiness'. That maxim could be updated for the Auto-Tune/ Melodyne era: 'We have grown used to connecting machines and soulfulness.' And that perhaps is the lingering mystery – the extent to which the general public has adapted to hearing overtly processed voices as the sound of lust, longing and loneliness. In another meaning of 'soul', we could also say that Auto-Tune is the sound of blackness today, at least in its most cutting-edge forms, like trap and future-leaning R&B.

Finally, people have claimed that Auto-Tune irrevocably dates recordings, thereby eliminating their chances for timelessness. In 2012, musician, sound engineer and recording studio owner Steve Albini groused about the lingering legacy of 'Believe', a 'horrible piece of music with this ugly soon-to-be cliché' at its heart. He recalled his horror when certain friends he thought he knew opined that they kinda liked that Cher tune, likening the syndrome to zombification: 'A terrible song that gives all your friends brain cancer and makes shit foam up out of their mouths.' Concerning Auto-Tune's widespread use, Albini declared that 'whoever has that done to their record, you just know that they are marking that record for obsolescence. They're gluing the record's feet to the floor of a certain era and making it so it will eventually be considered stupid.'

The counterargument is to simply point at phases of dated-but-good scattered all through music history, where the hallmarks of period stylisation and recording studio fads have an enduring appeal partly for their intrinsic attributes but also for their very fixed-in-time quality. The examples are legion: psychedelia, dub reggae, eighties electro with its Roland 808 bass and drum sounds, the short sample-memory loops and MPC-triggered stabs of early hip hop and jungle. Even things that might have annoyed the typical alternative music fan at the time – like the gated drums on mainstream eighties pop-rock – have now acquired a certain charm. One wonders also how Albini can be so damn sure the records he's been involved in making have escaped the sonic markers of their epoch. At this point, whatever his intent, I'd bet that the high-profile records he produced for Pixies, Nirvana, PJ Harvey and Bush all fairly scream 'late eighties/early nineties'.

247

*

The Auto-Tune anti-stance expressed by Albini and countless others is rockism's standard operating procedure: naturalise the core aspects of the genre – distorted electric guitars, raw-throated roar, un-showbiz performance – and in the process elide the technological contrivance and inherent theatricality that were always already there. Fuzztone and wah-wah guitar effects, then, cease to be heard as what they originally were (innovative, technological, artificial, futuristic) and seem authentic and time-honoured, the golden olden way of doing things.

In the 2000s, though, some figures from the alternative rock world were sharp enough to think past rockism and realise there was something fresh and timely about Auto-Tune – that here was a potential field of artistic action. Radiohead were one of the first, appropriately during the sessions for *Kid A* and *Amnesiac*, their own intensive project of self-deconditioning from the rockist mindset. In 2001, Thom Yorke told me about how they used Hildebrand's invention on 'Packt like Sardines' and 'Pulk/Pull Revolving Doors', both for the classic 'dead in-pitch' robo-effect and to talk into the machine. 'You give it a key and it desperately tries to search for the music in your speech and produces notes at random,' Yorke explained.

In 2011 Kate Bush revisited her 1989 song 'A Deeper Understanding', a prophetic parable of the alienated lifestyle of the approaching digital age, this time using Auto-Tune to make the Siri-like voice of the computer sound like a guardian angel offering surrogate solace and counterfeit company: 'Hello, I know that you're unhappy/I bring you love and deeper understanding'.

Anti-rockist to the core (remember their manifesto about never being photographed or appearing on stage in T-shirts?), Vampire Weekend were unsurprisingly early adopters –

tweaking the effect full-strength on 'California English' off of 2010's *Contra*. The previous year, Vampire Weekend's Rostam Batmanglij dedicated a whole side-project, *Discovery*, to diabetic coma-triggering levels of Auto-Tune super sweetness, including a tooth-enamel-corrosive remake of the Jackson 5's 'I Want You Back'. Less expected was neo-folk songwriter Sufjan Stevens's 'Impossible Soul', twenty-six minutes of deliriously fluttered singing in full Auto-Tune effect, from 2010's *The Age of Adz*.

Probably the most surprising indie embrace of pitch-correction was Justin Vernon's. His work as Bon Iver had been synonymous with soul-bared intimacy and acoustic honesty. But on 'Woods' and the album *22, A Million*, his music found the missing link between the Band's 'Whispering Pines' and Kraftwerk's 'Neon Lights'. A twinklescape of multitracked, glassily processed harmonies, 'Woods' conjures an atmosphere of solitude and self-care, a retreat from the ceaseless stimulation of a wired and worry-making world: 'I'm up in the woods/I'm down on my mind/I'm building a still to slow down the time'. Kanye West loved the song so much that he borrowed its hook and chorus for his own 'Lost in the World' and recruited Vernon to join him. West's lyric is more ambivalent, or confused: complaining about feeling 'lost in this plastic life' but still being up for some empty hedonism. West and Vernon also appeared in 2016's 'Friends' by Francis and the Lights, but here the vocal glisten came from a device called Prismizer. Around this time Bon Iver collaborated with James Blake, dubstep's prince of weepy and warped vocals, resulting in the extraordinary 'Fall Creek Boys Choir' – imagine a choir of ketamine elves imitating Michael McDonald.

All these moves by alt-rock figures were examples of sonic slumming: highbrows flirting with the lowbrow (and thereby bucking the consensus of the middlebrow), burnishing their cred by the counterintuitive gambit of venturing into the

commercial and gimmicky world of mainstream pop. I use
the word 'slumming' advisedly, since disdain for Auto-Tune
is a class reflex that can be indexed to similar attitudes that
favour vintage aesthetics, weathered and distressed textures,
the handmade and the antique, organic and locavore produce,
and the whole realm of heritage and history itself. The further
down the class spectrum you go, the more shiny and new
things get, whether you're talking about clothes, furniture
or sound production. Auto-Tune correlates with a lower-class
attraction to man-made fabrics, spaceship sneakers, box-fresh
clothes and an interior decor aesthetic somewhere between
Scarface and *MTV Cribs*.

That's why Auto-Tune has been most fervently embraced
in either the ethnic-majority urban zones of America and the
West generally, and throughout the developing world: Africa,
the Caribbean, the Middle East, India. Along with its hyper-
gloss allure, Auto-Tune may also resonate as a signifier of
ultra-modernity: globalisation as an aspirational aim, rather
than an imposed hegemony to be resisted.

For critics on both the left and right of the political spectrum, this kind of standardisation – popular music regimented
around a Western idea of proper pitch – would be reason
enough to abhor Auto-Tune. Conservatives would mourn the
erosion of tradition; Marxists would tend to focus on the rap-
acity of capitalism as it runs rampant across the world, with
pop music simultaneously propagandising for the Western way
of life while also raking in revenue for its musical commodities
and for its sound-shaping technology. But one of the surprising things about Auto-Tune is how it has been twisted by its
non-Western users, intensifying musical differences rather than
erasing them.

When it was first embraced by Western audiences in the
eighties, African music tended to be associated with qualities

like rootsy, earthy, authentic, natural – in other words, values fundamentally at odds with Auto-Tune. Actually, this was a mistaken – and, dare I say, rockist – projection. Most early forms of Afro-pop, such as highlife or *juju*, were slick, the work of highly professional bands not averse to a little bit of razzle-dazzle. There was nothing particularly rural about this sound, which was to a large degree associated with an urbane, sophis-ticated, cosmopolitan audience. Nor was it particularly 'pure' in the way that Western world music enthusiasts seemed to crave: it always eagerly incorporated ideas from black America, the Caribbean and the outside world, from King Sunny Adé's Shadows-style twangy guitar to the synths and drum machines in eighties Ethiopian electro-funk.

So it makes perfect sense that twenty-first-century Afrobeat would embrace the latest in sonic modernity. At the same time, Auto-Tune exacerbates rather than erodes the pre-existing hallmarks of African pop, intensifying the sing-song melodies, the interplay of glinting guitar and chirruping bass, the lilting rhythms. Auto-Tuned singing – lead voice and backing harmo-nies, all treated to different degrees of pitch-correction – drapes the groove in criss-crossing patterns, like strands of maple syrup and honey drizzled across a pancake. The sweetness and lightness inherent to African music becomes dizzying, at times cloying to the point of nausea, like you've eaten a whole pack of chocolate chip cookies in a single sitting.

With Nigerian singers like Flavour and Tekno, Auto-Tune enhances the delicacy of the vocal delivery, making it even more dainty and shimmering, like a hummingbird dipping for nectar. On Flavour's 'Sake of Love', every syllable of 'Baby you're my ecstasy/You are my fantasy' is deliciously clipped and distinct. But Auto-Tune is also used to make Flavour sound hilariously delirious on 'Alcohol', where each iteration of the title phrase gets more mush-mouthed, three syllables

degenerating into a single-phoneme warble. 'Ur Waist' by
Iyanya, who won the TV singing contest *Project Fame West
Africa* presumably without any technological assistance, bubbles over with pitch-perfected geysers of mystic bliss. Regarded
by some as the craziest musician in Nigeria, Terry G's tunes
are closer to dancehall: on tracks like 'Free Madness Pt. 2' his
raucous rasp rides the choppy hard-bounce of the beats, the
Auto-Tuned-to-the-max voice ranging from a parched roar to a
fizzy froth.

Head north from Nigeria and Ghana to Morocco, Algeria and
Egypt, and the Auto-Tune gets even more overdriven. As critic
Jace Clayton noted in his book *Uproot*, pitch-correction made
a perfectly (un)natural interface with the existing traditions of
vocal artifice in Arabic musical traditions, with its serpentine
curlicues of melismatic ornaments. 'Sliding pitches sound
startling through it,' Clayton wrote. 'A weird electronic warble
embeds itself in rich, throaty glissandos.' Listen to Algerian *raï*
or Egyptian popular song, and the often long tracks seem riven
with electric streaks of ear-dazzling intensity, like cork-screwing
bolts of lightning. If there is music that is more heavily Auto-
Tuned than this on the planet, I'm not sure I'm ready for it.

In 2009's 'Death of Auto-Tune', Jay-Z boasted 'my raps don't
have melodies' and claimed that his music made people 'wan'
go commit felonies', even comparing the track to 'assault with a
deadly weapon'. In other words, unlike all that pop-friendly rap
with R&B choruses and heavy Auto-Tune in the T-Pain style,
this was the raw shit – uncompromising and street-real. Proper
hip hop.

A decade on, in an ironic turnabout, it is hip hop at its most
melodious and 'cooked'-sounding that is the most gangsta and
hardcore in its themes. Trap is hard to define as a genre –
even the trademark rapid-fire hi-hats are not always present

in every track – but one widespread characteristic is the way
that MCs dissolve the boundary between rapping and singing.
And that development owes a huge amount to Auto-Tune.
To borrow a phrase from T-Pain's debut album *Rappa Ternt
Sanga*, Auto-Tune turns rappers into singers – or something
unclassifiable in between. Accentuating the musicality already
present in rhythmically cadenced speech, pitch-correction
technology pushes rapping towards crooning, encouraging MCs
to emit trills and melodic flourishes that otherwise would be
outside their reach. Auto-Tune works as a kind of safety net
for vocal acrobatics – or perhaps the equivalent of the harness
and pulley ropes that enable stage performers to fly.

'We're getting melodies that wouldn't exist without it,' says
vocals producer and sound-engineering wizard Chris 'TEK'
O'Ryan, who may prefer the more intricate programming
software Melodyne for his own 'vocal design' work for pop
superstars, but who thinks 'Auto-Tune is a good thing in rap'.
Listening to the Auto-Tuned and otherwise effected versions
of themselves on headphones as they record in the studio
booth, MCs like Quavo and Future have learned both how
to push specific extreme effects and to work within this rap/
melody interzone, exploiting the glistening sinuosity inherent
to Auto-Tune. As Future's engineer, the late Seth Firkins, put
it, 'because Auto-Tune pegs him to the right pitches, he can try
any shit, and it'll still sound cool'.

One of the arguments against Auto-Tune is that it's created
an impersonal pop landscape by homogenising vocal timbre.
But in trap, the opposite has happened – Auto-Tune has
become a medium through which personality flexes itself even
more vividly. Just look at the different approaches and feels of
the genre's leading artists.

One legitimate complaint about Auto-Tune could be that it
has stripped the blues element out of popular music – all those

253

slightly off-pitch but expressive elements in singing – in favour of a remorseless flawlessness (which is why so much pop and rock today feels closer to the musical theatre tradition than to rock 'n' roll). But Future goes the opposite direction. He's reinvented blues for the twenty-first century, restoring it not just as a texture (raspy, rough-toned) or as a style of delivery (somewhere between speech and singing) but as a mode of feeling, an existential stance towards the world.

'My music – that's *pain*,' Future told MTV.com. 'I come from pain, so you gonna hear it in my music.' He's talking here about his past, a childhood of poverty in the thick of the drug trade. But it equally describes his present, as captured in the disjointed stream of consciousness of his lyrics, which depict a treadmill grind of emotionless sex and numbing drugs, a lifestyle of triumphs and material splendour that feels strangely desolate. Take the extraordinary 'All Right', off 2016's *Purple Reign*, on which Future rap-sings, 'I got money, fame, I got enemies/I can feel the pain of my enemy/I been downin' Percocets with Hennessy/I can hear the hood sayin' they proud of me'. You're not entirely sure here whether he's gloating about the jealousy of haters, as is the rap norm, or whether he's so sensitised and tuned in to external emotional vibrations that he really does *feel* the pain of those he's defeated. The 'pride' that pops up repeatedly and dissonantly in the lyric (see also 'gave her two Xans, now she proud of me') speaks of an inside-out world where socially destructive and personally dissolute acts become glorious and heroic. But then, that's just like rock 'n' roll, isn't it – at least in the Stones/Led Zep/Guns N' Roses sense.

Wielding Auto-Tune like the twenty-first century's equivalent of the electric guitar, Future has explicitly differentiated his way of working from T-Pain's, saying that 'I used it to rap because it makes my voice sound *grittier*'. According to Seth Firkins, the Auto-Tune was always on, from the start of any

Future session, because 'that's how we get the emotion out of him . . . It's an integral part . . . of his sound and his delivery.' The performer and the technical interface merge into a synergy system, a feedback circuit. Over the course of his vast discography of mixtapes and studio albums, Future has learned how to work the technology, conjuring the cold-inside shivers that run through the marrow of the hook in 'Wicked', the chirruping gasps of self-rapture in 'I'm So Groovy', the ecstasy of triumph, abandon and carelessness in 'Fuck Up Some Commas', and the groggy whimper of 'Codeine Crazy'. In the last of these, Future's voice seems to fizz like the mixing of Sprite and codeine-laced cough syrup, to create 'lean' (also known as purple drank on account of its colour), the potent dissociative drink that is many rappers' and rap fans' favourite way to get high. Four of the most powerful sonic statements of this second decade of the twenty-first century, these songs couldn't have existed without Hildebrand's invention. A technology designed to glaze over deficient performances with posthuman precision has become – with Future – a rehumanising noise-generator, a distortion device to better reflect the aching mess of dirty souls.

Paradoxically, Auto-Tune's most flagrantly artificial effects have come to signify authenticity at its most raw and exposed. 'I was going to lie to you but I had to tell the truth', as Future put it on *Honest*. Oddly, yet logically, Auto-Tune parallels the effects of the prescription meds endlessly referenced in Future's songs. Just as the painkillers and anxiety-deadeners seem to simultaneously numb him and unloose him emotionally, Auto-Tune works in Future's music as a mask-on/mask-off device – at once shielding and revealing. Through the 'lie' of its distancing mechanism, Future can tell the truth.

As Future's own drug-soaked output testifies, Auto-Tune isn't just the fad that won't fade; it's become the sound of getting faded. Auto-Tune and other forms of vocal effecting are the primary colour in the audio palette of a new psychedelia. Appropriately for these dispiriting and despiritualised times, it's a hollowed-out and decadent update, oriented around razing rather than raising consciousness. Trap and its local subsets like Chicago drill represent a kind of debased transcendence: struggle and sleaze gilded through the prismatic perceptions generated by a polydrug diet of Xanax and Percocet, cough syrup, weed, MDMA and alcohol.

Which is one reason why Chicago drill pioneer Chief Keef comes over on his recordings like some strange composite of mystic and monster, saint and savage: he sounds serenely detached even as he's rapping about putting silencers on guns and hotties riding him like a Harley. Keef's goblin glint of a voice drones deadpan from amid beats whose synth-orchestrations and tinkling bell-sounds resemble Christmas trees draped in fairy lights and baubles. On tracks like 'Know She Does' and 'On the Corner' off 2016's astonishing *DP Almighty* mixtape, delay effects multiply Keef into rippling after-images, like selves receding in a mirrored hotel elevator. Auto-Tune and other FX seem to mineralise his vocals, as if he's turning into a half-mammal/half-glass creature out of J.G. Ballard's phantasmagoric catastrophe novel *The Crystal World*.

There's a similar iridescence to Travis Scott songs like 'Pick Up the Phone' and 'Goosebumps'. From the bizarrely underpraised *Rodeo* and *Birds in the Trap Sing McKnight* to the bizarrely overpraised *Astroworld*, Scott's albums could easily be filed under 'ambient' as much as their logical genre location, rap/R&B. If there's a through line to his work, it's voice processing: not just Auto-Tune but delays, stereo-sculpted chorusing and harmony structures, phasing and God knows what else. The result is a panoply of ear-tantalising tingles: the ghostly flutter of 'Pornography' and 'Oh My Dis Side', the gaseous moans and Seefeel-like sighs of 'First Take' and 'Sweet

Sweet', the Escher-style vocal architectures of 'Way Back' and 'Who? What?'

Where vocal weirdness is the audio thread running through Scott's work, decadence redolent of The Weeknd is the unifying lyric theme and mood-tone. Sure, the singer-MC-producer *claims* not to do that many drugs, but everything in the music appeals to the drugged ear, or, perhaps, aims to make our ears *feel* drugged. If all the talk of pill-popping and 'psychedelics got me going crazy' and his electric producer-tag 'it's lit!' is just a pretence, an attempt to go along with the current rap mood and style, that might well mean Scott is the Electric Prunes of the new psychedelia, rather than its Syd Barrett-era Pink Floyd. But as gorgeous frauds go, it's a beguiling one to hear oozing out of the radio like fluorescent vapour.

Early in his career Travis Scott worked with Alex Tumay, better known as Young Thug's sound engineer. Even without the involvement of technology, Thug would be the maven of voice mutation – rap's equivalent to Tim Buckley circa *Starsailor*. His vocal equipment – throat, palate, tongue, lips and nasal cavities – amounts to a formidable machinery for the mangling of sound and sense. His mouth is a bubbling font of babble, a zoo-music menagerie of uncaged moans, gibbering whoops, creaky croaks, throttled vowels, and drooling 'n' gnashing noises like an Amazonian shaman tripped out on DMT.

So Thug doesn't really need any help distorting and distending his voice, but he gets it nonetheless from Tumay and his bag of technological tricks. Reacting on the fly, the engineer throws in delays, Harmony Engine doublings and other plug-ins so that the MC hears and responds to them live in the booth. Indeed, Thug apparently hates it if effects are added after the event, invariably rejecting these additions and alterations. Listening to *Slime Season 2* tracks like 'Beast' and 'Bout (Damn) Time', you can't really distinguish the MC's mouth-music virtuosity from the engineer's treatments. The man-machine merger peaks with the chopped-and-screwed 'Love Me Forever', where Thug's molten wheezes resemble strings of iridescent ectoplasm being drawn out of his mouth. As a crush-collision of vocal eccentricity and woozy beauty, the track is rivalled only by 'Tomorrow 'til Infinity' off *Beautiful Thugger Girls*, Thug's 'singing album'. Here Thug invents a machine-boosted hyper-falsetto, a frail wavering warble that sounds like he's coming with every note. Folding ecstasy upon ecstasy into the word 'infinity', Thug reaches piping peaks comparable to Al Green at his most sex-mystical.

Where Thug is on a solo trip to the stars, Migos get there collectively. On the Atlanta trio's *Culture* and *Culture II*, trap goes choral. Tracks like 'T-Shirt' and 'Auto Pilot' work as honeycomb lattices of voices keyed to mesh with doo-wop-like perfection, while also being differentiated texturally by contrasting degrees of Auto-Tune – a range from almost naturalistic rapping Auto-tweaked for a subtle melodious sheen (Takeoff) right the way across to otherworldly abstraction (Quavo). In these terraced voicescapes, the focal rapper on each verse is shadowed by antiphonal layers. At the first level, there's the continuous flow of ad libs echoing or commenting on the lyric, or syncopating against the groove as non-verbal grunts, whoops and voice-percussion effects (that also serve as Migos audio-logos, like their famous tyres-skidding sound of 'skrt-skrt-skrt'). One layer lower than the ad libs, there are gurgling ripples of wordless vocal, Auto-Tuned for zero-speed pitch-correction. This Migos trademark has a medieval flavour, a holy rolling drone faintly redolent of the chanting of Benedictine monks. Where Migos lyrics conjure a profane cartoon of bitches, brutality and boasting, these blissed-out backing vocals create an effect like stained glass, transfiguring lowlife into highlife.

258

The mood of the two *Cultures* and the Migos-and-friends compilation *Quality Control* is different not just from their trap contemporaries, but from their own earlier mixtape incarnation. Then, the trio's hyped-up jabber emphasised how hard they worked for success and its spoils. Now, the vibe is imperturbable nonchalance, heard at its utmost on the glistening glide of 'Slippery' and 'Top Down on da NAWF'. That feeling of glazed buoyancy was captured perfectly by writer Jordan Rothlein when he described hearing his own Auto-Tuned voice through headphones for the first time: 'I immediately felt superhuman. The best comparison is walking through an airport and stepping onto one of those conveyor-belt walkways, where suddenly you're walking twice as fast as everyone else with the same amount of effort.' Which is why on the ethereal, almost effete wafting of 'MotorSport', Quavo raps 'I feel like I can fly', while Offset goes further, declaring, 'No human being, I'm immortal'.

The most striking thing about the Migos sound is its sheer splendour, which really does seem to drip and splash with rivulets of light. However hard-hearted and cold-souled the lyrics seem on tracks like 'Narcos' and 'CC' – endless variations on women as sexual disposables to be smashed and dismissed, foes and snitches shot in the face and condemned to a closed-casket funeral, and a persistent leitmotif about not being able to cry – the exuberance of the vocal interplay and its ecstatic texturising speaks to something else: a vulnerability to bliss. Quavo, so phonetically proximate to 'quiver', is the perfect name for the Migos MC most ecstatically merged with Auto-Tune technology. He and Offset seem entranced by themselves, lost in an auto-erotic swirl, draped in a jouissance that seems to seep out of their own bodies as a mist of Auto-Tuned droplets, a self-swaddling canopy of shivers and moans . . .

*

The story of Auto-Tune and its commercial rivals in pitch-correction and vocal design is part of a wider phenomenon: the emergence of the voice as the prime area for artistic adventure and innovation in the twenty-first century. Spanning all the way from Top 40 radio to avant-pop experimentalists, from local dance undergrounds like footwork to internet-spawned micro-genres such as witch house and vaporwave, doing weird shit with the human voice has been the cutting edge for well over a decade now: slowing it down and speeding it up, queering it and mutilating it, micro-editing and resequencing it into new melodic and rhythmic patterns, processing it into amorphous swirly texture-clouds or smearing it across emotional landscapes.

The basic rhythmic grammar of music has not changed as much as we might have expected after the surging advances of the nineties. For the most part, beat-makers have been modify-ing or stretching the groove templates spawned in the late twentieth century: electro, house, techno, jungle, dancehall, post-Timbaland nu-R&B, the Southern style of drum machine driven rap. Instead, the axis of invention has been in the domain of sound-design – the intricate gloss of high-definition production, now achievable more easily and cheaply than ever before – and in the area of vocal manipulation: treating a singer's performance not as a sacrosanct emotional expression to be kept intact but as raw material to be sculpted and, at the extreme, overwritten with new emotional content.

The question that remains is: why? Why is Auto-Tune in particular, and vocal manipulation in general, so pervasive, so epoch-defining? Why does it sound so good? (To some ears, at least – usually younger ears; while other, generally older, ears recoil still from its artificiality.) Finally, why does it sound so right?

It must be because the Auto-Tune sparkle suits the feel of our time. When everything else in the culture is digitally maxed out and hyper-edited, how could the human voice stay unscathed? The sheen of Auto-Tune fits an entertainment landscape of high-definition screens, retina-wrenching 3D camera movements, motion-retouching, and grading that sands down skin-tones into porcelain perfection and makes colours 'pop' with hallucinatory vividness.

When our emotional and social arrangements increasingly occur via info-mechanisms – DMs and FaceTime, Snapchat and Tinder, Instagram and TikTok – and when we habitually use editing and processing to tint and tidy up the image we present of ourselves to the world, it's easy to see why we've got used to pop stars using artificial processes to disguise their imperfect selves, from their videos to what was once thought of as the singer's most intimately innermost possession and deepest per-sonal truth: the voice. It makes absolute sense that Auto-Tuned singing – bodily breath transubstantiated into beyond-human data – is how desire, heartbreak and the rest of the emotions sound today. Digital soul, for digital beings, leading digital lives.

Pitchfork, 2018

BACK TO THE GARDEN: The Eternal Returns of Ambient and New Age

When it comes to chilling out in Los Angeles, you can't do much better than the Central Garden of the Getty Center Museum. Its sloping lawn, winding stream and waterfall were originally landscaped to be a living artwork by Robert Irwin, a Californian artist whose immersive site-specific installations were associated with the Light and Space movement. The Getty garden is unusually halcyon this particular September Saturday: serene synth melodies emerge from the foliage, as part of a celebration for the reissue of Mort Garson's 1976 album *Plantasia*. Back in the seventies the record was only available from a hippie horticulture hang-out on Melrose Avenue called Mother Earth's Boutique, which included a copy of the LP with every purchase of a potted houseplant. Garson's mellow Moog was meant to work as sonic fertiliser.

As with much of the past decade's hipster embrace of New Age sounds, the Getty event hovers in a blurry zone between ironic and earnest. Sideshows include a macramé workshop, a demonstration of plant-aura Kirlian photography, and the opportunity to coax sounds out of a Moog yourself. But there's also a series of performances from serious ambient musicians who've been given the brief to make sounds to nurture plant life. Playing on a stage flanked with shrubs, Gregg Kowalsky's jittery pulses seem more likely to make vegetation slither back into the soil. But when Emily A. Sprague – a member of the aptly named Florist – takes a solo turn, you can practically see the foliage quivering with pleasure at the shimmery sounds she caresses from her synth.

Ambient and nature have long been entwined. *On Land*, the most innovative and amorphously eerie of Brian Eno's ambient albums, was inspired by memories of the 'empty landscapes' of his childhood in Suffolk, England. The association has not always been considered positive: one American *On Land* reviewer sneered, 'I'll bet plants love it.' The implication is that tranquillity is soporific and safe, a middle-aged retreat from the urban edge and restless energy of true youth music.

But this past decade has seen increasing numbers of young listeners turning on, tuning in and dropping off to the sounds of ambient and New Age. And the pastoral motif resurfaces frequently, with a discernible note of desperation in the hankering for some kind of restorative sanctuary of sound. For instance, Huerco S. – one of this decade's leading ambient producers – told *The Fader* that although he records his albums in his Brooklyn apartment, 'it's me wanting to make these sounds for myself that gives me an escape into the nature'. This bucolic impulse has featured outside the bounds of ambient music too: early in 2019, Solange Knowles released the inward-looking *When I Get Home*, an album influenced by *The Secret Life of Plants*, Stevie Wonder's synth-laced soundtrack for a 1978 documentary based on a New Age book about 'the physical, emotional, and spiritual relations between plants and man'.

The connection between ambient and the rustic outdoors goes deeper than the longings that inspire the artists or the kind of imagery they use to title tracks and albums. The slowly and subtly shifting patterns in the music itself have a kinship with natural phenomena: drifting cloud-shapes, the way a breeze ruffles leaves and sways trees, the trickles and flickers of moving water. 'Soft fascinations' like these have been proposed by some therapists as a brain-massaging remedy, a respite from the frantic pace and fixated attention of our digitally overstimulated lifestyles.

In this moment of social media churn and political news overload, the idea of a soniferous panacea that filters and purifies the atmosphere of our living environment as effectively as a potted plant has renewed appeal. So too does the idea of music that induces in the listener a kind of vegetative bliss, that slows down your metabolism and deepens your breathing. Across town from the Getty, in LA hipster haven Highland Park, Leaving Records – a bastion of the nu-New Age – hosts regular Tree Music events, where you can listen to ambient music outdoors. As Leaving founder and ambient musician Matthewdavid says, 'being present and deep listening is very much needed now'.

At first glance, the dominant story in electronic music this past decade is digital maximalism. The 2010s started with EDM in the ascendant: festival headliners like Skrillex and Deadmau5 blitzed audiences with ultra-brite, buzzed-up noise closely synched to retina-scorching CGI animations. Cooler versions of the same absurdly awake sound came from Rustie with the hyperreal euphoria of *Glass Swords* and PC Music with their Top 40 simulation pop. From Iglooghost's kawaii fantasia to Flume's baroque intricacies, there was a common aesthetic of overworked production and overkill effects designed to grab your attention.

And yet you could just as easily construct a counter-narrative of the 2010s in which a completely opposite set of minimalist values – reduction, uneventfulness, calm, whatever the opposite of 'in your face' is – has been ascendant. Wander the internet

265

and you'll find dozens of flavours and substyles of ambient music. Idyllic and glinting in the classic lineage that runs back through nineties chill-out to Eno, Harold Budd and Steve Hillage. Space music in the Steve Roach and Sky Records tradition. Back-to-analogue modular synth wooze. Dark drone with an eldritch pagan feel. Work that feels vaguely liturgical and pre-modern, with devotional vocals and acoustic instrumental textures. And that's before you even drift into adjacent genres that share ambient or easy-listening qualities (vaporwave, hauntology, nu-shoegaze) or that encompass ambient subgenres (postmetal, the psychedelic trance side-genre 'psybient').

If digital maximalist dance is like mainlining a syringe full of Monster Energy drink, this counter-current of ambient and nu-New Age is like a steady intravenous drip of chamomile blended with valerian.

Alongside this sprawling array of contemporary exponents, ambient's foundational legends have been newly active as legacy artists: Eno's run of releases for Warp; The Orb, with a string of albums including *COW (Chill Out, World!)*; Ryuichi Sakamoto's acclaimed *Async*. There's also been an archival drive that made heroes of forgotten figures like Laraaji, K. Leimer, Midori Takada, Suzanne Ciani, Ernest Hood and Ariel Kalma. Reissue labels and album-sharing blogs have reactivated dormant concepts like Fourth World and exotica, and placed New Age, Japanese 'interior music', and library records into the canon of essential listening for young enquiring ears. This influence pool is already shaping an emerging generation of musicians, changing their value-set so that 'soporific' is not an insult but an ideal – an artistic objective, even.

One of the most appealing and endearing aspects of ambient and New Age is that it simply wants to pleasure the listener: these musicians aren't afraid of pleasantness and prettiness. The audio palette encompasses soft-focus sounds, gentle pulses

and chiming textures that carry an idyllic childhood aura
(via music boxes, ice cream vans and so forth). It's a radically
different conception of what music is for than the lineage of
punk, industrial, noise and the harder kinds of techno, where,
as William Thomas of the New Age archival blog/label Sounds
of the Dawn puts it, 'there is a strong tendency to see what is
soft, beautiful or soothing as not artistic, authentic or "real"'.

Hallowed classics they may be now, but on their original
release Eno's early ambient records were generally dismissed
by the punk-era rock press for lacking urgency, relevance and
street cred. For his part, Eno distanced himself from rock
rebellion, the lineage that led from the Stones to Sex Pistols.
Rather than perpetuating adolescent notions of 'intensity',
upheaval or commotion, ambient is a break with youth culture:
it's more like music for babies and children, its twinkling
cycles of sounds resembling an audio equivalent of a mobile
gently gyrating above an infant's crib. Either that or it's like a
hip version of easy-listening music in the Mantovani and Les
Baxter tradition; a kind of elective Muzak for the middle-aged
to destress themselves.

Although New Age was in some ways the ultimate do-
it-yourself music – made by individuals in home studios,
distributed through retail networks outside the record industry
such as headshops – it had no truck with what we generally
think of as a DIY aesthetic: rough-hewn, lo-fi, dirty, distorted.
On the contrary, the production aspired to be limpid and
luxurious. This decade's rehabilitation of New Age chimes with
an across-the-board shift in underground music that started
with chillwave's simultaneously ironic yet sincere appreciation
for yacht rock and has carried on with vaporwave. Words
like 'smooth' or 'slick' no longer have a negative charge; the
polished patina of professionalism in mainstream pop-rock of
the eighties is an aspirational ideal rather than something to

267

kick against. Spencer Doran, who compiled 2019's celebrated *Kankyō Ongaku: Japanese Ambient, Environmental & New Age Music 1980–1990* and makes a modern version of that sound in the group Visible Cloaks, pursues 'high-quality sonics' and says that the equation of lo-fidelity sound with 'authenticity or grit . . . has always felt really disingenuous and phony, like a pair of pre-ripped jeans'.

Designed to work as a form of exquisite audio-decor, Japanese interior music caught Doran's ear around a decade ago, resulting in a pair of celebrated online mixes titled *Fairlights, Mallets and Bamboo*. He also started the imprint Empire of Signs (the title comes from a Roland Barthes book about Japanese culture) to not so much reissue as make available in the West for the first time albums like Hiroshi Yoshimura's *Music for Nine Post Cards*. Alongside the *Kankyō Ongaku* compilation, the culmination of Doran's Japanophile ardour came with this year's *Serenitatem*, a collaboration between Visible Cloaks and veteran musicians Yoshio Ojima and Satsuki Shibano.

Serenitatem is Latin for serenity. The title emerged when Ojima and Doran discussed the hard-to-translate Japanese concept *shizukesa*. 'It can mean tranquillity, stillness or even silence,' explains Doran. 'I have this pet theory that there is this *shizukesa*-like essence in early European pre-classical music forms, that then fell away in the baroque era as things became more bombastic and grand.' But in the twentieth century, composers like Erik Satie and Arvo Pärt discovered medieval forms of monastic music like plainchant. Doran believes that in the late twentieth century both Western and Eastern music started separately 'circling back to this hidden, underlying sense of stillness or serenity encoded deep within our traditions' – an escape from the pressures of modernity itself.

*

New Age's rehabilitation actually started a little over a decade ago in the late 2000s, within that spectrum of DIY sounds variously dubbed hypnagogic pop and chillwave. James Ferraro, hypnagogic pioneer and vaporwave godfather, named his cassette label New Age Tapes. Kindred spirits like Spencer Clark, Emeralds, Dolphins into the Future and Oneohtrix Point Never drew on the wafting synthesiser sounds of Klaus Schulze and Tangerine Dream, as well as Krautrock artists like Manuel Göttsching whose rippling, effects-laden guitar patterns were by the late seventies verging on the New Age zone. Early in the 2010s, blogs like Crystal Vibrations emerged that were specifically dedicated to archival New Age and made long-lost and virtually unfindable recordings available to curious ears.

Alongside these unofficial excavations came a series of landmark double-disc compilations from the Seattle reissue label Lights in the Attic: 2013's *I Am the Center: Private Issue New Age Music in America 1950–1990*; its 2016 Europe-focused sequel *The Microcosm*; and the Spencer Doran-compiled project *Kankyō Ongaku*. Numero Group, another leading archival label, pulled off a conceptual coup by reissuing the entire series of *Environments* albums (originally released by Irv Teibel and his Syntonic Research imprint from the late sixties onwards) as an app that allowed you to immerse yourself in Teibel's pristinely recorded natural soundscapes via your phone. The Environments app wasn't ambient music so much as the ambiences of real-world spaces and weather conditions – a spring afternoon in an English meadow, dusk in a Georgia swamp, a thunderstorm in a pine forest – and it chimed with an uptick in interest in field recordings, nature sounds and even avian music, such as Sub Rosa's reissue of Jean C. Roche's *Birds of Venezuela*. Numero Group's repackaging-without-any-packaging of *Environments* pulled off a double whammy: at once environmentally sound (no carbon footprint from production or transportation) and a canny circumvention of the increasingly fraught business of selling box sets and lavish vinyl reissues.

One of the major New Age archival blogs, William Thomas's Sounds of the Dawn, has evolved into a record label, but it's not in the reissue business. The imprint instead releases new music in the dulcimer-chiming, flute-infused tradition, by artists like Hybrid Palms, a Russian producer whose glinting *Pacific Image* is one of the ambient highlights of the past decade. In addition to fostering contemporary exponents, Sounds of the Dawn also indirectly contributed to spawning the London chill-out club New Atlantis. Co-founder India Jordan describes the blog as 'a huge inspiration' that sparked their interest in the genre. The club/ label's name comes from a cassette they found on Sounds of the Dawn: *New Atlantis*, a 1984 cassette of meditational music by the English musician Frank Perry based around chimes from Tibetan singing bowls, gongs and bells. Perry himself took the name from Francis Bacon's *New Atlantis*, his 1626 novel about an island utopia – mostly likely because of the famous passage about 'sound-houses' in which sounds and harmonies are gener- ated that are 'sweeter than any you have, together with bells and rings that are dainty and sweet'.

New Atlantis the club is itself a mini-utopia in the gritty heart of South London. Taking place on Sunday afternoons at the Peckham record store Rye Wax, it's a place to recover from the stresses of the working week and the excesses of Saturday night alike. 'There's sofas, a rug on the floor,' says Jordan. 'They serve food. People go there to chill, not to get deafened. I actually prefer it not too busy, because if it's rammed you can't hear the music and people start shouting over each other, and then you lose the intimacy and it often drowns out the live acts.' The live performers and DJs mostly play beat-less music ('we do very occasionally let a bpm into the party!' laughs Jordan) and the mixing approach emphasises 'smooth transitions, blends and effects'. Jordan might take their own club-oriented 140 bpm tracks and play them at 30 bpm, 'using effects like reverb and reverse to make new sounds'. Accompanying the emollient music are beatific projections of images that Jordan has collected over the last few years, themed into seasonal sets like Spring or Winter. There are a lot of whales (their life-long favourite animal, but also New Age aligned via the seventies fad for whale-song recordings) along with imagery sourced in 1970s film animations or from the website of Iasos, creator of the 1975 New Age landmark *Inter-dimensional Music*.

The approach to sound and visuals at New Atlantis and at similar ambient events springing up all over recalls the original chill-out culture of the nineties: peripatetic events like Telepathic Fish's ambient tea parties, or the Big Chill, which started out at a North London church but quickly evolved into a huge summer outdoor festival. The first-wave chill-out scene flirted with New Age and hippie ideas in a tongue-in-cheek way, reflected in titles like The Orb's 'Back Side of the Moon', at once a confession of secret Pink Floyd love (then still an embarrassment for the postpunk generation) and a deflation of any cosmic mystic tendencies. You can see a similar sort of playfulness on New Atlantis's first compilation with track titles like 'Gran's Orgasm' by Pre-Emptress and 'Dianetics over MIDI' by L'Ron.

'There's definitely some humour in it,' says Jordan. 'It's important we don't take this too seriously, as it can become quite exclusionary.' Yet Jordan combines nineties-redolent irony with earnest spiritual leanings. Immediately before getting into New Age, they had been exploring meditation and the therapeutic properties of sound baths. 'It's very much a part of New Atlantis. Most people who are involved in it meditate or are spiritually creative in other ways.'

271

Leaving's Matthewdavid likewise is a seeker who's explored esoteric thought: Robert Anton Wilson, Alan Watts, Aleister Crowley, Gurdjieff and the theosophist movement. When I first saw that he'd titled an EP *Ashram*, I assumed it was a joke – but the record was literally recorded at an ashram in Indonesia. 'When we were living there, we had access to this meditation cave, and I would play flute in the cave and record.'

Where New Atlantis's roster is all contemporary producers inspired by the original New Age, Leaving puts out releases by first-wave artists as well as their modern descendants. Sun Path's *Dream Music* is a replica edition of cassettes originally released by Jeff Berry in 1980 and 1984: self-described 'Alternative Realities' music recorded in New Mexico and blending together Prophet synth, a Peyote ceremony water drum, Native American cedar flutes and field recordings of streams and snowstorms. Leaving has also put out exquisite repackagings of self-released 1980s tapes by the prolific New Age composer Laraaji. Creator of *Day of Radiance*, one of the original four Ambient Series LPs produced by Eno, Laraaji is also renowned for his laughter-meditation workshops. He's become a friend and mentor to Matthewdavid, who in turn has promoted Laraaji concerts at the Lodge Room in Highland Park. It's quite a trip to see the seventy-five-year-old African-American performer and his partner Arji OceAnanda stroking rippling chimes from their array of zithers and other metallophonic instruments, while hundreds of young people sit reverently on the hall's floor.

Matthewdavid initially moved to LA to participate in the Low End Theory beat-scene of artists like Flying Lotus. But crate digging in bargain basements led him to pick up prerecorded New Age cassettes from the 1970s and '80s, lured by both their off-the-map obscurity and their garish artwork. He found himself falling for even the most kitsch subgenres of the music: 'Pan

flute music, Celtic Heart music, Spa Music'. Although he made
(and still makes) beat-based and glitchy music, he created an
alter ego – Matthewdavid's Mindflight – for his ambient releases
like *Trust the Guide and Glide*. The goal was, he says, to 'really
hone in on New Age as an identity and try to reinvent or update
what that could mean now'. Leaving has become an outlet for
similarly aligned figures in the LA area like modular synth freak
M. Geddes Gengras and the devotional-vocal artist Ana Roxanne,
whose recent and wonderful LP contains songs with titles like
'I'm Every Sparkly Woman' and 'It's a Rainy Day on the Cosmic
Shore'.

Although people are tuning into the nu-New Age vibration all
over America – Sounds of the New Dawn is based out of Michigan and there's the nomadic event series Ambient Church in
New York – Los Angeles does seem to be a hub. Kaitlyn Aurelia
Smith, for instance, lives in Glendale, on the east side of the city,
and earlier this year did her own event at the Getty's Central
Garden: a performance of *Tides: Music for Meditation and Yoga*
('bring your own mat' urged the invitation), a work written
for Smith's mother that weaves electronics and field-recorded
nature sounds together. Ancestral figures live in the city, too,
like Harold Budd, famed for his soft-focus Satie-style piano as
heard most famously on the Eno collaboration *The Plateaux of
Mirror*, and Jon Hassell, conceptualist of Fourth World Music
and another Eno accomplice.

California is the historical well-spring for New Age thought,
the focus for most of the experimentation with consciousness,
spiritual research and esoteric therapy that Theodore Roszak
characterised as 'the Aquarian Frontier' in his 1975 book
Unfinished Animal. That same year saw the publication of
Ecotopia, Ernest Callenbach's science fiction near-future vision
of a West Coast that's broken away from the rest of America

to form a green-conscious, non-competitive society. These are the same states who currently form a rebel alliance against Trump's attempts to roll back environmental protections and open up Federal lands for the extraction and logging industries.

Yet California is also associated with a dot-com libertarian ethos spawned out of Silicon Valley. Promulgated from the early nineties onwards in magazines like *Wired* and *Mondo 2000*, it's been called the Californian Ideology: an evangelical mania for the exciting new frontier of maverick individualism that information technology would open up.

It's as though the counterculture split in two, with one strand (drives towards freedom, adventure, exhilarating chaos) going down the disruptor path and the other (the peace and spiritual-surrender impulses) going into the contemplative withdrawal and self-healing of New Age.

Looking at the modern world, you might almost say that the stresses and psychic toll resulting from the global triumph of the first set of impulses *require* the solace and recuperation of the second strand.

'I feel uneasy about the wellness movement broadly, as it's inherently linked to individualistic ways of healing under capitalism,' says India Jordan. 'The idea that a £5-a-month Headspace subscription' – they're referring to a smartphone app that offers guided meditations – 'will cure the overbearing pressure we feel trying to survive under a non-sustainable and destructive system – it feels like a bit of a plaster over a bigger issue.' For his part, Matthewdavid rejects the notion that New Age music or meditation is a mere escape, preferring to see it as a necessary coping mechanism. 'It's remedial because it helps me find my centre, so that I can manage my stress and proceed in the world without anxiety. This music helps facilitate that state from which I'm able to feel better about interacting in this current world.'

Whether the impetus is entirely personal or a semi-conscious response to the runaway train of geopolitical instability, many people involved in ambient and New Age see the music as something close to self-medication. Sounds of the Dawn's Thomas says his New Age conversion coincided with 'a stressful time in my life. I came upon Constance Demby's *Starborn* tape at a Salvation Army resale shop . . . It helped calm me down and put me in a better place mentally. So after that I just started looking for anything like that.' M. Geddes Gengras quipped on Twitter that 'I make ambient music because I was too scared to go to therapy for 20 years & synthesizers seemed cheaper.' Framing his Optimo label's Fourth World compilation *Miracle Steps*, DJ Twitch spoke of escaping into 'musical dreamworlds' as a necessary response to 'completely messed up times'. Last year ambient veteran K. Leimer released *Irrational Overcast*, an album explicitly framed as a remedial response to the toxic 'clouds of baseless beliefs and simplistic ideologies' choking our culture and straining nervous systems to snapping point.

Beyond the boom in blissed-out soundscapes, the 2010s has seen a sort of ambient-ising of other genres – including some that would seem to be politically and philosophically about as distant from New Age values as imaginable, such as trap and its variants like UK drill. Lyrically, it's toxic masculinity a-go-go: the same old shit of egomania, misogyny, commodity-fetishism and violence. Yet the music has an undeniably ambient quality, draping glistening wooze over the hard beats-and-bass, with wistful melody-riffs looping endlessly in a way that recalls the more idyllic kinds of nineties IDM. In many ways, trap is one of the last bastions of minimalism on the radio.

You could call it Ambien Music, after the sedative-hypnotic prescription drug, given the way that trap MCs incessantly reference painkilling, anxiety-deadening drugs like Percocet and Xanax. Although these pills are ostensibly taken as illegal highs, you have to wonder why this genre's defining affect is a kind of insulated numbness, why so many of the MCs seem glazed and oddly passive. Auto-Tune etherialises rappers like Quavo, Lil Uzi Vert and Playboi Carti (with his famous 'baby' voice) to the point where they sometimes seem barely there: angelic boy-men whose ego-boundaries are melting in the dissociative drug haze. The generic nature of the beats and the restricted range of timbres . . . the relative indistinguishability of MCs, which is further exacerbated by Auto-Tune . . . the repetitious themes and tropes and vocal tricks . . . these are not bugs but features. Achieving its effects through accumulative sameness, trap is designed for immersive and inattentive listening: it's purpose-built to slip back into being background music, the soundtrack to driving or chilling.

But then streaming seems to turn almost everything into background sound. You are generally listening to a streaming service on a device (a computer or smartphone) that practically forces you to multi-task, making it irresistibly tempting to plug into parallel culture-streams or obsessively follow the newsfeed. There is an inbuilt tendency towards partial attention and distracted listening, which in turn subtly encourages you to avoid things that demand full-on engagement. Last year saw a spate of investigative pieces in magazines exploring the partnership between Warner Bros. and the German company Endel to create customised soundtracks to everyday life, or discussing the implications of Spotify's mood-based playlists. Some of these playlists are overtly characterised as 'chill' modes for relaxation or as an aid to sleep, while others promise enhanced focus in the work situation or a peppy soundtrack to activity. The rise of what Liz Pelly characterised as a personalised form of 'emotional wallpaper' certainly has an unsettling and insidious aspect to it, seeming to represent a new kind of Muzak that is not imposed by bosses looking to increase productivity but actively embraced by the individual in the name of self-optimisation.

Yet, in a way, we've always used music to drug ourselves – to alter our moods, to transform the vibe in a social setting, to accompany activities like driving or housework or (since at least the invention of the portable music player) exercise, and to dull the ache of solitude. The Scottish postpunk group Fire Engines released a mini-LP of 'background beat for active people' titled *Lubricate Your Living Room* way back in 1981, a high-energy punky riposte to Eno's ambient series.

Still, there is something unnerving about the idea of ambient and New Age uncoupled from any higher purposes and applied to the task of self-repair. Like power yoga or micro-dosing, it is taking an agent of change that was originally part of a culture of liberation and discovery and putting it in service of the status quo. As David Toop, author of ambient bible *Ocean of Sound*, wrote, 'if ambient music only serves as an app to incentivise or a backdrop to productivity, networking and self-realisation, then it has no story of its own, no story worth hearing'.

There are already signs of a backlash against this therapeutic notion of ambient from musicians, or at least a redefinition that enlarges the scope of what ambient can encompass. In a recent Resident Advisor podcast, Huerco S. declared his desire to 'push back' against the idea of ambient as 'some sort of "cure-all", by making the music 'darker, more unpleasant, less forgiving, less holistic'. Sold, in her own RA podcast, argued that 'sometimes ambient isn't about self-care, sometimes it's about self-obliteration'. This shift-to-sinister echoes a similar turn that took place within the nineties ambient scene. Reacting against an overload of blissed-out beatific soundscapes from labels like Fax, artists moved into zones of eerie emptiness that

277

the producer/critic Kevin Martin (now best known as The Bug) dubbed 'isolationism'. The paradigm example of this evolution was the leap between Aphex Twin's first *Selected Ambient Works* album in 1992, with its idyllic melodies and fluffy textures, and the shivery sound-vapours of its 1994 sequel, *Selected Ambient Works Volume II*. From chill-out to chilly . . .

It's another sunny Saturday in LA and Leaving Music are holding one of their Tree Music parties. The location is a charming little public garden on the edge of Highland Park called La Tierra de la Culebra. 'Listen to music outside in the daylight under a tree,' the flyer suggests. Sure enough, the sound system and performance space are directly underneath an enormous canopy of dense leaves. Listeners gather on blankets under the branches or nestle in the hillside alcoves of mosaic stone. Birdsong from inside the trees blends beautifully with the purring and chirruping sounds coming out of the speakers. Leaving Records T-shirts are suspended from a low-hanging branch, available for purchase. A 'psychedelicatessen' offers vegan dosas and tea laced with powdered medicinal mushrooms that supply 'mental clarity' but leave a bitter tang in the mouth.

The vibes and sounds at Tree Music trigger a pleasant sense of déjà vu as I flash back to chill-out afternoons and illbient nights I attended in the 1990s. I get a similar atemporal feeling listening to this decade's ambient and nu-New Age. The juxtaposition of so much high-quality reissued material with the prolific outpour of contemporary exponents exacerbates this sensation: it's often hard to tell whether a record was made in the 1970s, or the 1990s, or the 2010s. Take Celer's 2018 *Coral Sea* – a gorgeous record, one of the decade's best, but in its texture and mood, not necessarily a huge advance on Eno's *Discreet Music* from 1975, even though its mode of construction is probably quite different.

'There's a good Eno quote, "I guess I want music to do the same thing to me, but to do it in a different way",' says Droid, who co-hosts the Dublin-based net-radio show *No Place Like Drone*. When the fundamental function of the music is abiding, the most effective ways of achieving those ends get discovered quite early and settle into place as relatively invariant features: a palette of textures and atmospheres that includes tuned-percussion chimes, piano shrouded in a halo of pedal echo, lambent synth pads, billowing drone-tones, dainty daubs of texture like Japanese calligraphy, reverberant space and shimmering horizons.

Droid regards the 2010s as a boom time for ambient and its sonic relatives, in both quantity and quality. He estimates that 40 per cent of all the ambient ever made was recorded during the 2010s. Digital technology – from distribution platforms like Bandcamp to laptop-producer-friendly programs like soft synths – has eliminated many of the obstacles and production costs that might have deterred earlier aspiring ambient composers, resulting in a DIY explosion. But amid the overload and redundancy, Droid also detects a bustle of invention and fresh directions. Notable developments include an increased number of women (including Grouper, Ekin Fil, Juliana Barwick, Áine O'Dwyer, Sarah Davachi, to name only a few) making this music, many using their ethereal or mystical-flavoured vocals prominently. Conversely, there's been what Droid half-jestingly calls 'manbient' or 'power ambient', as purveyed by the likes of Ben Frost – 'tunes that start quiet and get really noisy and distorted, or have a heavy emphasis on over-the-top sound design'. But Droid is not sure that either of those trends, or others like the boom for modular synth hardware, constitutes progression as such. 'It's more like an amalgamation or an accretion.'

Given that a fundamental impulse within this whole area of music is to suspend time, it kinda makes sense that

279

the genre wouldn't evolve in any kind of discernibly linear fashion. Rather it would logically work through cycles that recur inexactly, resulting in incremental changes and gradual growth. 'Maybe the function of the music itself is mirrored by an amorphousness in how the genre develops: stasis in form, function and content,' muses Droid. Each ambient piece in its edge-of-motionlessness is a microcosm of the slow movement of the genre as a whole.

The 'new' in New Age was always something of a misnomer, given that it proposed a flight from modernity, the rediscovery of lost spiritual wisdom, the recovery of a way of living at once grounded yet tuned into the transcendent. In the seventies, New Age music offered listeners, trapped in the urban rat-race, audio capsules of pastoral peace to transform their homes into havens. Today the internet and social media form a kind of postgeographic urban space, an immaterial city of information whose hustle 'n' bustle is even more wearing and deleterious to our equilibrium. Little wonder that some of us are wistfully turning to sounds that reconnect us with a world where 'tweet' simply signified a sound issuing from the beak of a bird.

As Laurel Canyon denizen Joni Mitchell once sang, 'we've got to get ourselves back to the garden'. In the meantime, a potted plant, an edible and a hammered dulcimer LP will have to do.

Resident Advisor, 2020

CONCEPTRONICA

Conceptual electronica has been in the ascendant for most of the 2010s, but in many ways its peak arrived with producer Chino Amobi's 2017 opus *Paradiso*. Baroque with details, and teeming with the voices and instrumental contributions of over twenty collaborators, the album had Amobi drawing direct inspiration from epic narratives like the *Odyssey* and Dante's *Inferno*, along with complex videogames like *Final Fantasy 7*. Like many of his conceptronica peers, Amobi's ambition sprawls laterally into parallel forms. As he explains from his Richmond, Virginia home, he envisions merging *Paradiso* with his current project – a book/soundtrack titled *Eroica*, based on his Fine Arts master's thesis – and developing the composite into spin-offs in other media: a film, a graphic novel, a theatrical play, an art exhibition, even garment production. 'It's like these layers upon layers,' he says.

The term conceptronica came to me way back in 2006 when reviewing a Matmos album. But concept-driven electronic music wasn't a particularly new thing even then. In the nineties, the Frankfurt label Mille Plateaux named itself after the French title of *A Thousand Plateaus: Capitalism and Schizophrenia*, a deliriously dense philosophical work by Gilles Deleuze and Félix Guattari. The label's best-known outfit Oval could spiel with intimidating rigour about the cultural ramifications of digital technology. Another Mille Plateaux artist

Terre Thaemlitz released a series of covers albums dedicated to iconic synthpop artists like Kraftwerk and Gary Numan, accompanied by queer-theory-infused polemical essays.

Still, it certainly feels like electronic music's conceptual bent went into overdrive during the 2010s. At some point I noticed a steady stream of press releases started arriving in my inbox that read like the text at the entrance of an art exhibition. I also became aware that the way I engaged with these releases actually resembled a visit to a museum or gallery: often listening just once, while reading reviews and interviews with the artist that could be as forbiddingly theoretical as a vintage essay from *Artforum*. These conceptual works rarely seemed like records to live alongside in a casual, repeat-play way. They were statements to encounter and assimilate, developments to keep abreast of. Their framing worked as a pitch to the browsing consumer, not so much to buy the release but to buy *into* it as valid and timely.

Conceptronica isn't a genre as such, but more like a mode of artistic operation – and audience reception – that cuts across the landscape of hip music, from high-definition digital abstraction to styles like vaporwave and hauntology. It's a macro-genre, where the coherence of the field isn't related to shared sonic features so much as the value system, procedures, assumptions and expectations of musicians and listeners. Concept-driven projects offer a way for artists to compete in an attention economy that is oversupplied while reflecting their enthusiasm for a vast array of ideas. Most of the leading conceptronica artists have been through art school or postgraduate academia, and they're comfortable speckling both their work and their conversation with references to critical theory and philosophy. During our interview, Chino Amobi brings up everyone from the black studies and performance scholar Fred Moten to the 1990s theory collective Cybernetic

Culture Research Unit. Hyperdub producer Lee Gamble
likewise enthuses to me about the inspiration sparked by
listening to an unofficial audiobook of Deleuze and Guattari's
A Thousand Plateaus.

This high-powered discourse contrasts with the relatively
down-to-earth vernacular of nineties IDM luminaries like Aphex
Twin's Richard D. James and Luke Vibert, whose records
were more likely to be daubed with puerile humour and porn
references than concepts from poststructuralism. Another major
difference between conceptronica and old skool IDM is that the
latter could be used as a relaxing background shimmer, a spur
to unthinking reverie rather than intellectual musing.

For sure, there had always been intellectuals involved
in techno-rave, people with philosophical interests or who
came from art backgrounds. Still, electronica in the past was
predominantly non-verbal: it *sonified* more than it signified.
Even when techno artists made works that addressed a 'theme'
(Wolfgang Voigt's Gas, Jeff Mills, Drexciya), the sonic outcome
tended to be open-ended and abstract. But with the conceptronica of the 2010s, the textual element is so imbricated with
the sonics that a work's significance is far more predetermined.
The listener's role is to be the recipient of a meaning placed
there by the artist.

Fluent in the critical lingua franca used in art institutions
and academia worldwide, conceptronica artists know how to
self-curate: they can present projects in terms that translate
smoothly into proposals and funding applications. Which is
handy, because what sustains these artists is not revenue
from record releases but performances on an ever-growing
international circuit of experimental music festivals, along with
subsidised concerts at museums and universities. Often trained
in the visual arts rather than music theory, conceptronica artists increasingly resemble figures like Matthew Barney, whose

work involves multiple media and is staged on a grand scale, more than IDM pioneers like Autechre, whose focus has always been overwhelmingly on sonic experimentation.

Despite these differences, 1990s IDM and 2010s conceptronica are similarly positioned in terms of their relationship with the electronic dance mainstream. IDM was a minority-interest adjunct to the drug-fuelled rave culture. Its producers took aspects of functional styles like techno but muted their dance imperative to create something that worked as introspective home-listening. Or they would push the formal features of genres like jungle – the chopped, sped-up breakbeats – towards dysfunctional extremes, making them both challengingly avant-garde and slapstick silly.

Conceptronica, likewise, often has a warped-mirror relationship with contemporary dance styles: hence the rise of the term 'deconstructed club'. Associated with Berlin's PAN label, a hub for conceptronica artists, Amnesia Scanner and M.E.S.H. have both gleaned inspiration from the bombastic Eurotechno sound known as hardstyle. Fellow PAN artist Stine Janvin's *Fake Synthetic Music* is an oblique homage to rave based entirely on manipulating the sound of her own voice. Others warp and mutilate hedonistic rap and R&B styles: Venezuelan producer Arca's early track 'Doep' resembled 50 Cent slipping into a coma.

Where IDM was a running commentary on rave and club trends as they went down in real time, conceptronica is also able to ransack the archive of dance history. On tracks like 'The Shape of Trance to Come', Lorenzo Senni, an Italian producer who's recorded for legendary experimental electronica labels Warp and Mego, remodels the Euro style that filled nineties superclubs with fluffy euphoria. Lee Gamble's 2012 debut for PAN, *Diversions 1994–96*, consisted of memory mirages of jungle raves in the English Midlands – not period-precise retro recreation but more like a ritual conjuring of the intensities he experienced during his misspent teenage years.

Conceptual electronic music still draws sustenance from dance music at its most mental and mindless – beats purpose-built for druggy all-night bacchanals. But although it uses the rhythmic tools of body music, it doesn't primarily aim to elicit a physical response. It's music to contemplate with your ears, to think about and think with. In that sense, it's closer to an art exhibition of photographs or video taken at a bygone club than actual club music. Gamble's *Diversions*, in fact, closely parallels the visual artist Mark Leckey's celebrated found-footage work *Fiorucci Made Me Hardcore*, an elegy for British working-class dance cultures like rave and Northern soul.

Amnesia Scanner – the Berlin-based duo Martti Kalliala and Ville Haimala – bring up a visual artform, albeit a lowbrow and pulpy one, when describing their work: videogames. They compare Amnesia Scanner to 'a game-design studio'. The idea of 'point of view' guides them during the recording and mixing process, in which they use binaural elements to simulate 360-degree surround sound. 'While it's us building this world, we are not in the centre of it,' says Haimala.

'World-building' is one of the buzz terms of 2010s left-field music, popping up in interviews and reviews so frequently it's verging on cliché. There was even an album titled *World Building*, by the enigmatic dark-ambient artist White Goblin, released via the international netlabel Quantum Natives. Several artists on Quantum, like Recsund's Clifford Sage, work in game design and 3D animation: their music is conceived in tandem with the videos they place on YouTube and is meant to be experienced as a single unified artform.

The ambition to build worlds clearly owes a lot to the pervasiveness of games as a generational youth pastime. It also connects with the popularity of young-adult fiction and dystopian-fantasy franchises in television and film. Digital audio software provides similar superpowers to CGI: the user can conjure the illusion of moving within a realistic yet fantastical alternative reality, immense in scale and impossibly detailed. Hubris and grandiosity – if not an outright god-complex – seem like occupational hazards.

Immensity of scale applies to not just the physical dimensions of these virtual worlds, but their propensity to extend themselves through time. In his book *Digimodernism*, the critic Alan Kirby identifies 'onwardness and endlessness' as hallmarks of twenty-first-century culture: page-turning propulsiveness, the unfolding of saga-like narratives teeming with plotlines, characters and locations, spawning prequels and sequels galore.

Thinking big has become endemic in marginal music. Vaporwave godfather James Ferraro is working on an epic project entitled *Four Pieces for Mira*: a cycle of four records, plus a prelude EP, accompanied by a 600-page text. Lee Gamble is halfway through a trilogy – or, as he prefers to put it, a 'triptych' – for Hyperdub: an audio-allegory about late capitalism bearing the cryptic title *Flush Real Pharynx*. Released early this year, the first instalment, *In a Paraventral Scale*, gets its name from a type of snake scale, which doubles as a reference to a nineties jungle classic (Source Direct's 'Snake Style') and a sideways allusion to 'the way capitalism works – slick, shape-shifting, seducing you with beautiful objects'.

Merging sound and vision, dance and concept, into a work of 'total art' is a longstanding aspiration that goes back through the multimedia happenings of the 1960s, via the idea of *Gesamtkunstwerk* – 'total artwork' – popularised by German composer Richard Wagner in the nineteenth century, all the way to the

286

ancients with their indivisible blends of poetry, drama, song, dance and ritual. Rave embraced lights, lasers and projections as a way to enhance and amplify the culture's escape into a hallucinatory asylum from reality. But in the 1990s the visuals were generally only a loosely coordinated accompaniment to what the DJs or live performers were doing. Music remained the main attraction.

What's striking about electronic dance culture in the 2010s is the audio-visual turn that has taken place across the board, from the crowd-pleasing mainstream to the arty margins. EDM behemoths like Skrillex provide pulpy thrills by splaying across giant screen towers a spectacle of CGI animation and projection mapping to match the music's rollercoaster spills. Meanwhile, on the experimental festival circuit, the visuals are more abstract and abject – mutational grotesquerie, dissolving forms – courtesy of collaborations between the likes of Arca and video-maker Jesse Kanda. This cross-contamination between the visual arts and experimental electronica has become such a hot zone that PAN have started an imprint, Entopia, dedicated to music written for art, film, theatre, dance and fashion.

Indeed, there is something of an audio-visual arms race going on within what the writer Geeta Dayal mischievously dubs 'the festival-industrial complex': musicians competing with each other not just to wow audiences but for places on the line-ups. Festivals increasingly look not just for someone who can deliver a slamming DJ set or sonically stunning performance, but for world-exclusive premieres of a new show that impacts with the avant-garde equivalent of razzle-dazzle.

'The idea of going on stage with a laptop and lighting done by some person you've never met before – that just doesn't make any sense at this point,' says Gamble. 'The expectation is a lot higher than that.' That puts more pressure on artists to create visuals that work in tandem with the music. But it's not like a sound-art exhibit in a gallery, something to be appreciated in a low-key, ruminative way. Gamble adds, 'At a festival, you need that immediacy and impact, something that can hit people fast and hard.'

Gamble realised a while back that, alongside limited-edition vinyl and streaming services, the festival stage is the primary place where his work lives, but also the main way he makes a living. Accordingly, he has teamed up with Quantum Natives' Clifford Sage, who works with world-building gaming software, to create a show around *In a Paraventral Scale*. For the track 'BMW Shuanghuan X5' – thematically inspired by a Chinese black-market copy of a BMW and incorporating Doppler-effect samples of the vehicle in motion – Sage developed a video accompaniment in which virtual car components assemble themselves in response to Gamble's sonic triggers. The sound and visuals bring out the themes of the record: the seductive mystique of brands, and the way that consumer desire cannot distinguish between the authentic original and the fakesimile but still mystically believes there is a difference worth paying for.

A quest for another sort of authenticity – the paid-for privilege of being present at an Event – fuels what Amnesia Scanner call 'the experience economy' of today's festivals. Just as much as bottle-service raves on cruise ships or EDM gatherings like Electric Daisy Carnival, experimental music festivals are selling exclusivity and a sense of occasion. There's a seemingly ever-growing number of these gatherings – Unsound, Flow, RMBA, Supernormal, Decibel, Nuits Sonores, Supersonic and many more – along with all-year-round arts institutions like Somerset House in London. Some are funded by national or local government, or by arts and culture ministries; others draw financing from corporate sponsors.

'Europe is so full of these festivals now, and it's very often where our music happens,' says Amnesia Scanner's Haimala. 'Kids don't necessarily have so much money that they would buy individual tickets to concerts by our kind of artist, but they will invest in a festival ticket. So that's where the competition started between artists – everyone trying to do more ambitious shows.' He points out that many of these festivals have music by night and a conference element by day, with panels and lectures. This discourse in turn feeds into the theory-buzzing roil around conceptronica. The festival circuit, adds Kalliala, 'has created a demographic that can be marketed to'.

The audio-visual turn made by experimental electronica makes sense given its immersive ambitions: if world-building is your goal, then rather than just create the sounds that *inspire* mental movies, why not make the movies themselves too? With games and CGI-laden fantasies, the impetus behind world-building is leaving reality behind for a zone of adventures that are thrilling but *safe*. What's different about the recent wave of conceptronica is its engagement with the real world in all its alienation and danger. As much as world-building, the impetus is world-*changing*, or at least world-critiquing.

Alongside the conceptualism and the audio-visuality, there has been a political turn in 2010s electronic music: artists making explicit statements and striking committed stances, often rooted in minority identity based around race, sexuality or gender. This contrasts with earlier phases of dance culture, where the politics were more implicit.

House music came out of the gay underground and rep-resented values of pride, acceptance, unity and love, but as shared subliminal principles far more than declared positions. Jungle likewise expressed its worldview as vibe rather than ideology: its tense rhythms and menacing bass sonically expressed an attitude of militancy and street realism, which occasionally came into focus through roots reggae or gangsta rap samples about Babylon falling or the police, but generally avoided overt statements. As used in a whole swath of different scenes and subcultures, the word 'underground' itself was at once potent and vague: it evoked opposition to the corporate music industry and mainstream values, but fell short of a defined politics.

Informed by the self-reflexive awareness of its makers and their background in higher education, conceptronica is a lot more clear-cut and committed. This new politicisation partly reflects the urgency of the present. Having created purely abstract works that drew inspiration from his formative rave experiences or from arcane research into aural hallucination, Lee Gamble felt that everything changed in 2016. 'Brexit was happening, Trump was happening, and I was like, "Am I now supposed to make an ambient record for everyone to just zone out?"' he says. 'In these times, making music about escapism would be a cop-out.'

In some quarters, though, a shift was discernible well before the horrific lurch towards populist authoritarianism and xenophobia that has convulsed the world these past four years. This drive towards addressing real-world issues began during the Obama years, drawing on the same post-crash discontents about inequality, precarious work patterns, and the seeming impunity of the global financial class that fuelled the Occupy movement and the student protests in Britain.

In 2015, UK producer Jack Latham made what then seemed like an unusual intervention with his second album as Jam City. *Dream a Garden* featured for the first time his fragile vocals singing politically conscious lyrics that blended rage and sorrow. The video for the single 'Unhappy' consisted of a montage of shopping malls, armed police, advertisement hoardings, drone strikes seen from above, and gaunt models taking selfies against a backdrop of urban decay. At the end, Latham walks away from the camera with the slogan 'Class War' visible on the back of his jacket, then the inspirational message 'Stop Being Afraid – Another World Is Possible' flickers across the screen.

In interviews, Latham spoke of how the power structure wanted people to be miserable and isolated, atomised individuals competing for scraps left by the plutocracy and drugging themselves with narcotic entertainments. Reflecting this state of affairs, even dissecting it, wasn't enough: *Dream a Garden* was a paean to the power of collectively envisioning a better life.

This shift to earnest and somewhat heavy-handed polemic ('Love Is Resistance' was another Jam City slogan of this era) was all the more striking given how glossily surface-oriented Latham's 2012 album *Classical Curves* had been. That record was about the seductive power of 'the aesthetics of wealth' – fashion runways, status brands, velvet-rope glamour – with the sorcerous allure of artifice and illusion seemingly left unchallenged. Now, according to Latham, 'we don't really have the luxury to just be repulsed and fascinated' by the 'visual culture' of hyper-capitalism. Instead, it was time to 'really be clear about what side you stand on'.

Latham's trope of the garden as utopia cropped up later in 2015 on *THE GREAT GAME: FREEDOM FROM MENTAL POISONING (The Purification of the Furies)*, a collaboration between Chino Amobi and the Houston, Texas producer Rabit. What sounds like a female GPS voice on its 'professional British woman' setting repeatedly declares: 'We will find our way back to the garden.' Recalling the thinking behind the project, Amobi talks of a politically engaged music that is 'helping and healing' as much as angry and militant; when the newsfeed

291

pumps so much toxic stress through your system, a politics that only amplifies rage and dread is counterproductive.

The specific inspiration for the 'freedom from mental poisoning' concept, though, was 'this idea of overclocking', says Amobi, referring to tricks by which users can increase the computation speed of their technology. For Rabit and Amobi, overclocking served as a metaphor for a media culture and a digital way of life that was morbidly accelerated and over-stimulated – with not just distressing news and inflammatory views, but advertising and the habit-forming endorphin buzzes triggered by social media use.

Where Amobi and Rabit's music is cyberpunk and dystopian in vibe, Holly Herndon – the Berlin-based American producer who's the most well-known conceptualist in contemporary electronica – offers a more optimistic vision of 'science fiction politics'. Drawing on the expertise of a bevy of technocrats and futurologists when she makes records, she can come across a bit like the Elizabeth Warren of electronica, brimming with can-do confidence and problem-solving pluck. While she's keen to stress that there is a critical attitude to technology involved in her work, Herndon says, 'I'm all about trying to feel agency with the technology that I'm using, and trying to imbue my audience with a sense of agency. When things go down the purely dystopian angle, I start to feel kind of hopeless. That cedes control to those who are already in power, already driving the narrative.'

Proto, Herndon's latest album, builds a bridge between the choral church music of her Tennessee childhood and the congregations of sinners at house clubs and raves. Using the pooled voices of around 300 people – a core ensemble of experimental vocalists, plus the contributions of a live concert hall audience, plus the artificial intelligence program Spawn – *Proto* is all about tapping into 'some sort of shared release' and 'communal catharsis', says Herndon. 'That's what I've been craving. We have figured out a lot of ways to spend time with each other online, but I think people need to be emotional with each other in real time and real space.'

Besides the political concerns and the interest in music as a remedy for alienation, another thing that Holly Herndon, Jack Latham and Chino Amobi have in common is that they all stepped out in front of their own music. It's as though the politicisation of electronic music demanded visibility: putting yourself on the line, facially and vocally. Amobi started out making low-profile electronic noise as Diamond Black Hearted Boy, but ultimately decided that the artistic alias had been a mask behind which he no longer wished to hide.

Along with using his given name, Amobi placed his image on the front of *Paradiso*, whose cover is an identity card that certifies him as a citizen of Non Worldwide – as though the label was a transnational political entity of dissident dreamers. In contrast to Amobi's defiant stare, Herndon gazed into the far distance on the front of 2015's *Platform*, unblinking blue eyes trained on a brighter tomorrow. In electronic dance history terms, Amobi is Detroit techno unit Underground Resistance, embattled, but this time with the masks off; Herndon is Chicago house legend Joe Smooth, dreaming of the promised land.

The public positioning of oneself in terms of identity politics has become so intensified this past decade that it would be surprising if electronic music wasn't affected. Amobi observes that the 'post-blogosphere' of Twitter, Facebook and Instagram has introduced a new 'level of words and articulation. Certain people find the voices that they identify more with in social media, and they find support there. People feel more confident to speak and articulate.'

Amobi and Non Worldwide are part of a loose network of queer and trans electronic artists that includes Elysia

Crampton, Arca, Lotic and SOPHIE. All make music as genre-nonconforming as it is gender-nonconforming, blurring the boundaries not just between contemporary and archival dance genres but between the rave tradition and noise, industrial and *musique concrète*. Like Amobi putting his imaginary ID card on the front of *Paradiso*, these artists figure prominently in their own music, rather than standing to one side of it. They use their voices, they feature in artwork and in videos, and live, there is often a theatrical staging of the artist as a physical being that contrasts with the relatively faceless and disembodied way that left-field electronic music has tended to present in the past. Arca's current project – a four-part experimental cycle titled *Mutant; Faith* that blends theatre, technology, design and sound – shows how increasingly conceptronic artists are performers as much as producers.

SOPHIE's 'Faceshopping' is a striking example of the producer stepping forward to front her music. The 2018 song and video work simultaneously as a critique and a celebration of the idea of self-as-brand, drawing inspiration equally from twenty-first-century social media and from the tradition of flamboyant display in ballroom and drag. A digital simulacrum of SOPHIE's face – already a stylised mask of makeup – is shattered and reconstituted using computer-animation effects.

From 'Faceshopping' and *Paradiso* to Arca's recent vocally oriented work, another common quality is a sense of drama and expressionistic excess hovering in an undecidable zone between euphoria and dysphoria. Apocalyptic theatricality is a thread running through Amobi's work, from the courtly trap of 'The Prisoners of Nymphaion' to the baroque EBM of 'Blood of the Covenant'. And tracks like 'Power' and 'Distribution of Care', by the Berlin-based producer Lotic, are full of peaky dissonances and nerve-shredding, high-end sounds.

If a single sonic motif runs through a large proportion of conceptronica, it's the crashing drum – a dramatic effect that sounds ceremonial and regal, but also vaguely punitive, like the smash of a police baton, or evocative of urban unrest, like the tinkling of a shattered window or riot shield. This imposing but ungroovy approach to percussion – probably first heard on Jam City's *Classical Curves* – is a key factor in what the critic Matthew Phillips identifies as a 'neo-futurist' aesthetic in electronic music. Discontinuities and ruptures replace steady dance beats. This is how club music should sound, it's implied, in the age of drone strikes and tweetstorms: not lulling dancers into a hypnotic trance but placing them on red alert.

The agitprop sector within conceptual electronica is woke music, in all senses. 'Using cacophony and unusual sonics, I reject the passive experience of listening, and try to use sounds that are active to wake the listener up and to bring them into the moment,' Amobi has said. This rhetoric recalls the postpunk band This Heat, whose song 'Sleep' agitated against consumerism and entertainment as mass sedation. In conceptronica and postpunk alike, there's a similar interest in demystification and seeing through the blizzard of lies: when Lee Gamble uses the late theorist Mark Fisher's term 'semioblitz' – the desire-triggering, anxiety-inciting bombardment of today's infoculture – I'm reminded of Gang of Four's 'Natural's Not in It' and its line about advertising as 'coercion of the senses'.

But you can also sense some of the same problems that afflicted postpunk, especially in its later years, when it reached an impasse. With conceptronica, there can be a feeling, at times, of being lectured. There's the perennial doubt about the efficacy of preaching to the converted. And there is also a disconcerting disjuncture between the anti-elitist left politics and the class-bound reality of the milieu, so heavily embedded with and dependent upon higher education and arts institutions.

As stimulating as conceptronica can be, something about it has long nagged at me. If its subject, in the broadest sense, was liberation, why then did I not feel liberated listening to it? It rarely provided that sense of release or abandon that you got with nineties rave or even from more recent dissolute forms like trap, whose commodity-fetishism and sexual politics are counter-revolutionary but which sonically brings the bliss.

I also wonder whether edification is really what I'm looking for from music. Certainly, with music at least notionally tied to the club and rave tradition, the desire is much more about the brain being temporarily disabled by a flood of sensation, about being overwhelmed by the physicality of sound. Conceptual electronica references those traditions of ritualised collective abandon but rarely provides that function itself. Listening, I'm viscerally aware of its non-visceral quality: that gut impact gestured at in old rave terms like banging, slamming and above all the jungle term 'brock out'. What once would have been called the Dionysian: the intoxication of sacred frenzy. In Nietzsche's *The Birth of Tragedy*, this is a force of pure musicality that shreds language, pushing lyrics to the edge of indecipherable opacity and rhythmatised non-sense (as with the MCs so important in ardkore, jungle and UK garage).

Speaking to the makers of conceptronica directly and starting to see their music as a contemporary equivalent to postpunk helped me both understand and also 'feel' it more. Alongside its political commitments, post-punk was also a critical commentary on rock itself – what had started out in the sixties, in Lester Bangs's words, as a 'program for mass liberation' had become a controlled and controlling leisure industry, siphoning youth's idealism and energy into a system that safely dissipated it while generating revenue for its owners. Setting itself in opposition to this decadence, postpunk could not allow itself the freedom and cutting-loose of early rock, a wildness now tamed and put into service. Postpunk *had* to be tense and fractured, it had to embody alienation in its sounds and rhythms, if it wanted to be authentic.

Conceptronica has a similar relationship to dance music. It is drawn to the residual disruptive power that still feels latent in archival underground genres like jungle, ballroom and gabber, as well as contemporary sounds like grime, trap and drill. Conceptronica wants to take the unwritten manifesto of emancipation and solidarity within these musics and articulate it crystal clear. Amobi talks about wanting to create critical art but combine it somehow with dance culture's ecstatic communion. It's a difficult balancing act, and a noble ambition.

Pitchfork, 2019

CODA: SONIC FICTION
(An Investigation in Two Parts)

PART 1 – 'If This Is the Future, How Come the Music Sounds So Lame?': Science Fiction at the Cinema

I can remember my memory clearly – the original memory, the false one. My favourite scene in *Star Wars* is the shady bar, known to buffs as Cantina, in the 'pirate city' of Mos Eisley. Entering this den of intergalactic lowlife, Luke Skywalker and Obi-Wan Kenobi meet and hire Han Solo and Chewbacca to fly them off the planet Tatooine. I saw the movie as a fourteen-year-old when it originally came out and was captivated by the bar band of dome-headed, insect-eyed aliens who played freaky-sounding music on futuristic-looking instruments.

Catching the movie again on television as a grown-up some years ago (but prior to its reconfiguration as *Star Wars Episode IV: A New Hope*), I was startled to realise that the music I'd remembered as so out-there was in fact positively musty with old-timey quaintness. No longer an impressionable teen but an adult with learned ears, I instantly recognised the alien music as pre-Second World War jazz – *Star Wars* composer John Williams doubtless aiming to play upon our received associations of the Prohibition-era speakeasy as depicted in countless

299

Hollywood gangster movies. As for the 'weird' instruments, they turned out on close inspection to be just superficially snazzed-up and plasticised versions of the saxophone, trumpet and clarinet.

Conceiving the piece, which he titled 'Mad about Me', Williams imagined 'several creatures in a future century finding some 1930s Benny Goodman swing band music . . . and how they might attempt to interpret it'. Watching the scene yet again for this article, I noticed that the music isn't a completely retro reproduction antique. There's a steel drum, of all things, bubbling in there as rhythm-pulse, and the bassline appears to be played on a synthesiser. But the essence of the tune is more or less the same as the music you'd hear in a Woody Allen movie or indeed the gangster-spoofing nostalgia musical *Bugsy Malone*, released a year before *Star Wars* in 1976. It sounds archetypal to the point of seeming *déjà entendu*, plagiarised from something famous you can't quite place. Williams's lame attempt at futurising it imparts a fusion-tinged gloss which has the unfortunate effect of double-dating the music to the seventies as well as the thirties. It sounds like something Weather Report might have done at their absolute creative nadir . . . or, worse, like The Manhattan Transfer.

This jarring experience – the fondly remembered freakadelic music revealed as not the least bit alien – did plant a seed in my mind, however: a mounting curiosity about science fiction's spotty record when it came to imagining the music of the future. There are two areas, adjacent but separate, up for investigation here: soundtrack composers and their valiant (if arguably always pre-doomed) attempts to come up with 'tomorrow's music today', and S.F. novels and short stories where music features either prominently or passingly. As a former science fiction fanatic who abruptly jilted the genre for punk and the rock press at the age of sixteen, I felt ideally placed to spot the overlap between my two youthful obsessions, S.F. and music. When I came to think about it, however, out of the hundreds of novels and story collections I'd read in my early teens, borrowed from Berkhamsted Public Library or bought with odd-job money, I could hardly recall *any* that had dealt with music – impressively *or* dismally. Cyberpunk, a genre I'd checked out when my interest in S.F. made a slight return in the nineties, certainly felt rock 'n' roll in vibe and often manifested a self-consciously flashy hipness when it came to pop culture references. But it was also hard to recollect many instances of cyberpunk stories where music (either as a sonic experience or in terms of its social function) was imaginatively projected into the future.

As it turns out, there *is* a submerged but reasonably substantial lineage of S.F. writing that deals with music. That is something I'll explore in the second part of this essay; here, I'm going to focus on science fiction movies and their soundtracks.

To expect contemporary composers to somehow reach beyond the horizon of present sonic possibility and bring back music that really is 'of' the future is a tall order. Still, there are soundtrack composers who have attempted precisely that, and they're the heroes of this essay. For the most part, though, S.F. movies have been scored pretty much as the action and suspense movies they generally are beneath the futuristic or extraterrestrial trappings. John Williams is the archetype and apogee here, his scores sticking with the symphony orchestra's sound-palette and using the vocabulary – all tempestuous majesty and swashbuckling derring-do – of the late-Romantic composers of the second half of the nineteenth century and first few decades of the twentieth (Mahler, Strauss, Holst, Elgar, Dvořák et al). In particular, Williams revived a device used in Wagnerian opera, the leitmotif, a recurrent phrase

301

associated with particular characters, moods or 'moral forces'. Williams's neo-Romanticism is perfectly suited for the job in hand, given that genre connoisseurs don't even regard *Star Wars* as true science fiction but as a 'space opera' or a sword 'n' sorcery epic, closer to J.R.R. Tolkien's *Lord of the Rings* than Philip K. Dick's *Valis*. Despite the Death Star and space fighters, it's an essentially medieval reality – all princesses and pirates, knaves and loyal servants (the droids). Its core revolves around the Manichean struggle between the Force and the Dark Side, as represented by the pure-hearted Jedi knights and the minions of the Evil Empire; there's even swashbuckling hand-to-hand combat in the form of the light-saber jousts. The retro-ness of the Cantina scene music is of a piece with the throwback aspect of the entire movie, something blatantly signalled by the opening legend 'a long time ago in a galaxy far, far away' but also apparent in echoes of the pulpy heroics of *Buck Rogers* and *Flash Gordon*. (George Lucas had in fact earlier attempted to buy the remake rights to *Flash Gordon* but they were out of his price range.)

Close Encounters of the Third Kind is actually considered one of John Williams's more modernistic scores, darker, venturing here and there to the brink of atonality. But there's a famous and much-loved scene in the movie, in which music plays a direct role in the story rather than just accompanying the action, that's inadvertently comic if you know even a smidgeon about the history of twentieth-century music: the duet between the human reception committee at Devil's Tower mountain in Wyoming and the alien mothership hovering a few hundred feet above the landing strip. The chief technician mutters 'If everything is ready here on the dark side of the moon, play the five tones' and the young keyboard player strikes up that famous euphonious motif, selected by Spielberg out of some 350 candidates prepared by Williams. The aliens respond with a basso-profundo ostinato, opaque and sub-melodic, forbidding and yet familiar (since its timbre is essentially that of the tuba). After a minute or so of tentative interplay, during which the aliens hit a bottom note so deep it shatters the glass in an observation tower, the 'jam' suddenly takes off and the technical crew struggle to keep up:

Chief Technician: 'Give her six quavers, then pause.'

Expert #1: 'She sent us four quavers, a group of five quavers, a group of four semi-quavers . . .'

Keyboard Operator: 'What are we saying to each other?'

Chief Technician: 'It seems they're trying to teach us a *basic tonal vocabulary*.'

Expert #2: 'It's the first day of school, fellas.'

Expert #1: 'Take everything from the lady. Follow her pattern note for note.'

The ensuing piece – titled 'Wild Signals' by Williams – is frantic and dense, the intertwining patterns of Mankind's arpeggios and Alienkind's counterpoint only brushing elliptically against anything you'd call a melody. Yet even someone like myself, a layperson when it comes to the evolution of classical music during the twentieth century, can tell that this 'basic tonal vocabulary' is no further advanced than, at most, the 1920s. It's amazing enough that the alien civilisation, which is capable of traversing the light-year distances between galaxies and sundry technological marvels beyond human fathoming (like keeping air pilots kidnapped in the 1940s from ageing), just so happens to use the exact same octaves and intervals favoured by the Western classical tradition. But why has their development halted somewhere in the vicinity of Stravinsky and Shostakovich (composers that Williams was partial to as a youth – funny that!), instead of vaulting through the twelve-tone scale and serialism on to the abstract sound-sculpting of post-WW2 electronics, with its total

303

control of timbre, duration, attack and all other parameters of the sonic event? It could be that the alien ambassadors are just talking down to us, speaking our lingo. But since it's 1977 and America, why don't they sound like . . . The Eagles?

The first great attempt to evoke Absolute Nonhuman Otherness for a science fiction movie was the soundtrack for 1956's *Forbidden Planet* created by the husband-and-wife team Bebe and Louis Barron. Although five years earlier, on *The Day the Earth Stood Still*, Bernard Herrmann had prominently deployed the ethereal whinnying of the theremin – a sort of proto-synthesiser activated by moving one's hands within a field of radio frequency oscillations – his soundtrack was largely orchestral. The first entirely electronic score in movie history, the Barrons' soundtrack must have been mind-blowing and hair-raising for audiences at the time. It still sounds impressively out of this world today. Historically, it's on a par with contemporaneous works by pioneering electronic composers like Vladimir Ussachevsky, Tom Dissevelt, Dick Raaijmakers and others beavering away in the experimental units of national radio stations in Europe or music departments of American universities. The Barrons were in contact with many of these people, thanks to their friendship with John Cage, whose milieu they fell into when they moved to Greenwich Village in the early 1950s and who became something of a mentor figure. Both Barrons had studied music at university; hubby Louis was also an electronics buff. In the late forties they were given as a wedding present by a German friend one of the very first tape recorders imported to America and immediately began to explore the same kind of techniques then being developed in Paris by *musique concrète* pioneers Pierres Schaeffer and Henry. Mr and Mrs Barron experimented with slowing the tape down, playing it backwards, adding echo, and in 1950 produced what is thought to be America's first musical work entirely based around the manipulation of magnetic tape, *Heavenly Menagerie*.

Louis Barron was fascinated by the theories of Norbert Wiener as outlined in books like *Cybernetics: Or, Control and Communication in the Animal and the Machine* and *The Human Use of Human Beings*, concepts such as positive and negative feedback, which the duo began applying to their fledgling experiments with electronic circuits, such as the ring modulator, that Louis cobbled together. Talking about the early years just prior to getting the *Forbidden Planet* commission, Bebe recalled how 'the same conditions that would produce breakdowns and malfunctions in machines, made for some wonderful music. The circuits would have a "nervous breakdown".' They soon started to see their activity as a kind of laboratory for the hatching of sound-creatures that appeared to have an uncanny life of their own. In a perturbing analogy with the kind of research that enrages animal rights activists, Barron talked of 'mimicking those experiments done to animals to put them into a state of stress . . . we would do basically the same things to these circuits, and you could hear them literally shrieking. It was like they were alive, and with a lifespan of their own.' Effects and timbres seemed to spawn themselves spontaneously and independently, 'and then we would change them by giving them more or less wattage – we used very primitive ways to bring around change. The sounds would seem to get wildly excited on their own, and then die down. And you could never revive them again! It was like watching a primitive life form come into existence and then fade away.'

After a few years of scoring experimental films and theatre pieces, the Barrons landed the *Forbidden Planet* gig by having the chutzpah to introduce themselves to the head of MGM, Dore Schary, at an art opening for his wife. In the process they displaced the original candidate for the soundtrack,

Harry Partch, the maverick composer whose menagerie of self-invented instruments and personally devised micro-tonal scales would have made for an equally out-there score in some parallel universe's alternative history of Hollywood. *Forbidden Planet* the movie has survived better than many of its fifties counterparts on account of its spectacular set design, but is perhaps less interesting in science fiction terms than as a prime example of the way that cod-Freudianism seeped into Hollywood and American popular culture during the 1950s and '60s (see also *Marnie* and Hitchcock passim). A human colony on the remote planet Altair IV is being marauded by mysterious monsters that are both invisible and indestructible. It turns out that the planet's previous inhabitants, a highly advanced species called the Krell, reached such a peak of civilisation and technology they created a machine that could materialise their thoughts and desires. But, as one character puts it, 'the Krell forgot one thing! . . . Monsters from the id!' The invisible Godzilla turns out to be the incarnation of the father character's unconscious desire for his own daughter. Its footsteps, incidentally, were created by the Barrons when they took an original source sound and slowed it down one hundred times, the crunching ponderousness of the noise evoking the way its colossal feet sank into the sand, leaving behind the footprints that proved it wasn't a mere hallucination.

In an interview for the *Re/Search* book *Incredibly Strange Music Volume II*, Bebe Barron wryly noted a syndrome that could easily be seen as a perennial hallmark of avant-garde music: 'in those days it was hard to do pretty things; it was much easier to do ugly things'. I wouldn't describe the *Forbidden Planet* soundtrack as ugly, but it is certainly forbidding: abstract, virtually atonal, its repertoire of drones, shrieks, groans and pulsations seems to reverberate from the coldest, most pitch-black recesses of deep space. *Time* magazine was in no doubt of the score's radicalism and significance, profiling the married composers under the headline 'Music of the Future', while noting that the Barrons 'refuse to consider their compositions music, partly because they cannot be sure before the tape is finished just what it will sound like'. Actually, the real reason was to avoid getting into trouble with the Musicians' Union, a powerful force in Hollywood; the Barrons' work crossed demarcation lines by effectively combining the functions of the sound department, the special effects department and the music department. So the Barrons were credited ambiguously with 'electronic tonalities' and as a result were eligible for an Oscar neither for Best Soundtrack nor in the special effects category.

Yet *Forbidden Planet*'s soundtrack is definitely music, as opposed to an arsenal of startling effects and sinister cues, as can sometimes be the case with the Barrons' closest counterparts, the BBC Radiophonic Workshop and their 'special sound' contributions for programmes like *Doctor Who*. This was largely down to Bebe, the more composerly half of the partnership, whereas Louis was the technical wizard. Indeed, in their own, rather more interesting way, the Barrons were updating – or radically futurising – the leitmotif idea that John Williams would later revive in his conventionally orchestrated works. As they wrote in the sleevenotes for the soundtrack album, 'in scoring *Forbidden Planet* – as in all of our work – we created individual cybernetics circuits for particular themes and leitmotifs, rather than using standard sound generators. Actually, each circuit has a characteristic activity pattern as well as a "voice".' Some circuits were 'characters' and given names, like 'Chloe', chosen because the plaintive sounds reminded them of a 'lost swamp girl'.

Amazingly, this was the couple's only Hollywood soundtrack; they reverted to the avant-garde world, doing scores for experimental films and for ballet (for some reason, modern dance troupes were particularly partial to electronic music in the sixties, with one avant-garde choreographer, Alwin Nikolais, actually making his own 'choreosonics' using *musique concrète*'s tape-editing techniques), interspersed with the occasional TV commercial and corporate commission. *Forbidden Planet* has long been available on CD, but with the exception of their backings for the necromantic spoken word of Louise Huebner's *Seduction through Witchcraft*, the rest of the Barrons' oeuvre – surely worthy of and long overdue for box set treatment – languishes out of our earshot.

By my reckoning, the next really notable science fiction soundtrack came a full dozen years later, and, interestingly, it shunned electronics. Could it be that synthesised sounds were already beginning to seem passé, a clichéd representation of tomorrow's music? I'm talking of course about *2001: A Space Odyssey*. After commissioning and then discarding an orchestral score from Alex North, Stanley Kubrick went back to the famous nineteenth century and not-so-famous twentieth-century pieces he'd used as temporary guide music during the early stages of production. Some of these already-renowned tunes, like Johann Strauss's *The Blue Danube*, became indelibly wedded to their movie images (in this case, the graceful gyrations of the Spaceport). Others, like the tympani-pounding 'mountain sunrise' sequence of Richard Strauss's Nietzschean symphony *Also Sprach Zarathustra*, became iconic in a way that completely erased their original context and effectively turned them into *2001*'s 'theme song'. The most interesting outcome of Kubrick's music choices, though, was the rise to worldwide fame they afforded an avant-garde composer called György Ligeti, otherwise likely destined to be a highly respected but relatively obscure figure.

Excerpts from four works by Ligeti appeared in *2001: A Space Odyssey* and each time they accompanied one of the most unsettling and sheerly memorable sequences in the entire movie. 'Atmospheres' scores the scene in which primordial man encounters the black monolith left by the aliens. Written for a large orchestra, its 'sound mass' of shimmering and shivering textures constituted one of Ligeti's early explorations of a self-devised technique he called 'micropolyphony', which the computer-music composer David Cope defined as 'a simultaneity of different lines, rhythms, and timbres . . . [that] resembles cluster chords, but differs in its use of moving rather than static lines'. Even more gorgeously hideous is the piece that soundtracks the second appearance of the monolith, this time on the moon. 'Lux Aeterna' is an a cappella choral work, sixteen voices incanting text from the Latin requiem in a style related to medieval canon singing. The effect is like a sinister textile billowing and crinkling in a zero-gravity chamber. The choral voices seem to ascend, fall, recede and veer close all at once, as if the fabric of the space-time continuum itself is undergoing some terrible curvature and infolding. This unearthly wavering creeps into our hearing during the spacebus journey of a team of scientists to the excavation site (the mono-lith having been found buried beneath the lunar topsoil and only detected on account of its intense magnetic radiation). The undertone of unease generated by 'Lux Aeterna' contrasts with the mundane chit-chat of the men as they inspect photographs while bantering about the lunar base's improved quality of vit-tles (sandwiches filled with ersatz ham and cheese). The Ligeti piece resurges to a soul-harrowing pitch as the space-suited experts descend a ramp into the excavation site and confront the mysterious artefact. In a moment of absurd bathos, they pose for a photo in front of the monolith, then a massive peal of high-frequency sound – signifying perhaps a burst of radiation from the monolith – sends them staggering and clutching their space helmets like housewives with migraine.

A sort of medley of Ligeti pieces – 'Requiem', 'Atmospheres' (again) and 'Aventures' – provided the score to the most disorienting and 'trippy' sequence of *2001*, the part titled 'Jupiter and beyond the Infinite', when the astronaut David Bowman encounters another monolith in orbit around Jupiter and gets propelled down a kind of intergalactic tunnel (known to fans as 'Star Gate') in a kaleidoscopic whirl of speed-streaked colour. A series of dream-like sequences ensues in a Louis XVI-style bedroom, in which Bowman sees future versions of himself, including decrepitly aged and doddering on death's doorstep. Throughout the soundtrack are the whispering, gasping, gibbering and cackling voices of 'Aventures' – which Ligeti dubbed a 'mimodrama' and is something like an abstract opera, devoid of libretto. In the movie this bedlam babble is rendered even more opaque and deranged by the application of an electronic effect, heavy echo, that wasn't part of the original piece. Ligeti, in fact, was not consulted about the use of his music in *2001: A Space Odyssey*. A settlement was reached and retroactive consent given, but while Ligeti benefited enormously from the exposure, he disliked the cosmic associations that were now permanently glommed onto his music.

Kubrick's avoidance of electronic sounds may not have been a conscious decision, but it proved to be a shrewd move because the movie's score has avoided the period stamp that so much early synthesiser music carries. The Ligeti pieces in particular are perfect for the movie because they combine the 'timelessness' and majesty of classical music (through their reliance on the timbral palette of orchestral strings and choir) with the anguished and alienating non-traditionalism of post-WW2 composition. Ligeti had actually dabbled with electronic music in the late fifties, after coming into contact with pioneering figures like Karlheinz Stockhausen, Herbert Eimert and Gottfried Michael Koenig, and being invited to work alongside

310

them at the Electronic Music Studio of WDR (West Germany's state radio station). In Cologne, he created two short but impressive pieces entirely based on tape-editing techniques, 'Artikulation' and 'Glissandi'. But the dalliance was short-lived and Ligeti soon became dissatisfied with the new medium. 'I am in a prison,' he once declared. 'One wall is the avant-garde; the other is the past. I want to escape.' Still, it seems likely that being exposed to the virgin frontier of beyond-human tonalities and mind-wrenching spatial effects then being explored at WDR affected him in terms of his ambitions as a composer. He would attempt to reach similar extremities of sound and emotion using the traditional instrumental palette but devising new techniques like micropolyphony.

Electronic music does make a brief appearance in *2001: A Space Odyssey*, however, in the form of the ditty 'Daisy Bell', or, as it's popularly known, 'A Bicycle Built for Two', as sung by supercomputer HAL 9000 (the absurdity quickly turning to terrible pathos as HAL's voice starts to decelerate in tandem with the disintegration of his mind). The rendition – the first computer to sing a song – originated as a pioneering experiment in voice-synthesis conducted by Bell Laboratories. For a telecommunications company, there were obvious commercial applications for voice-synthesis, but Bell had also done some groundbreaking 'pure research' in electronic sound, including creating one of the first computer programs able to play music. That had been developed in 1957 by Max Mathews. Four years later he would program the accompaniment to the IBM 7094's rendition of 'Daisy Bell'. The author of *2001*, Arthur C. Clarke, happened to be visiting a scientist friend at Bell Labs around this time and was blown away by what he heard; when it came to writing the screenplay several years later, he included the song in the sequence where David Bowman dismantles HAL's brain circuit by circuit.

311

The massive success of *2001: A Space Odyssey* in 1968 kicked off a boom in 'serious' science fiction films (as opposed to B-movie flicks in the vein of *The Astro-zombies*), with an early-seventies spate of movies including *The Andromeda Strain*, *THX 1138*, *The Omega Man*, *Silent Running*, *Slaughterhouse Five* and *Soylent Green*. Many of them drew inspiration from the look and sound design of *2001*: the sterile space-age decor of man-made materials and plasticised surfaces; vaguely menacing expanses of voluminous but enclosed space; a stillness and silence tremulous with subliminal mechanical hums, drones and subdued computer burble.

Visually stunning, *THX 1138*, the 1971 dystopia directed by George Lucas, looks something like a blend of *2001* and François Truffaut's movie of *Fahrenheit 451*, albeit set entirely within an utterly denatured interior space that's alternately claustrophobic and agoraphobic, and sometimes both at once. Sonically, though, it's completely original and even more powerful. The movie was an expanded version of Lucas's student film, *Electronic Labyrinth: THX 1138 4EB*. The first part of that original title is far more evocative than the Hollywood remake's, distilling not just the theme of the movie (a near-future society of total surveillance) but its look and its audio ambience. The latter was created by Walter Murch, who's credited with 'sound montages' and whose electronic and tape-based effects run in parallel with the official soundtrack by Lalo Schifrin (a sombre orchestral score, impressive in its own right). Murch also co-wrote the screenplay with Lucas, resulting in a unique synergy of sound and vision that permeates the entire movie. As much as the camera, it's the sound design (incidentally, a term that Murch is credited with coining) that creates the spatiality of the movie: the electronic labyrinth in which the nameless and numbered citizens are trapped, like rats in a behaviourist's maze, for every waking moment of their day. As Murch once put it, 'I tend not to visualise but auralise, to think about sound in terms of space. Rather than listen to the sound itself, I listen to the space in which the sound is contained.' Interestingly his obsession with how space affects sonic perception was catalysed by a scene in an earlier science fiction thriller, John Frankenheimer's *Seconds* (1965), which concerns a mysterious Company that helps people kill off their old identity and start their lives again, and is said to have so traumatised the already fragile Brian Wilson that it contributed to his inability to finish *Smile*!

THX's actual storyline and futuristic scenario are, in science fiction terms, fairly derivative, mish-mashing together elements of *1984*, *Brave New World* and *We* (Yevgeny Zamyatin's 1920 dystopia about a totalitarian One State presided over by the Great Benefactor, where there are no individuals, just numbers). There are also a few lifts from Ray Bradbury's *Fahrenheit 451*, via Truffaut's exquisitely visualised if somewhat inert film: the robo-cop outfits in *THX* recall the kinky-campy uniforms of *451*'s firemen, and both movies feature informer mailboxes where you can incriminate your neighbours anonymously. *THX* depicts a total-control world of computerised panopticon-style surveillance. The citizenry are pacified with tranquillising drugs; sexual love is banned and fetuses are incubated in glass jars. Men and women are either bald or cropped to a millimetre, and in some cases don't even have eyebrows. The TV announcer bestows the viewers with 'blessings of the State, blessings of the Masses' and exhorts 'let us be thankful we have Commerce . . . Buy more now. Buy and be happy.' Some of the inversions are quite witty: in this future reality, it's 'drug evasion', not drug-taking, that's criminal, the citizens being required to dose themselves regularly with sedatives to keep them docile, unquestioning and libido-less. But overall, we've seen and we've read it all before.

What makes the movie gripping is the superb decor and camerawork, and Murch's sound montages, which – as with the Barrons' on *Forbidden Planet* and BBC Radiophonic Workshop's work for *Doctor Who* – operate in the interzone between 'special sound' for dramas and *musique concrète*. Murch was later nominated for an Oscar for his film editing and sound mixing on *The Conversation*, Francis Ford Coppola's contribution to the 'paranoia cinema' genre of the mid-seventies (see also Alan J. Pakula's trilogy of *Klute*, *The Parallax View* and *All the President's Men*). Although set in the future, *THX 1138* is very much part of this sensibility, allegorising in typical S.F. fashion some absolutely contemporary anxieties. *THX* is riddled with abrasively processed sounds: sourceless shudders and judders, abject squelches, android death-rattles, shearing-metal groans, buzzing sound-sweeps like a bionic mosquito flitting around your earhole. Murch's use of electronic treatments to garble and distort the voices of officials, especially those involved in monitoring the citizenry or other bureaucratic positions of power, looks ahead to the vocal processing you'd hear a full decade later on Cabaret Voltaire records or on David Byrne and Brian Eno's *My Life in the Bush of Ghosts*. Like the harsh white spaces and frigid synthetic surfaces of the film's decor, Murch's sonic vocabulary conjures up the sense that this is an utterly inhospitable environment for human emotion.

Robert Wise's *The Andromeda Strain*, an S.F. thriller about scientists investigating a lethal supervirus of extraterrestrial origin in an isolated underground laboratory, was released the same year as *THX* and has a similar post-*2001* look: the sinister sterility of technocratic space. In the early seventies people still thought tomorrow's world would look plastic-coated and vaguely fetishistic, as opposed to the cyberpunk-and-after vision of the future as seedy and disordered. But, unlike *THX*, this time the official soundtrack itself is fully electronic.

Indeed, it's the most uncompromising effort of its kind since *Forbidden Planet*. Composer Gil Mellé was a jazz saxophonist who'd written music for television shows like *Ironside* and had developed an interest in electronics engineering when looking to expand his palette of sound. His theme tune for *Night Gallery* was the first completely electronic title music for an American TV show. Commissioned to compose the score for *Andromeda Strain*, Mellé explored *musique concrète* techniques to the hilt, going on field trips to gather found sounds – railroad noises, the roars and blasts of a jet propulsion laboratory, the ambient hubbub and clatter of a bowling alley – then transformed them through tape treatments. And he exploited the greatly expanded budget at his disposal by designing an electronic sound laboratory on the Universal Pictures studio lot. Here he built new instruments like the Percussotron III, an early form of drum machine, whose outlandish array of timbres are used to dramatise a sequence in the movie where the virus responds to X-ray bombardment by mutating into ever-more deadly forms.

As the seventies progressed, the clinical, hyper-controlled *mise en scène* of movies like *The Andromeda Strain* began to be replaced by more scuzzy and chaotic visions of the future. By 1979, even space travel had lost its Formica lustre and become grotty. That year's *Alien* debuted director Ridley Scott's penchant (see *Blade Runner* a few years later) for an implausible, if atmospheric, lack of lighting (hmm, so they can propel spaceships across the vast void between solar systems to transport mineral ore, but they can't afford a few extra 100 watt light bulbs?) and an incessant dripping of moisture (leaking pipes and trapped condensation in *Alien*, constant rain in the near-future Los Angeles of *Blade Runner*). One of the very last S.F. movies to conceive of the future as spotlessly clean and brightly lit was *Logan's Run*, a 1976 dystopia set in

315

what looks rather like a gigantic shopping mall bustling with youthful beauties – a scenario that would seem pretty utopian if it wasn't for the fact that everyone must turn themselves in for culling when they reach the age of thirty. *Logan's Run* does feature an excellent, partially electronic soundtrack by Jerry Goldsmith (also celebrated for his *Planet of the Apes* score), with thrillingly chilly tracks like 'Flameout' and 'Fatal Games'. Particularly stunning are the pornodelic pulsations of 'Love Shop', which soundtracks a short sequence in which the hero and heroine's escape route from termination takes them through a futuristic brothel, a strobe-like effect illuminating orgiastic tableaux behind the fleeing couple, who have to fend off the attentions of the nubile courtesans (called Wantons!) who work there.

A throwback to *Barbarella*'s softcore erotica (the swinging sixties projected into the outer reaches of the cosmos), the Love Shop in *Logan's Run* doesn't look the least bit sordid. But the general drift in S.F. cinema was towards decay and 'things fall apart'. Ahead of its time in this respect was *Solaris*, Andrei Tarkovsky's inspired 1972 interpretation of the classic novel by Stanisław Lem. The space station orbiting the planet Solaris, whose entire surface is covered by a sentient ocean, has definitely seen better days. This matches the way the discipline of 'Solaris studies' has fallen into neglect: once a zone of feverish research, scientists gradually lost interest as all of humanity's attempts to communicate with the ocean or penetrate its mystery have come to naught. But the real reason for the disrepair and scattered debris at the space station is because the crew have been driven to the edge of insanity by the sudden materialisation of people from their personal pasts. Phantasms of memory become material; these creatures – living replicas, exact down to every last birth mark and mannerism – seem to have been created by the ocean, which has

316

probed the deepest memory-strata of each crew member and offered these 'Guests' up (as gifts or taunts, or something else altogether, it's impossible to know). I'd be surprised, though, if Tarkovsky didn't draw some inspiration from the modernism-gone-shabby of Soviet ministries, perhaps during his visits to the State Committee for Cinematography to get permission to make *Solaris*. On the later *Stalker*, he produced a science fiction movie completely stripped of hi-tech. Based on *Roadside Picnic* by Arkady and Boris Strugatsky, this 1979 film is set in a wilderness that seems to have reclaimed a formerly inhabited area on the outskirts of a city: almost the entire action of the movie takes place against a backdrop of nettles, scrubland, rubble and partially crumbled buildings. Cordoned off by the government but infiltrated by treasure seekers, this is the Zone: an area once visited by aliens and now littered with mysterious artefacts and pockets of uncanniness where the normal rules of physics and reality don't apply.

Both Tarkovsky movies feature scores by Eduard Artemyev. His *Solaris* soundtrack is particularly impressive, its eerie vapours and muffled drones looking ahead to Eno's most radical ambient album, *On Land* (recorded over a decade later). Entirely electronic, the *Solaris* score was mostly made using an outlandish Soviet synthesiser called ANS that was housed in a studio above the Scriabin Museum in Moscow. Its method of generating sound was unusual, involving a photo-optic technique originally developed in cinematography that allowed for soundwaves to be rendered visually. ANS inventor Evgeny Murzin worked out how to do it in reverse: to draw the sine waves and then realise them as sound using a complex system of glass discs, light beams and photocells. ANS allowed for microtonality (as many as seventy-two intervals per octave), polyphony (it could play chords, including extremely rich and dense chords unplayable by human hands) and scientific synthesis (if you could work out the spectral composition of a real-world or instrumental sound, it could then be exactly reproduced). None of these things could be done by a commercially available synthesiser in the early seventies (they were still monophonic, incapable of playing chords).

ANS's name is an acronym for Alexander Nikolayevich Scriabin, a Russian composer obsessed with the correspondences between musical keys and colours. It's tempting to dub ANS a *synaesthesiser* (although many doubt that Scriabin actually had that confusion-of-the-senses condition). But certainly, in Artemyev's hands ANS generates a shimmering panoply of mingled sound-colours and is used very effectively on the *Solaris* soundtrack as a subliminal mood-tint, conjuring at different points the constant presence of the unknowable ocean below and the psychological malaise that grips the derelict space station above.

A different sort of future-gone-to-seed features in John Carpenter's *Escape from New York*. Although released in 1981, it's in some ways a quintessentially mid-seventies movie, capturing the turn towards paranoia and declining faith in progress registered in movies like 1975's *Rollerball* (set in a corporate-controlled Dark Ages of the near-future where the peon-like populace is kept distracted by gladiatorial contests). Written by Carpenter in 1976, *Escape from New York* taps into the post-Watergate atmosphere of cynicism about American democracy; it was also directly influenced by the hugely successful vigilante movie *Death Wish*, which portrayed Manhattan as a jungle of crime and urban decay. *Escape* transposes that contemporary sense of New York as a city on the verge of collapse into the near-future and dramatically amplifies it. It's 1997 and the entire island of Manhattan has been sealed off as a gigantic penitentiary without prison guards, a safari-style zoo in which all of America's life-sentence inmates are dropped and left to fend for themselves – until they manage to kidnap the President.

Unusually, Carpenter not only wrote and edited most of his movies but did the music and sound too. *Dark Star*, his wickedly witty 1974 spoof on *2001: A Space Odyssey* and its successor films like *Silent Running*, featured a synthesised score that managed – like the movie itself – to be both creepy and campy. *Escape from New York*'s soundtrack is one of Carpenter's best, transcending B-movie pulpiness with bloodcurdling, borderline-abstract sequences like 'The Crazies Come Out'. Carpenter's more melodic, synth-pulse-propelled style – represented on *Escape* by brooding themes like 'Orientation #2', which seems to glide along like an empty monorail car coldly surveying the ravaged city below – would, through its influence on pulp movies and straight-to-video nasties, become part of the gene pool of electronic dance music. A Carpenteresque vibe can be detected in the 'filmic' moments that flicker through tracks by grime outfits like Ruff Sqwad and Terror Danjah, or underground hip hop groups like Cannibal Ox.

Anticipating aspects of cyberpunk and actually cited as an influence on *Neuromancer* by William Gibson, *Escape from New York*'s gritty reimagining of S.F. urban space also helped pave the way for *Blade Runner*. S.F. author Robert Silverberg paired Ridley Scott's movie with Lucas's *THX 1138*, describing them as 'two of the most valuable science fiction movies ever made . . . They show the way the future looks . . . with such conviction, such richness of detail, such density of texture.' In this spirit, the highest compliment you can pay Vangelis's score is that it *sounds* like *Blade Runner* looks. It's a remarkable analogue of the Los Angeles of 2019 imagined by Scott, implemented by his squad of art directors, set decorators and special effects wizards, and captured by cinematographer Jordan Cronenweth. Melodically, Vangelis's themes drift back and forth between (and sometimes blend) languid sensuality, melancholy reverie and indeterminate exoticism, perfect for this twenty-first-century LA, now swollen into a Pacific Rim megalopolis where East Asian influences are hybridising with Latin American.

But it's really Vangelis's unique synth-palette of diaphanous timbres and his peculiar spatiality – a sense of immense expanses that aren't empty but somehow full, at once desolately distant yet cloyingly close – that so perfectly conjure the dream-like yet menacing megacity. In studio engineering terms, Vangelis's music has an incredibly 'wet' sound – everything is draped in a misty halo of reverb, so that you feel like you're dewy-*eared*, listening through a prismatic scrim of tears and rain. This production style was probably suggested by Scott's mood-manipulative but marvellously atmospheric use of near-constant downpour, steam rising from the street, and other *noir*-ish clichés. Canopies of synth seem to hang in the air like banks of glistening fog, or settle on the horizon's rim like tufts of fluorescent cloud; the pedal-kept-firmly-down piano ripples of 'Memories of Green' have the pitch-smeary indistinctness of Harold Budd's albums with Brian Eno. Apart from the occasional trickle of computer-gabble, and some no-big-deal-in-1982 sequencer pulses on the handful of propulsive, action-scene-oriented tracks, Vangelis's music isn't futuristic per se. It's often corny, in fact, from the wheezy curlicues of Parisian accordion rippling through 'Wait for Me' to the Clannad-like aria of wordless female ethereality that is 'Rachel's Song'. The single loveliest piece on the entire soundtrack, 'Love Theme', features a woozy saxophone solo (by Dick Morrissey) as its focal point. (But then beauty *is* cheesy, face it.) But in this respect, Vangelis's blend of electronic and acoustic instruments, heart-string-tugging manipulativeness and ambiguous unease, just fits the movie, which combines a futuristic scenario with retro elements: the hardboiled detective plot, the femdroid Rachel's 1940s hairstyle, the *mise en scène*'s constant echoes of film noir shadowplay.

These backward-looking elements were superimposed by Scott onto the source book, Philip K. Dick's *Do Androids Dream of Electric Sheep?* Indeed, *Blade Runner* could be slotted into the category of eighties movies that Fredric Jameson labels 'nostalgia mode' – films that aren't obviously set in the past but that 'regress', on the narrative and psychodramatic level, to the structures and character typology of earlier eras of Hollywood (Jameson's prime example is *Body Heat* but you could also include actual remakes like Scorsese's *Cape Fear*). Formerly a star director in the advertising industry, Scott had made his name with the iconic Hovis bread commercials of the early seventies that so effectively worked up nostalgia for the 1920s and 1930s, for small northern towns with cobbled streets and the associated Depression-era values of sticking together and sticking with it through hard times.

As theorised in his grand opus *Postmodernism: Or, The Cultural Logic of Late Capitalism*, Jameson's 'nostalgia mode' is not to be confused either with the nostalgia felt by an individual for their own past or with veneration and longing inspired by a remote-in-time golden age that seems preferable to the present. Rather it's a symptom of artistic and cultural malaise, an ability to innovate forms of narrative and modes of expression capable of representing the present, let alone projecting the future (as peak-era modernism achieved in the first half of the twentieth century). What I wonder is whether the onset of postmodernism in cinema (not just its 'highbrow end' – Tarantino, et al – but the mainstream's retreat to swashbuckling adventures and action movies, doofus comedies, franchises based on adapted Marvel and DC comic books, not forgetting the never-ending plague of remakes), whether this massive failure of nerve can also account for what appears to me to be an undeniable decline in the science fiction soundtrack?

Simply put, I can't think of an outstanding score after *Blade Runner*; with a few exceptions, I can barely think of an interesting one. *Liquid Sky* (1983) makes the grade with a wonderfully disjointed and aberrant-sounding score by Brenda Hutchinson and Clive Smith, who used the Fairlight sampler in a manner totally different from its uptake in hip hop and dance music subsequently. Their soundtrack is mostly original compositions apart from some adaptations of pieces by Carl Orff and baroque-era composer Marin Marais. This collision of fuddy-duddy and futuristic echoes the approach used by Wendy Carlos on Kubrick's *A Clockwork Orange* (1971), where the strangeness of the brand-new technology (in Carlos's case, Moogs and other early synths) seems to be felt most when applied to really old and really familiar music, the most classic pieces of classical extant, pieces by Purcell, Elgar, Beethoven.

Generally, though, the science fiction soundtrack pretty much ceases to exist as a category separate from other movie scores. Electronic sounds had been rendered commonplace thanks to their diffusion throughout popular music, starting with early-eighties synthpop but then spreading to R&B, dance-pop, techno and beyond. Increasingly, the once-startling sounds of the early analogue synths became trapped within the category of 'retro'. Our ears can't help automatically consigning those sorts of tonalities to a 'period', and as a result their bygone ability to conjure the future in either utopian or dystopian hues inevitably becomes contaminated with camp amusement. With that pathway to the future blocked off by our irony and condescension to the past, S.F. movie scores have become no different from the soundtracks to other Hollywood action or thriller movies – indistinguishable, and undistinguished. Either they're orchestral (at best, Gothic-ly foreboding, like Elliot Goldenthal's 1992 *Alien 3* score) or they're your bog-standard, blaring-and-pummelling collation of alternative, metal, industrial and the more rockified forms of techno-rave. A good example is the soundtrack for *The Matrix* (1999), where the line-up – Marilyn Manson, Ministry, the Prodigy, Rammstein, Rage Against the Machine, Propellerheads, Meat Beat Manifesto, Rob Zombie and Monster Magnet – would make for a hellish rock festival if you ask me.

Having highlighted the heroes and vilified the villains of the seemingly (for now, at least) lost art of the S.F. soundtrack, it's perhaps a little late to point out that none of these composers were, strictly speaking, attempting to make the music of the imaginary future world in the film they were soundtracking. They were *illustrating* – to the best of their ability, using the most advanced ideas or technology available to them – movies set in the future. Soundtracks and scores generally fall into a category that your cinema theorist calls 'non-diegetic sound': they're a mood-setting accompaniment to the moving images. Diegetic sound, which can include music but also covers effects and ambient audio, is sound that originates from *within the world of the film*. The music that the young people are grooving to in one of those sixties-movie nightclub scenes is diegetic. As is 'Stroll On', as performed by The Yardbirds in *Blow Up*, or Winona Ryder and her *Reality Bites* slacker friends bopping to 'My Sharona' in the convenience store, or any rock biopic that depicts a rehearsal, gig or recording studio session. Thinking about it now, though, I can't recall a single example of diegetic music in a science fiction movie, with the exception of the Cantina band in *Star Wars* and the climactic duet in *Close Encounters*. Certainly, I can't think of any movie that's made a serious attempt to depict the music of the future as an element within the narrative itself.

323

We can't fault the non-diegetic composers for their sterling efforts, though. If that paradoxical project – bringing you tomorrow's music today – appears to have withered away at some point in the mid-eighties, that's attributable to much larger, culture-wide shifts (the onset of postmodernity). That condition seems to be still with us; it's our predicament, the horizon of our culture as it presently stands, however much we might yearn and strain to break on through to the other side of it.

But what about science fiction as a literary genre? How do the writers fare on the 'diegetic' front? Are they as handy at projecting into the future with music (and the other arts) as they are with technology and science, geopolitics and society?

PART 2 – Sound, Envisioned: S.F. Writers Imagine the Music of the Future

You're familiar, I expect, with that old chestnut about how 'writing about music is like dancing about architecture'. But how much more absurd would it be to boogie to buildings that haven't been built yet, fantastical edifices that are just the fever-dream blueprints inside an architect's overheated brain? Yet that's what the science fiction writer who seeks to imagine tomorrow's music is attempting. It's enough of a challenge to describe already-existing music, but to take something inherently abstract and elusive, project forward from its present forms to the future, then try to evoke the flavour of these phantasmal sounds . . . well, the results are likely to be unconvincing, or embarrassing, or both.

My curiosity about the deficiencies (and rare triumphs) of the science fiction movie soundtrack was sparked by *Star Wars* and its famous scene in the lowlife bar where the alien band play really far-out music that turns out, on close inspection, to be just Benny Goodman-style swing. When it comes to S.F.

324

writers and their visions of sound-to-come, the intrigue started
with William Gibson and specifically *Idoru*, whose whole
storyline concerns pop but which strangely lacks a soundtrack,
as it were. Gibson's novels brilliantly imagine the near-future
but are oddly mute when it comes to music – even as a vague
'rock 'n' roll'-ness suffuses most every page. Interviewed about
Idoru when it came out in 1996, Gibson suggested that 'there's
never been a successful science fiction rock 'n' roll book, not in
my opinion'. An interesting assertion – and a candid admission,
given that the genre he helped to pioneer contains the word
'punk'.

I asked Bruce Sterling, who's collaborated with Gibson and is
considered cyberpunk's co-inventor, about S.F.'s difficulties with
music. The analogy he came up with was 'the old jazz muso'
who, interviewed by a journalist about where he feels music is
going next, replies: 'If I knew what the future of jazz was, I'd
be playing it already.' Sterling, whose own 1999 rock 'n' roll
novel *Zeitgeist* was set in the present, argued that while it's
'pretty easy to write about future models of the music *industry*
or future *roles* for musicians within future societies', describing
'what music *sounds like* in the future is kinda tough'.

Despite this, according to one encyclopedia of science fiction I
consulted, 'of the arts, music is the one most commonly featured in S.F.' And it's certainly true that the genre is littered
with passing references to outlandish instruments, from the
'three bass radiolyn' in Samuel Delany's *Out of the Dead City*
to the ultracembalo in Harlan Ellison and Robert Silverberg's
'The Song the Zombie Sang'. There are also a fair few appearances of alien music that is incomprehensible, traumatising
or simply inaudible to the human ear. Isaac Asimov's early
story 'The Secret Sense' features Martian music woven out of
the flickering patterns of electric current and therefore beyond
human perceptual thresholds. And in Samuel Butler's *Erewhon*

325

(1872) there are Musical Banks (all mercantile transactions are accompanied by music, albeit 'hideous to a European ear') and sinister Stonehenge-like statues sculpted with holes that catch the wind and produce an unearthly keening music, 'a ghostly chanting' such that 'however brave a man might be, he could never stand such a concert'.

Erewhon is strictly speaking about not an alien civilisation but an undiscovered land on Earth. A similar scenario underpins the much earlier utopian novel, Francis Bacon's *The New Atlantis* from 1626, a time when the voyages undertaken by the great explorers were that era's equivalent to manned missions into outer space. Europeans were only just making their first contacts with the mainland of Australia, and Bensalem, the new Atlantis of the title, is an unknown island in the Pacific west of Peru. Bacon's book contains a remarkable passage about what music might be like in a society that – while not technically of the future – is far more advanced than the European present:

> We have also sound-houses, where we practise and demonstrate all sounds and their generation. We have harmonies which you have not, of quarter sounds and lesser slides of sounds. Divers instruments of music likewise to you unknown, some sweeter than any you have; together with bells and rings that are dainty and sweet. We represent small sounds as great and deep; likewise divers trembling and warblings of sounds, which in their original are entire. We represent and imitate all articulate sounds and letters, and the voices of beasts and birds. We have certain helps which set to the ear to do further the hearing greatly. We have also divers strange and artificial echoes, reflecting the voice many times, and as if it were tossing it; and some that give back the voice louder than it came, some shriller and some deeper; yea, some rendering the voice, differing in the letters or articulate sound from that they receive. We have also means to convey sounds in tubes and pipes, in strange lines and distances.

In just 174 words there, we have microtonality, the synthesiser, hearing aids, an array of effects and processes equivalent to the modern recording studio, and the telephone. *The New Atlantis* passage about 'sound-houses' was famously tacked to the office wall of the BBC Radiophonic Workshop in 1958 by its co-founder Daphne Oram, to serve as a sort of mission statement defining the ambitions of the unit, which would use then state-of-art tape-editing techniques and sound-synthesis devices to create eerie special effects and incidental themes for radio dramas and (later) TV programmes like *Doctor Who*.

Written in the early days of the Enlightenment, *The New Atlantis* was a straightforwardly utopian vision of a society organised around rational principles. But by the twentieth century, science and planning were starting to take on a negative tint, suggestive not of high-minded reason but of high-handed authoritarianism: a technocratic elite who thought they knew best and imposed their rigid ideas on the population. The result was a series of novels that envisioned future societies that look utopian at first glance, or at least considered themselves to be achieved utopias, but are actually dehumanising and totalitarian. In two of the most famous examples of dystopian utopias, Yevgeny Zamyatin's *We* and Aldous Huxley's *Brave New World*, music serves as a potent instrument of social control.

Written in 1920 shortly after the Bolshevik Revolution, *We* was a precocious act of dissidence against the Soviet system: it circulated illegally among Russian writers during the 1920s and only saw official publication in the USSR a few years before the fall of communism. Zamyatin delineates a cold rationalist society in which every aspect of daily life is regimented and supervised. In the One State, presided over by the Benefactor, privacy has been abolished (people live in glass houses, literally), passion is frowned upon, and sex days are strictly rationed (you need a pink chit to schedule a shag). Everyone wears identical uniforms and is identified by number, not name. The main character, D-503, is an engineer working on building a spaceship, but like Winston Smith in *1984* he's seduced by an erotic dissident, I-330, a woman still in touch with human passion. Music in the One State has been ruthlessly rationalised and enlisted for utilitarian goals. It's made in a factory, the Music Plant, which churns out rousing march rhythms that get worker-citizens moving in lockstep, or generates serene patterns to quell agitations of the nervous system.

In one scene, a lecturer illustrates a talk on mathematics and music by displaying a device called the musicometer, explaining to his listeners that 'simply by turning this handle, any of you can produce up to three sonatas an hour. Yet think how much effort this had cost your forebears! They were able to create only by whipping themselves up to fits of "inspiration" – an unknown form of epilepsy.' An ancient instrument is then wheeled out – the piano – and a Scriabin piece is played to the bemusement and amusement of the audience. D-503 recoils from the 'senseless, hurried clattering', divining in it 'something savage, spasmodic, variegated, like their whole life at that time – not a trace of rational mechanical method'. He contrasts it with 'our present music . . . the crystalline chromatic measures of converging and diverging infinite series and the synthesizing chords of Taylor and McLauren formulas; the full-toned, square, heavy tempos of "Pythagoras' Trousers"; the sad melodies of attenuating vibrations; vivid beats alternating with Frauenhofer lines of pauses – the spectroscopic analysis of planets . . . What grandeur! What imperishable logic! And how pathetic the capricious music of the ancients, governed by nothing but wild fantasies . . .'

Brave New World resembles *We* in its portrayal of a 'negative utopia' (Huxley's term) in which passion and conflict have been eliminated through social engineering and conditioning. Unlike the puritanical world of *We*, though, sex is encouraged along with all forms of entertainment, distraction and sensual pleasure. The removal of tension promotes social stability, so promiscuity is mandatory while romantic obsession is deemed pathological. Drugs are readily available to smooth away every crease of anxiety, doubt and emotional pain. Music likewise is an agent of social tranquillisation. Huxley anticipates Muzak with his Synthetic Music Machines: the first one we encounter is 'warbling out a super-cornet solo' in a female dressing room; later, a Super-Vox-Wurlitzeriana fills the air 'with gay synthetic melodies' at a hospice for the terminally ill. As in *We*, music production is centralised, streaming out of a gigantic building in London that contains various Bureaux of Propaganda, floor upon floor of which house the 'laboratories and padded rooms in which Sound-Track Writers and Synthetic Composers did the delicate work'.

In *Brave New World*, there are also concert halls and night-clubs like the Westminster Abbey Cabaret, whose hoarding promises 'ALL THE LATEST SYNTHETIC MUSIC'. Two of the characters, Lenina and Henry, go there on a date, joining the crowd of couples 'five-stepping around the polished floor' to the complex rhythms of Calvin Stopes and His Sixteen Sexophonists. The band play standards like 'There Ain't No Bottle in All the World like that Dear Little Bottle of Mine': not a paean to booze but Huxley's twist on Al Jolson's maud-lin 'Mammy', for in *Brave New World* fetuses are hatched in glass wombs, to spare women the hassle of pregnancy and the agony of birth but also to avoid emotional attachment and all the neuroses created by the Freudian 'family romance'. Hence lyrics like 'Bottle of mine, why was I ever decanted?/ Skies are blue inside of you/The weather's always fine'. As the 'tremulous chorus' of sexophonists 'mounted towards a climax' the conductor 'let loose the final shattering note of ether-music and blew the sixteen merely human blowers clean out of existence'. After the band finishes, a 'Synthetic Music apparatus' pipes out 'the very latest in slow Malthusian Blues', leaving Henry and Lenina feeling like 'twin embryos gently rocking together on the waves of a bottled ocean of blood-surrogate'.

Elsewhere there's ecclesiastical music (or, in *Brave New World* terms, hymns and choral music for a Solidarity Service at the Community Singery), including fanfares from ersatz trumpets and haunting harmonies from 'near-wind and super-string' instruments. Music is also a crucial component of the 'feelies': an omni-sensory update of cinema in which smell and touch are stimulated as well as sight and sound. At one show, the 'scent organ', which Huxley may have borrowed from Huysmans's *Against Nature* (whose decadent aristocrat Des Esseintes composes symphonies with perfumes), plays a 'delightfully refreshing Herbal Capriccio – rippling arpeggios of thyme and lavender, of rosemary, basil, myrtle, tarragon; a series of daring modulations through the spice keys into ambergris; and a slow return through sandalwood, camphor, cedar and new mown hay (with occasional subtle touches of discord – a whiff of kidney pudding, the faintest suspicion of pig's dung) . . .' Meanwhile the music machine unfurls 'a trio for hyper-violin, super-cello and oboe-surrogate' which is joined by a synthesised singer, 'a much more than human voice . . . now throaty, now from the head, now hollow as a flute, now charged with yearning harmonics', which passes effortlessly 'from Gaspard Forster's low record on the very frontiers of musical tone to a trilled bat-note high above the highest C' (only once before hit by the opera singer Lucrezia Ajugari back in 1770).

All terrific fun, then, but for the most part the music in *Brave New World* is a technologically boosted, artificially sweetened version of the popcult fare of Huxley's day (the book was published in 1932). So Calvin Stopes and His Sixteen Sexophonists are a big jazz band à la Duke Ellington's Cotton Club Orchestra, while songs like 'Hug Me Till You Drug Me, Honey' are modelled on the Tin Pan Alley trifles of the twenties. At the feelies, the Synthetic Music machine operates using a 'sound-track roll' (an idea obviously inspired by the player piano, aka the pianola, at its peak of popularity in the 1920s but dating back to the 1870s). Even more unimaginative is the Super-Vox-Wurlitzeriana, inspired by the Mighty Wurlitzer pipe organ designed as a one-man orchestra and used in movie theatres to accompany silent films. Considering the talkies were taking over at the time when Huxley was writing his novel, this is frankly feeble as far as extrapolation and speculation go, especially taking into account the fact *Brave New World* is set *six centuries* in the future. Still, when asked if there is nothing he cares for at all in the modern world, John – the Shakespeare-quoting visitor from the Savage Reservation in New Mexico – concedes 'there are some very nice things. All that music in the air, for instance . . .'

Huxley imagined his benevolently behaviourist New Order of peace, plenty and pleasure having been constructed in response to the devastation of the Nine Years' War and a world economic collapse. But there's not a shred of extenuation for *1984*, George's Orwell's vision of a totalitarian society organised around perpetual war. Just like *Brave New World*'s caste system based around IQ, the Britain of *1984* (which is actually part of a superstate called Oceania) has rigid social divisions. There's the Party (the political class, itself split between low-level bureaucrats and an Inner Party who make all the decisions) and then there are the proles, 85 per cent of the population, powerless drones mired in squalor and pacified by mindless entertainment. This popcult pabulum is created mechanically, via 'mills' that churn out novels with stereotypical characters and prefab narratives. The same goes for music, with songs being 'composed without any human intervention whatever on an instrument known as a versificator'.

In one of the most famous scenes in the book, the dissident Winston Smith stares out the window of the love nest in London's proletarian quarter where he and his lover tryst, entranced by the sound of a prole housewife singing one of these assembly-line ditties – 'It Was Only a Hopeless Fancy' – while hanging nappies on a washing line. 'Whenever her mouth was not corked with clothes pegs she was singing in a powerful contralto . . . She knew the whole drivelling song by heart . . . Her voice floated upward with the sweet summer air, very tuneful, charged with a sort of happy melancholy . . . The woman sang so tunefully as to turn the dreadful rubbish into an almost pleasant sound.' Winston is confirmed in his belief that if there is hope it lies with the proles – still in touch with basic human emotions, still grounded in the earthiness of the primal and ageless. Like lions after slumber, in unvanquishable number, they'll rise and throw off the Party.

But later in the book, 'It Was Only a Hopeless Fancy' – the big hit tune that season with the proles – starts to be eclipsed in popularity by 'The Hate Song', the theme tune for the upcoming Hate Week, and which, from its description, sounds a bit like Oi! or the more shouty kinds of rap such as crunk. 'A savage, barking rhythm which could not exactly be called music, but resembled the beating of a drum. Roared out by hundreds of voices to the tramp of marching feet, it was terrifying. The proles had taken a fancy to it . . . The Parsons children played it at all hours of the night and day, unbearably, on a comb and a piece of toilet paper.' The rise of this ugly chant, even among the apolitical proles, seems to prefigure the grim conclusion of *1984*: the inevitable triumph of ideologies that feed off hatred and mob rage, the sinister Inner Party apparatchik O'Brien's vision of the future as 'a boot stamping on a human face – forever'.

Ray Bradbury's 1953 novel *Fahrenheit 451* fuses aspects of *Brave New World* (soul-eroding hedonism) with *1984* (the Party's ruthless drive to strip the poetic and emotionally expressive power from language and turn it into the instrument of ideology). The core of *Fahrenheit 451* is the black joke of the firemen of the future being sent out not to extinguish blazes but to flamethrower books, considered socially disruptive because they arouse the imagination, but still kept in secret private libraries by dissidents and eccentrics. As with Huxley and Orwell, music is considered to be on the side of sedation not sedition: it dulls the mind in tandem with TV, which in this near-future has evolved into surroundvision, via a four-wall mega-telescreen. Music can be peppy, an emptily effervescent upper so loud it drowns out conversation: 'the walls of the room were flooded with green and yellow and orange fireworks sizzling and bursting to some music composed entirely of trap drums, tom-toms, and cymbals'. But mostly it's bland and emollient, doping the listener just like the legal tranquillisers that Mildred, wife of the fireman Montag, constantly pops.

Mildred also wears 'audio-seashells' – tiny transistor-radio earpieces – all day long. One night, Montag returns home late and opens the bedroom door:

Without turning on the light he imagined how this room would look. His wife stretched on the bed, uncovered and cold, like a body displayed on the lid of the tomb, her eyes fixed in the ceiling by invisible threads of steel, immovable. And in her ears the little Seashells, the thimble radios tamped tight, and an electronic ocean of sound, of music and talk and music and talk coming in, coming in on the shore of her unsleeping mind. The room was indeed empty. Every night the waves came in and bore her off on their great tides of sound, floating her, wide-eyed, toward

333

morning. There had been no night in the last two years that Mildred had not swum that sea, had not gladly gone down in it for the third time.

Like *Fahrenheit 451*, Anthony Burgess's *A Clockwork Orange* reflects the anxiety and concern felt by educated people and the literati about people not reading books anymore on account of the rise of 'admass society' (J.B. Priestley's 1954 term for the complex of advertising, mass communications and consumerism). The quirk of *Orange* is to blame the advent of a pleasure-principled post-literate society not on Americanisation, the typical bogey-man in this scenario of popular culture as mass zombiedom, but on its Cold War adversary. Burgess's novel is set in a near-future Britain whose pop culture has been corrupted by 'subliminal penetration' from the Eastern bloc and where teenage slang is largely composed of pidgin Russian. (Of course, in *reality*, it happened the complete other way round: denim jeans and rock and Hollywood made Communist youth eager to Westernise.) Anti-hero Alex is the fifteen-year-old leader of a gang of 'droogs', who belong to a larger youth subculture that Burgess models on the teenage tribes of the early sixties. Fusing the yobbery of rockers with the razor-sharp elegance of mods, these dandy hooligans dress 'in the height of fashion' (at the start of the book, that's ultra-tight black tights through which show the bas-relief patterns of decorative abdominal protectors, plus lapel-less jackets with padded shoulders) and prowl the nocturnal streets, where they fight with rival gangs and brutalise defenceless citizens. Equally recognisable as early sixties is *Orange*'s urban landscape of high-rise 'flatblocks' and foreboding power stations.

In classic S.F. style, Burgess took the present – brutalist architecture, youth's new insubordinate arrogance, a rapid-fire turnover of fashion trends, rising crime and drug use, the popularity of milk bars and cafés as places for teenagers to

hang out and listen to jukebox rock – and exaggerated it.
In *Clockwork Orange*'s near-future, the milk bars sell state-
sanctioned psychoactive potions like 'synthemesc' and 'milk
with knives in it', Alex and pals' terms for a speed-shake that
puts them in the mood for ultraviolence. Pop music is naturally
central and like the teen argot mostly originates from the
communist bloc. In the Korova Milkbar, the jukebox plays
Berti Laski's golden oldie 'You Blister My Paint'; later, we
come across Russky pop stars like Johnny Zhivago, Ed and Id
Molotov, and Goggly Gogol.

Unlike his peers, Alex is not interested in all this pop pap.
In one of those curious expressions of authorial narcissism that
novelists often cannot resist, Burgess inserts, implausibly, his
own preference for classical music into his lead character. For
Burgess was a prolific composer who only turned to writing
as a second choice and who churned out Elgar and Holst-
influenced symphonies, concertos and fugues throughout his
life. Alex owns a fancy hi-fi stereo and a large album collection,
funded by muggings and burglaries. And he finds that the
tempestuous Romanticism of composers like Beethoven stirs
up the Dionysian emotions, stoking his appetite for destruction
and sexual cruelty.

In one scene, he hurries down to his local record store Melo-
dia (which happens to be the name of the state record label of
the former USSR) to see if a new version of the 9th Symphony
has arrived. A pair of ten-year-old, precociously sexual girls
tease him for buying such square and crusty stuff, rather than
the hit parade tunes they're into, like 'Honey Nose' by Ike
Yard and 'Night after Day after Night' which, sneers Alex, is
'moaned by two horrible yarbleless like eunuchs whose names
I forget' (I'm guessing the inspiration for Burgess here was
The Everly Brothers or The Four Seasons). Alex invites the
girls back to hear their teenpop platters on his mega-system

(like putting some horrible fizzy kid's drink in a fine wineglass, he complains). Then he whacks on Beethoven and, suitably stirred, subjects the girls to 'the strange and weird desires of Alexander the Large', leaving them 'bruised and pouty' and punching him with 'teeny fists' as they scurry out the door.

Despite Burgess's evident disdain for pop, *A Clockwork Orange* had a huge influence on pop groups. The Human League titled an early EP, *The Dignity of Labour*, after a mural in Alex's high-rise, while the offshoot band formed by Ian Craig Marsh and Martyn Ware took their name from *Orange*'s fictional group The Heaven Seventeen. Clock DVA derived its own name partly from Nadsat, the Russian teen-slang all the young droogs speak. Another group from the same Sheffield postpunk scene, Molodoy, had a whole look inspired by the Kubrick movie version of *A Clockwork Orange*, as did the punk group The Adicts. Other homages include the band Moloko (Nadsat for 'milk'), the record label Korova, and the New York-based, Factory Records-signed outfit Ike Yard.

Often, though, the S.F. novelists who feel most 'rock' on account of their influence on musicians seem to have given the least attention to music in their work. Philip K. Dick has inspired everyone from Sonic Youth and Royal Trux to the Human League and (via *Blade Runner*) countless techno and drum and bass producers. But I can't recall that many appearances of music *in* his books – which is odd, given that he was a music nut with a huge collection, worked in a record store, once entertained ambitions to compose, and even performed in an ensemble led by Harry Partch (albeit only playing the triangle). I only recall a wee thing in *The Three Stigmata of Palmer Eldritch*, where Earth is afflicted by chronic global warming: one apartment block's air conditioning fails, causing a resident's record collection to melt into a single blob. In *The Simulacra*, there's a pianist character who has the telekinetic capacity to play piano using his mind, and there's also an early short story, 'The Preserving Machine', about an inventor who aims to save the canonic works of classical music for all time via a machine that turns them into animals that can be loosed into the wild, with disastrous consequences.

J.G. Ballard had even greater impact on rock, influencing all the usual postpunk suspects (Joy Division, Cabaret Voltaire, Throbbing Gristle, Mute Records founder Daniel Miller who, as The Normal, wrote the *Crash*-inspired 'Warm Leatherette') along with Gary Numan, The Buggles ('Video Killed the Radio Star' is loosely based on his short story 'The Sound Sweep'), Radiohead, The Klaxons and dubsteppers like Kode 9. Yet Ballard often remarked on his lack of feeling for music, claiming to have a 'tin ear' and almost boasting of never having 'bought a single record, cassette, CD or whatever. I don't own a record player of any kind.' He enjoyed the cultural convulsion of punk, but his Desert Island Discs were barely middlebrow: 'The Teddy Bear's Picnic', a Bing Crosby and Andrew Sisters version of a Cole Porter tune, Noël Coward, Marlene Dietrich, various light classical pieces, plus 'The Girl from Ipanema'.

'There's no music in my work,' Ballard once declared. 'The most beautiful music in the world is the sound of machine guns.' Certainly there is a kind of hypertrophy of the eye in his fiction that makes all the other senses dim next to his monstrous visual intensity, from touch (*Crash* is about the arrangement of limbs and objects in compelling patterns, about geometry rather than sensuality) to sound. The Ballardian narrative is a machine for generating landscapes and tableaux: where Burgess was a frustrated composer, Ballard had originally wanted to be a painter like the surrealists he so admired.

That said, music and sound did feature here and there in his work, and when it appeared it was handled more

337

imaginatively than by many of his more musically sensitised
S.F. peers. Mostly it's early in his career, perhaps before
he realised precisely where his gift lay, with the drastically
transformed landscapes painted in post-cataclysm novels like
The Drowned World. Indeed, his very first published story,
'Prima Belladonna' from 1956, involved music. The protagonist
is the owner of a shop selling 'choro-flora', mutant singing
plants that typically have a twenty-four-octave range and can
hit notes like K sharp and high L. The story is full of delicious
wisecracks (references to 'mixed coloratura herbaceous from
the Santiago Garden Choir', the 'Kew Conservatoire' and so
forth) but also precociously features the unique Ballardian
atmosphere of uncanniness and psychological fixation, with its
narrative about the strange love/hate relationship that develops
between the 'specialty singer' Jane Ciracylides and a 'beautiful
but evil' orchid. Set in the same indolent-yet-eerie dreamscape
of Vermilion Sands, 1962's 'The Singing Statues' features
sonic sculptures that respond to the sounds of their immediate
environment, including the 'body tones' of their owners. 'Sonic
sculpture was now nearing the apogee of its abstract phase;
twelve-tone blips and zooms were all that most statues emitted.
No purely representational sound . . . a Mozart rondo or . . . a
Webern quartet, had been built for ten years.' The plot echoes
'Prima Belladonna' with its wealthy female art collector forming a morbid obsession with one particular sound-sculpture.

In between these two early Ballard shorts came 1960's 'The
Sound-Sweep', quite possibly science fiction's very best story
about music. It's set in the near-future, a few decades after the
discovery that sound leaves residues, like the build-up of scale
in a kettle, an after-resonance of staleness and agitation that's
bad for health and environment alike. Sound-sweeps, employed
by the Metropolitan Sonic Disposal Service, use Sonovacs to
suck up all the 'embedded sounds' in public spaces and private

homes. It's not always a simple process: some residues, such
as the seven centuries of Gregorian chants that have soaked
into a church, are like the picturesque weathering on a building's brickwork, and so a delicate restoration job is required,
retaining these 'tonal inlays' but removing the coughs and
rustlings left by congregations over the decades. The sound-
debris is emptied at a dump way out in the dunes on the edge
of the city, a sort of sewage plant for sound where the waste
frequencies are corralled in complex arrays of baffles. Cue for a
classic Ballardian landscape that's also, for once, a soundscape:
'a place of strange echoes and festering silences, overhung
by a gloomy miasma of a million compacted sounds . . . The
cacophonic *musique concrète* of civilization.'

This scenario ought to be sufficiently fertile to sustain a
forty-page story, but Ballard, in the full flush of his early
creativity, adds another layer: in this near-future, music as we
know it has been outmoded by the introduction of 'ultrasonic'
music, which employs 'a vastly greater range of octaves, chords
and chromatic scales than are audible by the human ear,
[providing] a direct neural link between the sound stream and
the auditory lobes, generating an apparently sourceless sensation of harmony, rhythm, cadence and melody uncontaminated
by the noise and vibration of audible music'. An ultrasonic
trumpet, for instance, is strictly speaking silent but its
'fantastic glissandos . . . like frantic eels' charge the air 'with
gaiety and sparkle'. Best of all, ultrasonics leave no stagnant
residue behind, the 'leaden and tumid' after-tang you'd get
from playing, say, a Mahler symphony. Ballard adds another
witty tweak: ultrasonics catch on with the general public and
completely replace audible music in part thanks to a further
invention, the short-playing record. Spinning at 900 rpm, the
SP condenses a forty-five-minute Beethoven symphony into
twenty seconds but delivers the same amount of 'neurophonic'

pleasure – indeed, it's distilled into a deeper hit of bliss, the classical music equivalent of the crack high perhaps.

The actual plot of 'The Sound-Sweep' (and the bit that semi-inspired 'Video Killed the Radio Star') is a *Sunset Boulevard*-like *mise en scène* involving a decrepit, delusional opera singer, Madame Gioconda, and her magnetic hold over the sound-sweep Mangon, who's somewhere between a vassal and a lover, and, for inverse symmetry, is also a mute. With Mangon's help, the prima donna attempts to relaunch her career and bring about a 'sonic revival'. Here's where, for all of Ballard's prodigious inventiveness, we encounter the familiar S.F. problem of imagining music of the future. The fact that the story's based around an opera diva and that Ballard imagines ultrasonics leading to not some unimaginable form of post-music but the re-scoring of the established classical canon (complete with new-old instruments like the ultra-tuba and triple bass) indicates how hard it is to think beyond the musical limits of one's era.

Things remain equally date-stamped as we reach the psychedelic late sixties. *Stand on Zanzibar*, John Brunner's 1968 classic, is set in an overpopulated early twenty-first century. As with most near-future S.F., everything is extrapolated from the trends of the day, from sexual permissiveness to then-recent scientific advances like genetics. Using a revolving cast of characters and large number of plotlines to offer a panoramic view of this world at every social level and in many corners of the globe, Brunner's execution is generally inspired. *Zanzibar* features a number of cute and imaginative ideas about music, albeit mostly just tantalising hints. We follow a night-time walk through a megalopolis, music coming 'from everywhere, mostly hits from the current pop parade in which two or even three disparate rhythms clashed randomly on semitonal discords'. Some of these sounds issue out of

340

'radio-dresslets': garments fitted with tiny speakers. There's
a passing reference to grooving on 'the random sounds of a
Whyte Noyse generator'. At a party, someone talks of visiting
Detroit, now a ghost town full of abandoned car factories and
whose only living inhabitants are squatters, and going to a
squat party with 'a zock group playing full blast under a steel
roof five hundred feet long. Didn't need lifting [drugs] – just
stand and let the noise wipe you out.' That sounds more than
a little like an illegal rave, and in Detroit, the historical
birthplace of techno, too. Not bad at all, Mr Brunner. But, um,
'zock group'?!

The party is a retro-theme event thrown by society hostess
Guinevere, a queen bitch who's decreed that anyone caught
wearing something that dates after the turn of the millennium must pay a humiliating forfeit. The retro idea is itself
pretty prescient, since in 1968 it was barely discernible as
an undercurrent within pop culture (indeed the word 'retro'
is not actually used in that chapter of *Zanzibar*). It's also a
cool manoeuvre that allows Brunner to recap some of the pop
cultural fads of the intervening decades. So the soundtrack
is seventies, with 'divisible-by-two rhythms' that seem 'banal
and boring' after the more complex rhythms like 'five against
eleven' that emerged in the eighties and nineties. There's a
reference to a currently popular style of 'chants sans paroles' in
relatively 'bland monotonous rhythms of five against four and
seven against eight'. Guinevere catches a guest doing the zock
– a 'this minute dance' and, worse, the perpetrator's doing it
with 'the genuine, free-fall touch' – and the poor sod is forced
to do it with a dish of honey between his elbows.

Later, there's a whole chapter about 'zock'. It's split into two
columns, Aud and Vid, to convey the musical and visual aspects
of this hybrid entertainment form. Here's an extract of the Aud
channel:

FUTUROMANIA

Trackin hiss
Pick up 7-beat bass below aud threshold
Synch in five-beat
WAH YAH WAH YAH
WAH
Sitar picks up 5
7 beats express takeoff
Octave up bass
Bass up 2nd octave
Bring in at 4-beat intervals tympani, Lasry-Bachet organ, pre-cut
    speech tape
MANCH/total recall/SHIFT/man that's really someth/WHIP/ah
    whoinole cares anyway/GARKER/garker/GARKER/garker (ad lib)
Snatch of Hallelujah chorus
Leader talks over gp:
YOU GOT THE OFFYOUR ASS FOR BOTH OF US MY SPAREWHEEL
    AND ME AND SHIGGY MAKES THREE
Las-Bach FFF waltz-time
Acceleratube passes by
Resume speech tape
I GOING BUST MY
SKULL
Kiss loudens synch with
Resume bass, sitar . . .

The visuals meanwhile are a colour-saturated blur of nudity
and simulated sex ('shiggy fondles own breasts', 'shiggy sucks
the longest glass column of 'the Las-Bach organ') plus random
psychotropic imagery.

It's the sitar that gives the game away: this is all just an
amped-up version of 1967 and '68 . . . Hendrix, Jefferson Air-
plane, the White Album. Coloured-oil projections oozing while
Floyd go into 'Interstellar Overdrive' at the All Night Rave.

'Lasry-Bachet' is another period-piece reference, albeit fairly esoteric: it's a reference to the Crystal Organ, fifty-four chromatically tuned glass rods that produce sound when rubbed with wet fingers, which was invented in 1952 by Bernard and François Baschet and played by Jacques and Yvonne Lasry.

Written a few years after *Stand on Zanzibar*, Robert Silverberg's *The World Inside* grapples with some of the same contemporary anxieties as Brunner – overpopulation, mega-urbanisation, permissiveness – but is set four centuries into the future. The year is 2381 and most of the world's 75 billion population live their entire lives inside gigantic city-size skyscrapers that tower one thousand stories high; the rest of the planet's surface is devoted to agriculture to feed this ever-expanding population, which continues to grow because there are no restrictions on breeding and total sexual freedom is promoted. *The World Inside* is unique, I think, among S.F. novels for having a whole chapter devoted to a detailed description of a single soundcheck-cum-performance by a band. Dillon Chrimes plays 'vibrastar' in a 'cosmos group' that tours up and down the three-kilometre-high building, which is divided into forty-floor-tall 'cities' that bear names like Rome. Other instruments include comet-harp, orbital diver, gravity-drinker, Doppler-inverter and spectrum-rider.

Dillon and his band arrive at the auditorium on the 530th floor of Urbmon 116, which has a stage that hangs like a toadstool in the centre of the space and around which is concentrically strung a web on which the audience will nestle. The vibrastar is so heavy it requires a robot to manoeuvre it onto the stage: it's as if Silverberg couldn't imagine synthesisers ever getting any less unwieldy than the Moogy monstrosities prog-rock groups lugged with them on tour. The group's output is visual as well as audio, and in full improvisational flight that night the effect is like a planetarium reprogrammed by acid heads to make the trip as spectacular as possible. 'The spectrum-rider . . . skis off toward the ultraviolet in a shower of hissing crispness.' Then Dillon takes a solo: he 'coats the ceiling with dripping nebulae', gives the audience 'the stars in one skullblowing rush', and on impulse lets rip with 'an eclipse of the sun – why not? Let the corona crackle and fry'. The climactic blast sends the 'flaccid data-stoned audience' apeshit: they give the band the ultimate ovation, slapping their own cheeks. As with Brunner's zock, all this noodly out-there-maaaan-ness is just the slightest of projections forward from what cosmic rockers like Tangerine Dream, Hawkwind and The Grateful Dead were doing in the late sixties and early seventies. As if to signpost this more sharply, the floor that Dillon and the group live on is called San Francisco and his wife Electra even paints 'psychedelic tapestries' for a living.

A decade or so later, cyberpunk would also reflect its moment. The term was coined in 1983 by Bruce Bethke, who used it as the title of one of his short stories, but it really took off with William Gibson's *Neuromancer* in 1984. Although *Village Voice* would hail cyberpunk as a 'hip, musically literate high-tech movement' that was rejuvenating an S.F. genre that had lost its edge in the pulpy post-*Star Wars* era, by the early-mid-eighties 'punk' as a reference point could hardly be described as cutting-edge. If anything it was played out, suggestive as much of London tourist postcards depicting spiky-haired punks down the King's Road or Billy Idol's lip-curl sneer on MTV, as of cooler inheritors like the Jesus and Mary Chain or Hüsker Dü. (Idol would actually attempt a career comeback in 1993 with the album *Cyberpunk*; at his insistence, journalists were obliged to read *Neuromancer* before interviewing him, although – it turned out – he hadn't actually read it himself.) But then the punk in cyberpunk wasn't really about musical allegiances but 'attitude': tough, speed-wired, affectless. There was also a punk-like minimalism to the hardboiled, clipped-and-stripped prose, while the genre's worldview and mindset, if not quite nihilistic, were certainly dark: the enforced cynicism and paranoid wariness of renegades in a world dominated by sinister corporate entities.

Mirrorshades, the 1986 short-story collection edited by Bruce Sterling, brought together all the luminaries of the young genre and featured several stories that directly dealt with music. Pat Cadigan's 'Rock On', a sketch towards her 1991 novel *Synners*, is set circa 2025, a time when rock 'n' roll's spirit has faded from the world apart from a handful of battered survivors from the olden golden age – like the protagonist Gina, who remembers being taken as a toddler by her mum to see the Rolling Stones' 1981 tour. By the third decade of the twenty-first century, rock has become an audio-visual entertainment fed directly into the brains of fans via sockets in the skull. But uniquely endowed individuals, people like Gina with a special feel for a-rockin' and a-rollin', are needed to mediate this stimulus before it can be turned into the tapes that fans buy and channel into their nervous systems. These 'sinners' – short for 'synthesizers' – seem to be something like a studio engineer or mixer, except they don't really have agency in the process; they're perhaps closer to a pre-amp, a prism that sharpens the signal. Young upcoming bands and entertainment conglomerates alike compete to get hold of one of this dying breed of rock 'n' rollers.

The scenario – a meretriciously flashy audio-visual distraction that needs the substance of true rock to give it any real life – looks suspiciously like the mid-eighties, when American radio followed MTV's lead and filled the airwaves with British pop tarts and flamboyant fake-rock like Mötley Crüe. There's even a give-away mention of Bow Wow Wow and Oingo Boingo, MTV one-hit wonders that Gina is just old enough to remember (while still preferring her mother's Hendrix and Who albums). Having the lead character be a relic from an earlier era is a neat ruse too, a way of avoiding imagining the music of the future.

Oddly enough, the *exact same ploy* is utilised in 'Freezone', the other main music-based story in *Mirrorshades*. Author John Shirley is widely credited as having pioneered cyberpunk with 1980's *City Come A-Walkin'*, which introduces the squalid yet glittering cityscape later familiar as the Sprawl of *Neuromancer* and other Gibson novels. *City* also has a rock 'n' roll thread running through it: its cast of characters includes a music club owner and a tough little rocker (called Catz Wailen!). Gibson hailed Shirley's book as 'less an S.F. novel set in a rock demimonde than a *rock gesture* that happened to be a paperback original'. Shirley didn't really need to write about rock 'n' roll because he *was* rock 'n' roll: former drug addict, the spiked dog-collar-wearing frontman of various punk bands (including Sado-nation, whose songs included 'Our Love Is Like a Death Camp' and 'Kill Myself'), a writer of lyrics for Blue Öyster Cult (he named his first novel after their 'Transmani- acon MC'). Gibson's adulation of this dude who walked it like he talked it gets pretty icky: 'I look at Shirley today, the grown man, who survived himself, and know doing that was *no mean feat*. A cat with extra lives.' And pretty yukky: he describes *City* as 'quite literally, a seminal work; most of the elements of the unborn Movement swim here in opalescent swirls of Shirley's literary spunk'.

Gibson pinpoints the proto-cyberpunk hallmark of *City Come A-Walkin'* as its *mise en scène*, 'a "near future" that felt oddly like the present (an effect I've been trying to master ever since)'. Written in 1985, 'Freezone' conjures a near-future (early twenty-first century) that feels oddly like its own recent past. Hero Rick Rickenharp is a 'rock classicist' who sings songs like

'Pain Is Everything', sports sunglasses after dark, and wears a battered leather jacket reputedly worn by John Cale when he was in the Velvet Underground. His band Rickenharp are on a downward trajectory: the nostalgia wave that had carried them peaked long ago; their latest holovid isn't getting airplay. So the band are muttering about changing their look (to 'minimono', streamlined and muted-toned) and style (to 'wire', a music form that is 'danced' by performers, with the movements triggering sounds in a manner possibly inspired by the theremin). We witness the wire act NewHope, a sexless, emaciated voidoid whose muscular contractions of limbs and torso are converted, via 'impulse-translation pickups', into 'long, funereal pealing' and 'bagpipe-like riffs'. The minimono-styled audience respond with appropriately complex geometric dance moves. Rickenharp tries to get into it, to accept it as 'another kind of rock 'n' roll' . . . but concludes: 'Real rock is better. *Real rock is coming back . . .'* He finds the music that minimonos dig mechanistic and inhuman: 'the stultifying regularity of their canned music banged from the walls and pulsed from the floor . . . you felt a drill-bit vibration of it in your spine'.

You don't have to be too sharp to twig that NewHope is mostly likely inspired by Gary Numan or maybe even the writhing dancer that Howard Jones used to have in his videos, while Rickenharp is a stand-in for Shirley, whose Stiv Bators-style punk has been outmoded by the NewRomance's synths and drum machines. As a practising rocker, Shirley is good at evoking the magic and chemistry of a gig when it all comes together for the band: Rickenharp, playing what may be their last show as a rock 'n' roll group, hit a righteous groove and slay an audience most of whom have never seen a live drummer before.

But overall, Shirley is happier writing about clothes and hair than sound. There's a fashion parade in 'Freezone' of near-future subcults: neutrals, flares, rebs, chaoticists, preps,

347

minimonos, retros. But even the most extreme of these (the chaoticists with their filed teeth, pierced nipples and skinhead crops with painted sides) are barely further out than the modern primitives of eighties industrial or the freaks of Leigh Bowery's Taboo scene. Similarly, William Gibson's *Count Zero* from 1986 – part of the Sprawl trilogy that started with *Neuromancer* – features style tribes straight from the early eighties: Gothicks, all lacquered hair and leather and 'grave-yard pallor', versus Kasuals, blonde and healthy in cottons and loafers. This mysterious persistence is all the more odd given that *Neuromancer* had featured an oft-quoted passage about the incredible rapidity with which fashion trends and subcultures germinate, blossom and disappear on a monthly basis within the youth population of the Sprawl, a conurban spread that's transformed the East Coast of America into a single gigacity.

But it's *Idoru*, Gibson's first and only book to put pop music centre-stage, that really flinches from the challenge of speculating about music's future. As he admitted in an interview, 'I was a little shy with that . . . I'm not a musician, I'm not musical enough.' In what looks to be a hallmark of the cyberpunk approach to music, a Gina/Rickenharp-like out-of-time rocker is the novel's central figure: Rez, ageing frontman of Lo/Rez, a guitar band who've released twenty-six albums in the decades since their debut for Taiwanese indie label Dog Soup. Lo/Rez are classic retro-rockers, quite possibly modelled on Black Crowes or Lenny Kravitz, as they seem to have been behind the times even when they emerged in the nineties. Asked on TV about the accomplishments of axe hero Lo, 'a venerable British guitarist in wonderful tweeds' declares that 'they hadn't really expected the next Hendrix to emerge from Taiwanese Canto-pop'. Kathy Torrance, an executive at the infotainment company Slitscan, regards Rez as 'a living fossil,

an annoying survival from an earlier, less evolved era'. Another
throwback band in *Idoru* is The Dukes of Nuke 'Em, whose
Billboard smash 'Gulf War Baby' caused 'diplomatic protests
from several Islamic States'. Appealing to the 'meshbacked'
audience (i.e., redneck, after the trucker-style caps), they play
Republican rock that's 'all about hating anything that wasn't
their idea of American'. Gibson's inspiration here, I suspect,
was the intolerant opinions expressed by raunch-metal groups
like Guns N' Roses and Skid Row.

Yet nothing musical actually *sounds* through *Idoru*'s pages.
The book's real subject is celebrity and fan culture. The plot
concerns Rez's decision to marry an idoru, a literally manu-
factured pop idol from Japan called Rei Toei, who puts out
records and videos and has fans, but who doesn't exist, is just
a software agent, a data-spun figment. The wedding appears
to be a mixture of publicity stunt, performance art gesture and
philosophical statement about the nature of fame. For Rez the
human being has long ago been subsumed within a fantasy-
figure superself, woven out of criss-crossing threads of publicity
and fan fantasy. Gibson has sharp perceptions here: he notes
how Lo/Rez's 'fan-base had refreshed itself over the years with
a constant stream of pubescent recruits, girls who fell in love
with Rez in the endless present of the net, where he could still
be the twenty-year-old of his earliest hits'. But what seems like
the most speculative and futuristic element in the book – Rei
Toei, the artificially engineered pop idol – was overtaken by
reality in the gap between his handing in the manuscript and
the book being published: there actually was a virtual idoru
known as Kyoko Date, with a website and animated videos.
Then again, you could say the cartoon pop group The Archies
got there first in 1969 with 'Sugar Sugar'.

Gibson legendarily wrote his books while watching MTV and
his fiction is littered with rock references (a spaceship called

349

Sweet Jane, an *Idoru* chapter titled 'Fables of the Reconstruction' after the R.E.M. album, phrases like 'meat puppets', etc.). But, as he admits, music rarely appears in the narrative, instead figuring as 'a kind of offstage influence'. Cybertheory academics go gaga for the passages in *Neuromancer* concerning the Rasta space station Zion, where dub basslines echo through sensi-scented corridors:

> When they'd strung the cables . . . they hung them with battered sheets of yellow plastic. As they worked, Case gradually became aware of the music that pulsed constantly through the cluster. It was called dub, a sensuous mosaic cooked from vast libraries of digitalized pop; it was worship, Molly said, and a sense of community . . . Zion smelled of cooked vegetables, humanity, and ganja.

When I first read this, I did wonder how come people were *still* listening to dub in the twenty-first century, a good fifty years at least after King Tubby invented the genre. Still, credit where credit's due, what Gibson describes *is* slightly ahead of the game: 'a sensuous mosaic cooked from vast libraries of digital-ized pop' doesn't sound like reggae in 1984 but like the *idea* of dub that emerged in the nineties, promoted by figures like DJ Spooky and Kevin 'The Bug' Martin via his *Macro Dub Infection* compilations: dub as process not genre, closer to remixology or sampladelia than a band-played form of music like reggae.

Fifteen years after *Neuromancer* came *Needle in the Groove*, science fiction that's not only all about a band and music-making but is deeply informed by the de-Jamaicanised notion of dub that emerged in the nineties. Author Jeff Noon's earlier novels like *Vurt* and *Pollen* offered a British post-rave coun-terpart to cyberpunk: urban grime, subcultural colour, drugs, musical references. A former musician himself, Noon had been involved in a late-seventies moment that pre-echoed all those

nineties ideals of musical boundary-crossing and mixing it up.
He played guitar in the Manchester postpunk outfit Manicured
Noise, whose singer Owen Gavin (now the journalist Frank
Owen) told me about the group's formidable experimentalism:
they'd lay down 'military beats, over which we'd recite poetry
by Mayakovsky' and combine that with elements inspired by
film soundtracks and primitive funk learned by copying Chic
singles slowed down to 33 rpm. Talking about the postpunk
era, Noon argued that the discovery by white youth of dub reggae's bass pressure and disorientating spatiality was the most
significant musical development in the last few decades: 'from
that moment comes everything we now listen to', by which he
meant electronic music, drum and bass, post-rock, trip hop,
Timbaland-style R&B, and so on. 'Everything' is stretching it a
bit, but those were the sort of claims being made for dub in the
mid-nineties, among a certain *Wire*-reading and *Wire*-writing
sector of the population. In the noughties, we'd hear less of
this kind of talk, but if he were making that comment today,
Noon could certainly add dubstep to the 'everything' list.

Needle in the Groove's acknowledgements section doffs its
cap to outfits like Autechre, Microstoria and others operating
on the post-rave/post-rock fringes of nineties music. Noon has
often talked about how he has 'such an intimate relationship
with music. My writing is all tied up with it. I listen to it
all the time, writing to the rhythms.' So how well does he
do, then, with *Needle in the Groove*? Noon didn't set himself
a massive challenge since the novel is set in the very near
future: *Needle* came out in 1999, and because of the main
character's age (twenty-four) and his time of birth (summer
1978), you can tell the story is set around 2002/2003. The location is familiar Noon territory, a Manchester where the streets
are named after bands or records (State 808 Street, Ian Curtis
Boulevard and so forth). The protagonist/narrator Elliott is an

ex-junkie bassist who joins a band called Glam Damage: like
Manicured Noise, a mixed-gender, experimental-but-danceable
outfit, but here updated for the rave era. There's the brilliant
enigmatic drummer 2spot, the sultry black girl singer Donna,
and the female DJ/sampler-whizz Jody, who throws scratches
and samples into the mix in real time, and is also a drug fiend.
The 'Needle' in the novel's title has a double meaning: the
turntable's stylus, the addict's syringe.

So far, so 1990s, then. The futuristic and speculative factor
added by Noon is that Glam Damage, through their patrons
Zuum (a club/label), have got access to a new recording format
that captures music in a liquid: a technology identified at various
points as 'wave recording', 'wave-sonic technology', 'aquamatics'
and 'hydrophonics'. Instead of a reel of tape or a DAT, there's
a golf-ball-sized vessel full of sky-blue gel veined with darker
strands (these hold the music). Like a child's snowscape, this
globe can be shaken, causing the music to remix itself in a
potentially infinite number of ways as the strands settle into
new patterns. And the harder you shake it, 'the deeper the mix',
explains DJ Jody. Elliott gives Glam Damage's 'Scorched Out
for Love' a good jiggle. What results is 'Elliott's Bad and Busted
Remix'. And a wodge of prose poetry (the first of several) that's
something like a William Burroughs cut-up using only issues of
Melody Maker from the early nineties:

the creeping two-shot spots of a flow-down drumfall and the rim
of skin-beat, in a snare-dancer's downtime rhythm-loop explode
lament/where all the rain cymbals sing/the contours of the voice,
waiting for the bass to steal, the sliced and crazy feel/shots of the
lost/the hidden sound chant knowledge caught and twisted, now
stretching guitar burst/a drag from the fingers/holding, releasing/
noise caressing the blade-song/I wonder what colours you'll burn,
when the bass returns/bruise of crackle-pattern, vinyl screech-pop

of string . . . incisions of chorus, made of mad magic/amplifies the heart crying out, injection dance/cuts of motherloading bass honey, off-kilter dripping deep, and then word by funky word, passion splinters the tragic splice tactics/on the caught samples singing it all away/all the tripwire scratching kaleidoglide of a strange groove/ deep jesus bass of music, catching the shimmer/the final crackle of silence/holding, releasing, dissolving.

There are loads of tricks you can do with this new plasmatic recording technology. At the Zuum club one night, where ravers trance out to 'cheapcore', 'fleshcore' and 'techzak' (terms indicative of Noon's professed disdain for the more functional forms of dance music), Jody puts vinyl versions of 'Scorched Out for Love' on both turntables and cuts back and forth, then uses an eye-dropper to siphon some of the liquid version of the same track out of the little blue orb, squirts it onto the 12-inches and scratches the needle over these wets spots. This makes 'the music slip away and slither/become a river', until the ravers are pounding on the glass wall of the DJ booth and screaming to know what the hell this freakadelic tune is. Cue more prose poetry from Jeff, aka the 'Club Zuum Remix':

Loop dancer dripping a deep lament
Of mad magic scatter honey
Found
Exploding bootleg skin splinters
Nerve poison scraped from the shimmer
Working a pop drag screech from the heart lost
And taking a hit from blade strings
Injection's dance fires up the groove glide
Along the decks of tripwire
Found
In the snare-time rain of cymbals drumfalling

Through scratches of rhythm stolen and kissed
Kaleidofunk dissolving
Lost in the tangle and crackle.

Wave-sonic music gets made illegal before the book's end, but
not before the band work out you can intravenously inject the
liquid. The samples in the track become portals through time
taking them back to when and where they were recorded (in this
case, the punkfest at the Electric Circus in Manchester, October
1977, as recorded for the live album *Short Circuit*). But is it just
a mind-blowing hallucination or actual time travel?

In interviews Noon talked about how 'the way we live now, I
call it Liquid Culture, and I think to find the prose equivalent
of that is great'. The concept/conceit of *Needle* is that the
method of its composition is in tune with the digital era's
cutting-edge music. Or at least the prose-poetical mix chapters
are, since it's those bits that have been sluiced through the
'Cobralingus Filtering System'. Noon characterised this writing
technique in terms of the array of effects and processes offered
by a studio mixing board or digital audio workstation. He
talked of channelling his prose through 'filter gates' (overload,
'ghost edit', 'add virus', randomise, decay) and 'drug'-like
treatments such as 'metaphorazine' and 'repititorphan'. But it
turns out that Cobralingus was closer to a randomised set of
instructions and options à la Brian Eno's Oblique Strategies,
except that Noon didn't bother to make them up as a pack of
Tarot-style cards: this technology of the imagination was a
purely imaginary technology, existing only as 'the strangely
twisted pathways inside [my] head'.

Noon had dabbled with literary counterparts to dub's version-
ing in his earlier *Nymphomation* and *Pixel Juice*. And after
Needle, he'd go further still, writing a whole book of 'remix
fiction' actually titled *Cobralingus*. Here he sampled text from

sources like Emily Dickinson, Thomas De Quincey and Ecclesiastes, then shoved the literary signal through 'a series of gates'. In one story, Shakespeare gets melded with Zane Grey. It all sounds a bit like Kathy Acker's iconoclastic remakes of canonical novels like *Don Quixote*, updated from the era of no wave and Cindy Sherman to the age of Warp-style electronica and all those 'remix albums' that cluttered up the latter years of the nineties and whose versions increasingly bore no resemblance to the original (and in some cases no *relation* either, since they featured not a single sonic shred of the supposedly remixed track).

A prototype version of *Needle* featured a female character called Toop (short for Tupelo). Bizarrely, Noon hooked up with David Toop to create an album based around his novel: *Needle in the Groove: if music were a drug, where would it take you,* released via Scanner's Sulphur label in 2000. Or not so bizarrely, really, given that Toop was the perfect choice, as one of the principal theorists for 'liquid culture' with his 1996 book *Ocean of Sound: Aether Talk, Ambient Sound and Imaginary Worlds,* which contained passages like this:

> Disco began to work on the principle of decomposing songs into modular and interchangeable fragments, sliced and repatched into an order which departed from the rules of Tin Pan Alley . . . Songs became liquid. They became vehicles for improvisation, or source material . . . that could be reconfigured or remixed to suit the future. In a humiliating way, musicians became technicians, alongside recording engineers, tape ops, editors and all the other technocratic laboratory assistants cleaning their glasses in the back room. At the front end of the medium was the DJ, ruling the disco, playing music and people as one fluid substance.

In terms of its S.F. premise and the storyline, but also at the level of the text itself, *Needle* attempts to implement this

355

very nineties and technotopian notion of dub/remixology as deliquescent and deterritorialising. For the resulting fictional music to be then realised as sound by Toop, one of the great theorists of 'sonic fiction' (Kodwo Eshun's term), made for a perfect circularity: what flows around comes around. It's also, as far as I know, the only time an attempt has been made to create the future-music imagined in an S.F. novel, and with the involvement of the author to boot.

So what does *Needle in the Groove: if music were a drug, where would it take you* sound like? Kudos to Noon for the cojones . . . but frankly, a little underwhelming after the 'remix' passages of the book, and after Noon's burbling in interviews about the 'mind-boggling' thrill of going into Toop's studio and being confronted by 'all this digital stuff they've got [nowadays] . . . they can do absolutely anything. They can manipulate the musical input, the signal, any way they like.' The track 'dubbedoutforlove (Dubgeist Remix)', for instance, doesn't sound ahead of its time but, if anything, slightly behind it: ambient chill-out infused with a fragrant tang of 'modern exotica', it's all a bit mid-nineties, in the vicinity of Mouse on Mars's *Iaora Tahiti*. The track sways on a gentle bass-pulse, draped with ripples of hand-percussion and twangy curlicues of steel guitar redolent of Eno's *Apollo* soundtrack, an album Noon listened to while writing *Needle*; bobbing like a corked bottle in the waves is a sing-songy Mancunian voice, Shaun Ryder's dotty uncle – Noon reciting lines like 'boomsonic boomsonic/kaleidofunkphonic'. This mellow, atmospheric approach was taken, Toop explained, because it's 'impossible to read in a flexible, expressive way over hard-edged dance music' but also because he 'heard something other than dance music in the book . . . a weird soup of skiffle, blues, hip-hop beats, Manchester rock and psychological noise'. Toop did take a stab at achieving something close to the liquid remixing in *Needle*:

he took 'a huge collection of fragments and jammed them all together in the computer'.

But the very idea of remixology was already past its freshness date by the turn of the millennium. Dance culture in the noughties would veer away from the totally unrecognisable remix version like a Music & Video Exchange bargain basement employee swerving to avoid toppling a stack of un-resellable 'remix albums'. Instead, there were vogues for 're-edits' (remixes that largely consist of the original song, but structurally resequenced – a reversion to how things were done in the eighties, in other words) and for mash-ups (chimera-like composites stitched together out of amputated parts from two or more highly recognisable tunes).

The album *Needle in the Groove*, like the novel, proves once again the difficulty of thinking ahead or outside of present conceptions of music. To imagine the music of the future and then convey that in prose you'd need to be a mixture of accomplished critic, musicologist and practising musician (and if you were the latter, as Bruce Sterling suggested, probably you'd be making the music already). Futurologists are no better at this game than S.F. writers. Take Ray Kurzweil, the inventor who pioneered optical character recognition, text-to-speech synthesis and a number of keyboard synthesisers. In his 1999 book *The Age of Spiritual Machines: When Computers Exceed Human Intelligence*, he drew up a timeline of breakthroughs that the twenty-first century was set to unfurl. He postulated that around 2009, a computer would have become sufficiently intuitive to be able to 'jam' with a human musician: a 'marvel' that dates him to the era of Carlos Santana and Jerry Garcia.

Futurologists and S.F. writers both tend to do much better speculating about technology, geopolitics and social mores than arts and culture. Especially with science and machines, the cause-and-probable-effect trajectories are far easier to

357

track; you can see the gaps in contemporary knowledge or technical capacity that could be filled, the breakthroughs that are required for the currently impossible to become possible. There are magazines and specialist journals that are all about speculating about developments, proposing goals and solutions. But art and fashion don't have a 'way forward' that you can map out in this fashion; there is no teleology, no immanent logic set to unfold in ways we could predict. The history of pop music, especially, is full of swerves, double-backs, bolts from the blue. Twenty-five years ago, at the height of synth-pop, or even fifteen years ago, at the peak of techno-rave, few would have predicted the massive revival of interest in folk forms and acoustic instrumentation that took place in the first decade of the twenty-first century. Similarly, people who heard 'Tomorrow Never Knows' and 'Are You Experienced?' when they first came out might have thought that rock music was just going to get weirder, more studio-phantasmagoric and drug-frazzled (John Brunner and Robert Silverberg certainly did). One or two strands of rock did pursue those trajectories, but most of it went into completely unexpected directions (the singer-songwriter boom, glam's warped echoes of fifties rock 'n' roll), and some of it deliberately went the opposite way (The Band, Creedence Clearwater Revival, country rock, et al). Music can offer a potent *sensation* of the future-now, but it is rarely an actual glimpse of the shape of sounds to come. And it is only looking backwards that you can see what were the harbingers of, or flash-forwards to, our sonic present: at the time itself, the germinative inklings and heralds of tomorrow's music were more often than not ignored, undervalued, unnoticed.

Perhaps the very idea of 'tomorrow's music today' is one of those Wittgensteinian wrinkles in language, a nonsense produced by the peculiarities of tenses and grammar. If it's made today, or even *conceivable* today, then by definition it's no longer *of* the future; it's already here. In music journalism, one of the standard-issue ways of praising something (usually old music, a reissue or something that deserves to be reissued) is to say it was 'ahead of its time', that a certain record 'looks ahead to' or 'anticipates' something much later, that with a particular song Band X 'invents' the much later Band Z. No actually existent music can really be ahead of its time but it is possible for popular taste – the general public, or a particular, wilfully backward-looking sector of it, like indie-rock – to be *behind its own time*.

What about the idea that music itself is the vanguard of culture, the furthest-extending promontory into the oncoming ocean of the future? This notion is aired in *Idoru* – 'popular culture is the test-bed of futurity', observes Mr Kuwayama, the boss of the company that created Rei Toei. As outlined in his classic book *Noise*, Jacques Attali's theory of music's evolution hinges on the notion that music is already in advance of the rest of culture, that its current forms are somehow prophetic of future modes of social organisation. The theory is too complicated to examine here, but the part that is most relevant and suggestive concerns the present era, what Attali terms the age of 'composition': after a long period of music being a specialist profession and consumers 'stockpiling' recorded sound and listening to it passively and mostly in private, the punters get to make their own music. Attali (whose latest book *A Brief History of the Future* doesn't mention music) wrote *Noise* in the mid-seventies and there have been various interpretations of what 'composition' would look like: some have pointed to punk and to the do-it-yourself/release-it-yourself culture of postpunk, others to the more recent micro-undergrounds of noise, improv, drone et al (where music is home-recorded and circulates in tiny editions of cassettes and CD-Rs among fans who are mostly likely practitioners themselves). But perhaps the most convincing candidate for 'composition' is DJ culture and related genres based around sampling. This is literally composition, the putting-together of shards of pre-existing music either in the DJ's mix or as a sample-collage, resulting in the reanimation of 'dead' energy trapped in stockpiles (aka record collections). But all these candidates for 'composition' fit Attali's theory in so far as you could see them prefiguring egalitarian social forms based around transactions within networks of autonomous individuals.

I really like this idea of music being the forward sector of culture: as someone who's dedicated his life to writing about music, it appeals to my professional patriotism. If music had the capacity to herald change (if not actually effect change by itself), that would certainly ratify the excessive importance that some of us have invested in music. The latent futurity of music would also go some way towards explaining why so many S.F. writers are influenced by music, why so many pop groups have been inspired by S.F., and indeed why so many rock critics started out as S.F. fans (Greg Shaw, founder of the pioneering rock mag *Who Put the Bomp* had a long history doing science fiction fanzines beforehand, as did Paul Williams, whose *Crawdaddy* is generally regarded as the very first magazine devoted to rock criticism). Part of the allure of being a music hipster is the idea of being *in on the future*. I don't know why I've never before connected my own interest in music's cutting edges with the fact that science fiction was the thing I was into immediately before I discovered punk and the UK rock press; before I wanted to be a music writer, I wanted to be a S.F. novelist. The big postpunk festival of the era, headlined by groups like Public Image Ltd and Siouxsie and the Banshees, was Futurama in Leeds, and it was originally billed as The World's First Science Fiction Music Festival.

This Attali-derived notion of utopianism as the latent content of music, or *some* music, actually fits the feelings that music, or *some* music, stirs up: the vertigo of limitlessness, inordinate hope, unstoppable energy. It's the same scary-euphoric rush that the best S.F. gives. But if music *is* the future-now, it only figures that dreaming up in prose the future form of that future-now is going to be a tall order.

Originally published as an essay series in issue 1 and issue 2 of
Loops, 2009 and 2010

AFTERWORD

Futuromania, as its title indicates, is a kind of sister book to *Retromania* – its inverted mirror image, its twisted twin. Where 'retromania' is clearly a malaise, 'futuromania' is more like an excessive vigour, an agitated excitement about anything and everything in the present that could be taken as 'tomorrow's music today'. It evokes a fanatical impatience and restlessness.

Lee Brackstone – once my editor at Faber & Faber, and with whom I am thrilled to be reunited now at White Rabbit – said of *Retromania* that it was the third instalment of a trilogy that began with *Energy Flash* and continued with *Rip It Up and Start Again*. That had never occurred to me, but it instantly struck me as astute and accurate – emotionally true, if not literally. The boy whose taste for the shock of the new had been awakened during postpunk by bands like Public Image Ltd and Talking Heads, and whose belief in musical modernism was recharged during the rave nineties – that would be exactly the person who'd write *Retromania* in gloomy response to a slowing down of innovation in the 2000s.

So *Futuromania* maybe makes it a tetralogy: the fourth book in an unofficial series, a celebration of the sort of sounds that stirred and sustained a taste for music that's forward-looking and future-bound.

363

Future-talk appeals to music writers partly because it positions the critic as a prophet. It's not really about prediction,
though; it's more like a boast that you are more advanced as
a listener than most everybody else. The critic who bangs on
about the future is really saying 'Catch up! Join us in the
vanguard . . . but hurry, because we'll soon be on to something else!'

But why *should* music always have to be breaking with tradition and hurling itself into the unknown? What's so virtuous
about being purportedly nearer the future than the majority of
the population? It's only music, after all. Or is it?

Futuromania is so constitutive of my musical being, so much
at the core of how I respond to and process sound, it feels
like a neurological affliction: an addiction to the sensations
of surprise and speed. But again, I'm not sure this really
has much to do with any putative future; it's more about
how things feel, how you feel, *right now*. Particularly during
the 1990s – my years of most intense raving to, and raving
about, electronic dance music – the imaginative function of the
Phuture (as we often spelled it then, to make it look more, er,
phuturistic!) was really all about creating a quickening in the
present. A quality of propulsive linearity coursed through all
the dancefloor electronica of the nineties – trance and techno
as much as my personal favourites like jungle and gabber.
A hurtling teleology, a ballistic sense of purpose, impacting
you as a battery of physical sensations: tempos grew faster,
beats got ever more brutal and fractured, textures escalated
in abstraction and noxiousness. Hearing these genres through
a massive sound system was onslaught and ordeal: a test for
dancers, forging new flesh. Each individual track was a microcosm of the entire culture's fast-forward drive. That was the
sense in which rave was a movement: not politically, but as a
sensibility, a sensorium, oriented around velocity. *Go*.

In the 1990s, digital music exuded a futuristic aura in part because everyday life was still largely an analogue affair. Personal computers were becoming widespread in work and were creeping into our leisure, but did not dominate our existence. Nearly everyone had dial-up rather than broadband; Wi-Fi was unknown, the smartphone still some way off into the future. YouTube, social media, satellite navigation, Siri and a dozen other commonplace 'superpowers' of today were either unimagined or a long way from being realised.

Music based around sequencers, sampling and electronic tonalities conjured an approaching world that seemed like it would be less human. Although it worked on the dancing body, techno felt radically disembodied, because of the relative dearth of audibly hand-played elements. Assembled using computer software with clicks and cursor drags shunting information around a screen, it rarely correlated with physical human actions in the way that sounds generated by an orchestra, jazz band or rock group did. That kind of music invited listeners to 'play along' mimetically with what they were hearing: you might have no idea how to play the instrument, but it could feel irresistible to mime air guitar or air drums. But it seems highly unlikely that anyone has ever attempted to 'air-sequence' or 'air-drum-machine-program'. Likewise, listening to techno, you didn't visualise the person(s) responsible for the sound; instead, you might picture an intricate, maze-like environment, or imagine a track as an abstract vehicle taking you on a journey.

Picking up on this (actually deceiving) posthuman quality to the music, critics like me wrote about the new sounds in a deliberately depersonalised way, to the point sometimes of attributing a purposeful sentience to the way that genres evolved and mutated. It felt appropriate and necessary but also desirable – sexy, even – to talk about music as if it was

365

independent and indifferent to human designs, governed
only by its own remorseless agenda. We wanted to match the
music's severity and abrasive strangeness, so we broke with
the older, more humane and humanist ways of describing and
valuing. We'd fail the test of our time if we didn't respond to
its challenge to formulate a new language – to invent a poetics
that was anti-poetic. Hence all the neologisms and portman-
teau terms, the tropes informed by chaos theory, astrophysics
and cybernetics. Kodwo Eshun redescribed the critic as a
concept engineer – a deliberately unromantic notion of writing
(although it echoed William Carlos Williams's 1944 description
of the poem as a 'machine made of words').

The musicians also seemed to be pushing this way of hearing and feeling the music, almost to the point of erasing themselves. Producers sheltered behind depersonalised names of a
numerical, scientific or industrial aura: Nexus 21, Electribe
101, T99, LFO, Cybersonic, Noise Factory. Some named themselves after specific pieces of technology, as if the machines had
created what you were hearing on their own: 808 State (after
the Roland 808 drum machine), Q-Bass (after the virtual studio
software Cubase).

For critics like me, theory played a big part too, in particular Gilles Deleuze and Félix Guattari's concept of the desiring
machine and Paul Virilio's writings about speed and technology
(shorn of his Catholic anxieties and recast from dystopian
dysphoria into apocalyptic exultation). Cyberpunk fiction and
cybernetic theory seeped into the mix, in particular Brian Eno's
concept of scenius: a pun on 'scene' and 'genius' that replaced
the Romantic notion of the individual artist with anonymous
collectives.

And let's not forget about the drugs. I remember someone
quipping that 'Desiring Machine' would be a great name for a
brand of Ecstasy pill.

Buzzing on D&G and MDMA, I still remained enough of
a humanist and socialist to have some concerns about the
wear-and-tear that rave's pleasure factory inflicted on its
flesh-and-blood components, while worrying about the potentially depoliticising effects of the culture. But nowadays, I tend
to think that the machine-talk was a kind of game we were
playing. It made things more exciting; it turned our era into
an adventure – something we felt uniquely equipped to capture
and convey using appropriately apocalyptic imagery.

Today, it seems rather obvious to me that nothing comes out
of technology – whether it's a sampler, Auto-Tune or AI – that
doesn't bear the imprint of human intention. For sure, tracks
like Rufige Kru's 'Terminator' or The Mover's 'Apocalypse Never'
sounded then and still sound like machines gone mad, pursuing
some radically unhuman agenda. No doubt that's why Goldie
titled 'Terminator' after the robo-killer beamed from the future
into the present to assassinate a child who'll one day grow up
to be the future leader of the resistance to the sentient war-
machines. But the track, like all the tracks of this era, is nothing
but an accumulation of human decisions. The music (or for that
matter the machines on which the music was made) would never
have existed without human ingenuity and human imagination
– *including* all those theories and fantasies about becoming-
machine, cold dark futures, the posthuman . . .

One of the curious aspects about future-music of the kind
celebrated in this book – from 'I Feel Love' through 'Acid Trax'
to 'Renegade Snares' – is that despite the passage of time, these
tracks and thousands like them continue to exert an imposing
fascination. They endure as monuments to the future, to use
the philosopher Fredric Jameson's term for the twentieth-
century modernist pantheon of artworks. When you listen, the
future-feeling emitted by them is as strong as ever. Despite any

personal memories that might attach to where you heard the track, in the moment of re-entry to its sound-space, the original abolition of nostalgia that this music instigated – it happens all over again. These tracks are still, somehow, 'the future' – even though in a literal chronological sense they belong to the past.

Looking to explain this apparent paradox, we might turn to Jameson's *A Singular Modernity*, which contains an acute analysis of how formerly radical, but now classic, artworks still give us that future-rush, even though we live in a present where the innovations they introduced have been assimilated and domesticated, such that they ought to be shorn of all unfamiliarity. According to Jameson, what defines the modernist artwork is a relationship to time. It enacts the break with the past forms of art within itself. 'The act of restructuration is seized and arrested as in some filmic freeze-frame' and thereby 'encapsulates and eternalizes the process'.

A concrete example of this at work within the music discussed in *Futuromania* would be the techniques of breakbeat science. In UK hardcore and jungle, there is a suspended clash between the analogue and the digital, between hand-played drumming and the micro-editing and processing of samples done using a digital audio workstation like Cubase. The uncanny time-warping of digital technique coexists with and permeates the real-time musicianship from decades earlier. The sweaty funk of flesh-and-blood drumming (with jungle's central breakbeat, the 'Amen', less than eight seconds of Gregory Coleman's lifeforce from The Winstons' 1969 soul tune 'Amen, Brother') mutates into something far beyond human playing capacity. It's superhumanised. Similar transfigurations take place with the vocal science of Todd Edwards's house (a hiccupping patchwork of micro-samples of ecstatic singing) and with the Auto-Tuned rap-sing delirium of trap artists like Migos and Playboi Carti. Jameson, again: 'the older technique or content

368

must somehow subsist within the work as what is cancelled or overwritten, modified, inverted or negated, in order for us to feel the force, in the present, of what is alleged to have once been an innovation'.

This dynamic is particularly potent within black music dance cultures: reggae and dancehall, hip hop and R&B, jungle and its hardcore-continuum successors like 2-step garage. The emphasis, though, is as much about continuity as it is the modernist-style break with the past. There's a richly resonant blend of 'roots 'n future', to borrow a song title from a rave-era UK group called – funnily enough – Phuture Assassins. Through sampling, lyric interpolation and the recycling of older rhythms, black music subcultures are able to bring the past into the present as a living thing, a functioning element in whatever today's sound is. The relationship to the past is neither overly reverent nor contrivedly iconoclastic; it doesn't aim to replicate but to reactivate. Temporally, it's a two-way street: always simultaneously harking forward and vibrantly haunted by its past. Whatever materials can be salvaged from history (a beat, a vocal lick, a keyboard timbre) get reinserted into a chronology that points ever forward (to Better Days) while continuing to know where it comes from. Retro doesn't come into it.

The idea of the future as an improvement on the present, or at least excitingly different, owes a lot to a Western and widespread (if perhaps now ailing) ideology of progress. Likewise, critics have often celebrated the futuristic currents in music as if they were indexed to similar progressive advances in politics and society. In truth, technology is neutral. Indeed, the cutting edge, on a technical level, in popular entertainment might actually be more often linked to regressive cultural forms: the kind of movies that win awards for special effects, editing, sound design, colour grading and so forth are often medieval or proto-fascist

369

in their subliminal ideology, peddling fantasies of heroism and destiny. Radical sonic techniques can occur in genres otherwise quite traditional in their musical structures and emotional affect. The engineering in a Top 40 hit might be super-advanced, but everything else in it could be conventional, or even reactionary. Conversely, the example of various folk revivals – as well as newer 'folk' forms like punk and indie – shows how traditional acoustic or electric guitar styles can be allied with left-wing politics, or progressive ideas about gender and sexuality, in a way that feels like a natural fit.

Still, for my generation, the equation of radical sounds and radical politics remains a default assumption; a deep-seated, if increasingly shaky, article of faith. That conflation in turn is often bound up with a love of the more challenging forms of science fiction. Many groups of the new wave era – especially electronic ones, like the Human League and Cabaret Voltaire – were inspired by new wave S.F. writers like Ballard and Dick.

Fanatical interest in pop music and science fiction is generally associated with youth. It comes, I think, from the adolescent's frustration with the stifling banality of their surroundings. It's the insufficiency of the world as is – and the inadequacy of the half-formed adolescent self – that drives kids into the fantasy-systems offered by science fiction and various forms of youth music. That man Jameson again talks of 'the desire called utopia' in his S.F. study *Archaeologies of the Future*. But you could just as easily talk about the 'desire called dystopia'. Dark futures – totalitarian scenarios or post-catastrophe aftermaths alike – offer heroic narratives of discovery and danger, the chance to dream yourself as extraordinary, with the mettle to face down extreme challenges. In the end, perhaps The Future is just a ciphered placeholder, the amorphous object for a yearning to be 'anywhere but here, anywhen but now, anyone but me'.

But this craving to escape to an absolute elsewhere, this refusal of limits and one's allotted self . . . is this, I wonder, something to grow out of? Certainly, as I get older and the actual future seems a less alluring prospect (the mass extinction event of climate ruination paralleling my own individual extinction), I am feeling the pull of another way of relating to time. In my sixties, I think back to a slogan of the 1960s, the decade in which I was born: a past era of optimism and anticipation, of the youthquake and rock's first flush. Be here now . . .

ACKNOWLEDGEMENTS

Thanks to my awesome agent Cathryn Summerhayes and her team at Curtis Brown.

Thanks to Lee Brackstone for his encouragement and guidance.

Thanks to Sarah Fortune, Sophie Nevrkla, Tom Noble, Kasimiira Kontio and everyone else at White Rabbit involved in making this book come out right.

Thanks to the magazines and editors who originally gave me the space in which to explore these ideas – in particular Pitchfork (Ryan Dombal, Mark Richardson) and *The Wire* (Tony Herrington, Rob Young, Anne Hilde Neset, Derek Walmsley, Joseph Stannard, Chris Bohn) but also *Melody Maker*, *Village Voice*, the *Guardian*, NPR Music, the *Observer Music Monthly*, Resident Advisor and others.

Thanks to the friends who've shared ideas and excitement over several decades: Paul Oldfield, David Stubbs, Frank Owen, Kodwo Eshun, Matthew Ingram, Mark Fisher, Bethan Cole, Sam Batra, Luke Davis, Droid, Geeta Dayal, Bat aka Anindya Bhattacharyya, Rupert Howe, Susan Masters, Craig Willingham, Kit Mackintosh, Paul Kennedy, the Dissensus massive, Carl Neville, Asif Siddiqi, Phil Knight, Julian House, Jim Jupp, Ian Hodgson and more.

Big shout to all the music makers and dreamers of dreams, the producers and DJs and label operators who've kept me 'living for the future'. Most, if not all, are in this book, but here are a few who warrant a special mention: A Guy Called Gerald, LFO, Ultramarine, Richard H. Kirk, Robert Haigh, Goldie, 4 Hero and the Reinforced Crew, Foul Play, Moving Shadow, Chris Macfarlane aka Potential Bad Boy, Steve Gurley, Dem 2, Marc Acardipane and the PCP clan, Moon Wiring Club, Mordant Music / eMMplekz, Ghost Box . . .

Last, but most – thanks to Joy Press, my companion and counsellor in this project as in all the ones before and those still to come. Big shout to my sons Kieran and Eli, each chasing and manifesting the future in his own different way.

MUSIC FOR FUTUROMANIACS

A Guided Tour, in Approximately Chronological Order

You can hear these tracks (well, *almost* all of them) on Spotify.

To listen to the Spotify playlist, you can scan the QR code or click the link below:

https://open.spotify.com/playlist/2SrmedUDoeNQjfg2Key028?s
i=83c9bebb1ba74160

Hugh LeCaine – Dripsody
BBC Radiophonic Workshop/Delia Derbyshire – Doctor Who
Tonto's Expanding Head Band – Jetsex
Donna Summer – I Feel Love (Patrick Cowley Megamix)
Kraftwerk – Trans-Europe Express/Metal on Metal/Abzug
Jean-Michel Jarre – Oxygene, Part IV

Yusuf/Cat Stevens – Was Dog a Doughnut?
Kraftwerk – Neon Lights
Donna Summer – Now I Need You/Working the Midnight Shift
Weather Report – River People
Sparks – Number One Song in Heaven
David Bowie – Ashes to Ashes
Suicide – Dance
Creation Rebel – Space Movement Section 4
Terry Riley – Desert of Ice
Tubeway Army – Down in the Park
Talking Heads – Seen and Not Seen
Thomas Leer – Tight as a Drum
Zapp – More Bounce to the Ounce
Human League – Love Action
Kraftwerk – Home Computer
Conrad Schnitzler – Metall I
Liaisons Dangereuses – Los niños del parque
D.A.F. – Verschwende deine Jugend
Cabaret Voltaire – Black Mask
Ryuichi Sakamoto – Riot in Lagos
Sylvian and Sakamoto – Bamboo Music
Japan – Ghosts
CTI/Chris & Cosey – Dancing Ghosts
Art of Noise – Close (to the Edit)
Man Parrish – Hip Hop Be Bop
Janet Jackson – Nasty
Mantronix – Needle to the Groove
Nitro Deluxe – Let's Get Brutal (Brutal Dub)
Mad Professor/Intense – On My Dub
Mantronix – Music Madness
The Young Gods – Fais la mouette
Phuture – Acid Trax
Phuture – Your Only Friend

Sleezy D – I've Lost Control

Royal House – Party People (B Boy National Anthem)

Mr. Fingers – Washing Machine

Rhythim Is Rhythim/Derrick May – Daymares, It Is What It Is

A Guy Called Gerald – Voodoo Ray

33⅓ Queen – Searchin'

Orbital – Chime

Beltram – Energy Flash

Ultramarine – Stella

Kraftwerk – Computer Love (The Mix Remix)

LFO – Mentok 1

Nightmares on Wax – Aftermath

Joey Beltram/Second Phase – Mentasm

Mescalinum United – We Have Arrived

Sweet Exorcist – Clonk's Coming

Rufige Cru – Menace

Underground Resistance – Death Star

Acen – Trip II the Moon, Part 1

Aphex Twin – Pulsewidth

Seefeel – Time to Find Me (AFX Fast Mix)

The Black Dog – Virtual

Blame – Music Takes You (2 Bad Mice Take You)

4 Hero – Students of the Future

Rufige Cru – Darkrider

Derrick May – Kaos (Juice Bar Mix)

Metalheads – Terminator

Foul Play – Open Your Mind (Foul Play Remix)

Omni Trio – The Original Soundtrack

LTJ Bukem – Atlantis (I Need You)

Drexciya – Wavejumper

Aphex Twin – Alberto Balsam

Blame & Justice – Anthemia (Heaven)

Renegade – Terrorist (P.A. Mix)

Omni Trio – Renegade Snares (Foul Play Remix)

Foul Play – Being with You (Foul Play Remix)

Code 071/Tek 9 – A London Sumtin'

Beenie Man – Who Am I (Sim Simma)

Boards of Canada – Roygbiv

Renegade Legion – Torsion

Reign – Light and Dark (The Next Dimension)

Inferno Bros – Slaves to the Rave

Pilldriver – Apocalypse Never

Superpower – Move: Don't Stop!

Wagon Christ – Scrapes

Gas – Königsforst 5

Resilient – 1.2

Monolake – Macau

Maurizio – M6b

De'Lacy – Hideaway (Deep Dish Remix)

Armand Van Helden/Sneaker Pimps – Spin Spin Sugar

Todd Edwards – Push the Love

Dem 2 – Destiny

Aaliyah – Are You That Somebody

Missy Elliott – Get Your Freak On

Daft Punk – Digital Love

Dizzee Rascal – I Luv U

Big E.D./Terror Danjah – Frontline

Burial – Southern Comfort

Pinch – Qawwali

J Dilla – Won't Do

Zomby – Mercury's Rainbow

Oneohtrix Point Never – Physical Memory

Actress – Supreme Cunnilingus

DJ Traxman – The Comeback

Kaitlyn Aurelia Smith – I Am Learning

Maria Minerva – A Little Lonely

Tinashe – 2 On
Sage the Gemini – Gas Pedal
Future – Fuck Up Some Commas
Young Thug – Constantly Hating
Chief Keef – On the Corner
Migos – T-Shirt
James Blake – If the Car Beside You Moves Ahead
Travis Scott – Goosebumps
Playboi Carti – No Time
SOPHIE – Faceshopping
Holly Herndon – Fear, Uncertainty, Doubt
Beatriz Ferreyra – Echos

FUTURE READING

You can find more related writing by me at the Futuromania blog: https://futuromaniac.blogspot.com/.

Here are some recommended reads written by other people:

Vince Aletti – *The Disco Files 1973–78: New York's Underground, Week by Week*
Jacques Attali – *Noise: The Political Economy of Music*
Franco Berardi – *After the Future*
Jack Chuter – *Storm Static Sleep: A Pathway through Post-Rock*
Julian Cope – *Krautrocksampler*
Kodwo Eshun – *More Brilliant than the Sun: Adventures in Sonic Fiction*
Mark Fisher – *Ghosts of My Life: Writings on Depression, Hauntology, and Lost Futures*
Jeremy Gilbert and Ewan Pearson – *Discographies: Dance, Music, Culture and the Politics of Sound*
Albert Goldman – *Disco*
Fredric Jameson – *A Singular Modernity: Essay on the Ontology of the Present*
Alan Kirby – *Digimodernism: How New Technologies Dismantle the Postmodern and Reconfigure Our Culture*

Janette Leech – *Fearless: The Making of Post-Rock*

Dan Leroy – *Dancing to the Drum Machine: How Electronic Percussion Conquered the World*

Kit Mackintosh – *Neon Screams: How Drill, Trap and Bashment Made Music New Again*

Tobias Rapp – *Lost and Sound: Techno, Berlin and the Easyjet Set*

Tara Rodgers – *Pink Noises: Women on Electronic Music and Sound*

Peter Shapiro – *Turn the Beat Around: The Secret History of Disco*

David Stubbs – *Future Days: Krautrock and the Birth of a Revolutionary New Music*

David Stubbs – *Mars by 1980: The Story of Electronic Music*

Dave Tompkins – *How to Wreck a Nice Beach: The Vocoder from World War II to Hip Hop, the Machine Speaks*

David Toop – *Exotica: Fabricated Soundscapes in a Real World*

David Toop – *Ocean of Sound: Aether Talk, Ambient Sound and Imaginary Worlds*

McKenzie Wark – *Raving*

INDEX